Sport, Professionalism and Pain: Ethnographies of injury

Sport, Professionalism and Pain considers these and other pertinent concerns as it questions whether, in the world of modern sport, it is the participants themselves or the sport's administrators who exert more control over athletes' well-being. It is asserted that because of the distinctive nature of sport, the power to transform medical practice and application of sports medicine lies not with physicians but within the practices of sport itself.

Sport, Professionalism and Pain bridges a perceived space in the literature between medical anthropology, medical sociology and sport studies, examining issues such as:

- the relationship between sports medicine, the body and culture;
- the power struggle between sport administrators and participants;
- the historical transformation of sports medicine.

P. David Howe is a Senior Lecturer in the Anthropology of Sport in the School of Sport and Leisure at the University of Gloucestershire.

Sport, Professionalism and Pain

Ethnographies of injury and risk

P. David Howe

Routledge
Taylor & Francis Group

LONDON AND NEW YORK

First published 2004
by Routledge
11 New Fetter Lane, London EC4P 4EE

Simultaneously published in the USA and Canada
by Routledge
29 West 35th Street, New York, NY 10001

Routledge is an imprint of the Taylor & Francis Group

© 2004 P. David Howe

Typeset in Goudy and Gill Sans by
Florence Production Ltd, Stoodleigh, Devon EX16 9PN
Printed and bound in Great Britain by
The Cromwell Press, Trowbridge, Wiltshire

British Library Cataloguing in Publication Data
A catalogue record for this book is available from
the British Library

Library of Congress Cataloging in Publication Data
A catalog record for this book has been requested

ISBN 0–415–24729–2 (hbk)
ISBN 0–415–24730–6 (pbk)

For my parents M.D. and T.S.P. with love

Contents

Illustrations

Figures

Tables

Acknowledgements

The genesis of the ideas that find their way into this book occurred when I suffered a serious sports injury as a Master's student at the University of Toronto in 1991. Since that time I have been concerned with exploring the relationship between medical treatment in sport and issues of professionalism and commercialism and the impact these have upon the sporting body. I am indebted to many people personally and professionally for taking time from their own busy schedules to listen to the thoughts and ideas I have had over the past decade regarding this project.

I would like to thank Doug Richards and Ed Ratz, who, through their treatment of my injuries at the University of Toronto, helped me to formulate the embryo of the ideas presented here. The bulk of the theoretical exploration was undertaken while I was a PhD student at the Centre for Medical Anthropology at University College London. For his insight and sense of humour I would like to thank Murray Last, who made thinking painful, rewarding and enjoyable and, most of all, helped me by believing in me during the process of my PhD research.

I am indebted to all the informants who have contributed to this study, notably the time and energy selflessly given by those at Valley Rugby Football Club, the athletics club and the Paralympians (the case studies). ('Valley' is a pseudonym for a club in South Wales, UK, that plays rugby union at the elite level.) Thanks must also go to Steve Pritchard, who has had the difficult job of being my coach and advisor for the past eight years. He has made me realise how much my mortal engine could really hurt and yet still survive, and for these experiences I am grateful. Also to Fatty, Jabba, Kip Kev and Rocket for going the distance and providing much food for thought.

Some of the material in this volume has appeared in a similar form elsewhere. I am grateful to Alan Tomlinson and Sage Publications for permission to reprint material from P.D. Howe (2001) 'An Ethnography of Pain and Injury in Professional Rugby Union: The Case of Pontypridd RFC', *International Review of Sport Sociology* 35 (3): 289–303.

Thank you to Samantha Grant and the sport and leisure team at Routledge, and to series editors Mike McNamee and Jim Parry, who took a gamble on a novice writer when suggesting this volume. I am hopeful it was worth the wait.

My family have always been very supportive of whatever project I undertake, and this book has been no different. In particular, I want to thank Stephen, my brother, who is my role model and friend, as well as my father for instilling in me a passion for sport, and running in particular, and not letting my impairment get in the way. Most of all, my thanks go to my partner, Carol, who has read every word, and improved this work with a delightful turn of phrase. Her understanding also gave me strength when the going was tough. It could not have been done without her. While her input no doubt improved the text, any failures in it are my own.

Introduction

This book is an anthropological study of the impact of commercialism on the professionalisation of sports medicine. In particular, it examines how the embodied practice of sport in a professional environment places stress on elite sporting participants. These individuals have better medical provisions than were available to the competitors of yesteryear. But they come at a price. The book investigates the relationship between commercialism, medicine and the body, in order to establish the importance of pain, injury and risk in the contemporary sporting world. Ethnographic case studies of Welsh rugby union players, British distance runners and a sample of Paralympians at the last four Paralympic games highlight the ways in which distinctive cultural environments in the process of transformation to professionalism have different approaches to the management of pain, injury and risk. The provision of sports medicine is, in a sense, a tool used by sports administrators and club officials to fast-track elite sporting performers (often prematurely) back into competition. In spite of the cultural differences, however, all three cases illustrate the fact that in an era of elite professional sport the health and well-being of the participant is ultimately a personal responsibility.

Like the interpretations of pain, injury and risk, the playing and understanding of games may be seen as culturally distinctive. The exact nature of informal games that are played varies between cultures. Nevertheless, it is widely thought that the playing of games is a cultural universal (Blanchard 1995). This notion, first developed in the work of Johan Huizinga (1950), has shaped the way the field of anthropology has addressed the concept of play. Anthropologists such as Bateson (1972) expanded upon the work of Huizinga by identifying both the cultural and the biological importance of play. First, the biological influence of play can be seen in the necessity of humankind to survive, and the manner in which traditional societies articulate lessons of this kind is through encouraging their children to play. Second, playing is one of the ways in which children in contemporary Western society escape from the rigour of studying traditional school subjects, and since Victorian times codified forms of play, such as sport, have also become part of the school curriculum.

Games may be mere pastimes for children, but the act of playing that is part of the lives of most people has an important function within society. The mechanism of play is employed by all cultures to eliminate the burden of concerns that are apparent in the real lives of people. Play is, in other words, a collection of symbolic actions that help remove social tension (Blanchard 1995). This is a functionalist analysis, of course; others are available in the diverse literatures of play. Yet while play may be seen also as an avenue for skill acquisition that can develop into life or sporting skills (or both), the possibility of 'getting hurt' is never absent. The risk society that Beck (1992) chronicles is predicated upon this notion of the possibility of hurt. Issues related to harm are articulated in sports medicine literature (Grayson 1999). Between the concepts of hurt and harm there is room for elite sporting performers, sports administrators and coaches to make decisions that could have a negative impact on the participants' well-being.

The playing of sport – the re-enactment of play-like behaviour in an environment where a codified set of rules and regulations are administered upon proceedings – may go some way to reducing the tension of everyday life.[1] It is the utterance 'Be careful!', all too familiar within our childhood, that is interrogated throughout this book in three elite sporting contexts. It is within the act of playing in a more formalised environment, while trying to 'be careful', that injury rears its ugly head. In the context of elite sporting practices the onset of hurt and related pain and injury are of crucial importance. Hurt can be seen as the cause of bodily or physical pain, whereas the harm that may confront the body is the agent of hurt. Although closely related, pain and injury are physically and conceptually distinct. Pain is a subjective phenomenon, and this has led to its exclusion from much discussion of injury, which may be seen as more objective. Injury can be understood as a breakdown in the structure of the body, a breakdown that may affect its function. Pain is the marker of an injury, and is an unpleasant sensory and emotional experience associated with actual or potential tissue and skeletal damage.

As elite sport rationalises formal play further, the inclusion of provision for sport science support to enhance performance (Blake 1996; Hoberman 1992) and the management of pain and injury through sports medicine have greater impact upon the cultural identity of sporting communities. The professionalisation of sport is a form of rationalisation, since the shift from amateur to professional ethos in sports may be a justification for elite sporting participants who spend so much time and energy in the pursuit of sporting excellence. The fact that involvement can increasingly cause harm to participants is largely ignored. This shift is not as simple as it first appears. While it is only recently that sports such as athletics and rugby union have come to be seen as formally professional, there have long been links between the amateur sports of Victorian gentlemen and the professional sporting participant.

The development of innovative technology, which has led to the enhancing of sporting performance, was the result of experimentation by professional sporting participants and their coaches. These innovations could be commercially exploited to provide the best equipment and methods for the recreational amateur (Park 1992a; Wigglesworth 1996). The development of scientific performance enhancement by professionals helped amateurs but created tension for sporting administrators in sports such as rugby union and athletics, who felt that the amateur sporting ideal was being eroded (Smith 2000). In other sports such as cricket, where the distinction between amateur and professional players remained clear, players from different socio-economic backgrounds could turn out for the same team and be playing within the rules of the game (Allison 2001).

Social, economic and political shifts in the approach to sporting practice from amateur to professional are central to this book, which is informed by the anthropological study of sports medicine. It is an attempt to explain the transformations that have taken place in three elite sporting environments where medical practice has assumed greater importance. As the title of the book suggests, this work is primarily concerned with issues of pain, injury and risk, but, importantly, it focuses upon how this triplex is transformed in the sporting world, which at the elite level has become increasingly commercialised. Pain and injury in the past meant missing competitions or taking a break from the rigour of training. In the world of commercialised sport, however, being injured and being unable to perform takes on a more significant meaning. The three ethnographic case studies included in this volume – Welsh rugby union, British club athletics and Paralympic sport – contextualise the new significance of pain and injury in the sporting environment, where results and performances matter financially sometimes more than they do emotionally for the participants. Injury can mean that an elite-sporting participant has to look for a new career, and such harsh socio-economic realities must have an influence on sporting habitus. I am using the concept of habitus as it is defined in the work of Bourdieu (1977, 1990, 1993). Specifically, I am referring to how an actor embodies the cultural convention of the social group of which they are a member.[2]

This text is very much a reflection of my life experience since, as a four-time Canadian Paralympian (1988–2000) who has trained as an athlete in the social environment of an athletics club in Britain, I have on more than one occasion been in severe pain as a result of injury. In both the environment of the athletics club and various disabled sporting festivals I have been well situated, physically, to undertake ethnographic research. In the case of Welsh rugby the association was more contrived. I spent several years in Wales investigating the importance of the professionalisation of sports medicine and the impact it had on the transformation of amateur rugby to a professional concern (Howe 1997) as part of the rites of passage of an amateur anthropologist. This research led me to examine more fully the importance of pain and injury in the world of club athletics and the Paralympic movement. Because of my personal commitment to the subject matter, the focus of this book is not dissimilar to that of the vast majority of ethnographic studies undertaken within the discipline of anthropology (Clifford and Marcus 1986; Marcus and Fischer 1986), which have led to the debate surrounding degrees of objectivity obtainable through social scientific research.

My interest in the medical anthropology of sport came primarily from personal experience as an injured elite athlete. I was born with mild congenital cerebral palsy that affects the functioning of one hemisphere of my body, which means that my running is not as efficient as that of an 'able' elite runner. While undertaking my Master's in anthropology at the University of Toronto I was also preparing to compete in the 1992 Paralympic Games, which were held in Barcelona, Spain. At this time I fell foul of an athletic injury (Achilles tendinitis) and began a year-long rehabilitation process that eventually laid the seed for this research. Visiting the sports medicine clinic, in the first instance for curative treatment and then for preventive measures, I began to consider the social implications of being an injured athlete. Literature searches followed but no ethnographic studies had examined the questions that I was asking myself – for example, 'What social impact has the professionalisation of sports medicine had upon an elite sporting participant?' and 'Do pain and injury and the way in which particular sporting cultures treat them have an impact on the development of a culture of risk?' As I came to terms with the frailty of my own body, I became concerned with the structure of sporting culture and how it is constructed to sideline or eliminate discussions of the issues surrounding pain and injury.

Work in the field of the sociology of sport (Curry and Strauss 1994; Nixon 1992, 1993a, b; White et al. 1995) had gone some way to illuminating a social understanding of the phenomena of pain, injury and risk. Research by Waddington (1996, 2000) and Hoberman (1992) was helpful in contextualising the social importance of sports medicine. In fact, it is the title of Hoberman's work *Mortal Engines* (1992) and his discussion of the body as an engine that first enabled me to conceptualise my personal experience of sports injury and risk, and that led to many of the observations in this book. When I turned to the anthropological literature on sport, however, it was limited, and no studies had addressed the issues that are central to this book. I felt that an ethnographic exploration of the issue would further enlighten these discussions (see also Howe 2001). What follows is a brief justification for ethnographic research into this particular aspect of the anthropology of sport.

Sport and ethnography

Anthropology, the traditional 'home' of ethnography, has been rather slow to examine the social milieu surrounding sport. The importance placed on the utilitarian nature of culture in traditional anthropology, as opposed to the expressive dimensions of culture, of which sport is a part, may help to explain this absence (Chick 1998). While early work by anthropologists such as Tylor (1896), Firth (1931) and Lesser (1933) examined the importance of sport in the social world, few have followed in their footsteps. Anthropologists such as Geertz (1973) and Foley (1990) have used the anthropological lens to examine sport, although sport was not their prime focus. The history of the anthropology of sport (see Blanchard 1995; Sands 1999a) is rather limited, but the adoption of ethnography as a cross-disciplinary methodological tool for furthering our understanding of the sporting world should be seen as a major contribution by anthropology to social research regarding sport. The related discipline of sociology has increasingly been the focus of high-quality research into the social environment surrounding sport,[3] some of which has adopted ethnographic methods.

Over the past decade there has been an increase in the use of participant observation as a primary ethnographic tool for detailing sporting communities. Important ethnographic studies have been produced by anthropologists such as Armstrong (1998) on football hooligans, Foley (1990) on American football, Klein (1991, 1993) on baseball and body-building, as well as several collections in the form of edited volumes (Armstrong and Giulianotti 1997; MacClancy 1996; Sands 1999b). Meanwhile, the work by Wheaton (1997, 2000) and Wheaton and Tomlinson (1998) on windsurfing, and that by Sugden (1996) and by Mennesson (2000) on men's and women's boxing respectively, are examples of how social scientists have embraced ethnography and put it to constructive use in describing and understanding the functioning of sporting cultures and in chronicling the transformation of these cultures.

One of the important advantages of the ethnographic method for the study of pain and injury in a unique sporting context is that pains can be recorded as they occur, and the ethnographer is able to observe their impact on both the individual concerned and the sporting communities to which they belong. Over time, the anguish of an acute pain and injury may be forgotten. This is a potential difficulty for researchers interviewing sportsmen and -women 'at a distance' from their injuries. Furthermore, if an acute pain develops into chronic pain, it becomes a private or semi-private experience, being usually shared by the player only with the club's sports medicine team and external 'others' such as the anthropologist assisting in the treatment room. I adopted numerous participatory roles while undertaking this research. I was, among other things, a 'water-boy' and general 'gofer' while exploring Welsh rugby; an elite distance runner while exploring the culture of distance runners; and both a competitor and a sports politician in the world of Paralympic sport. The manner in which data have been collected for this book highlights the distinctiveness of participant observation. It is the establishment of personal relationships that is the primary vehicle for the collection of data. Following the assertion of Last (1981), other research methodologies enable an exploration of the known social world of the 'natives', but the important element that ethnography can add to the research project is that it can facilitate an understanding of the hitherto 'unknown'[4] elements of a particular community because of the intimacy that participant observation can afford.

Ethnography has undoubtedly enhanced understanding of sporting cultures and communities. It is an approach, however, that has been subject to critique both within and without anthropology. Notably, the traditional view within anthropology of an objective social science has been brought into question, leading to a 'crisis of representation' within the discipline and elsewhere in the social sciences (Clifford and Marcus 1986; Marcus and Fischer 1986). This crisis made it clear that anthropologists must attend to the epistemological uncertainties of their writings. It has also made them acutely aware of the importance of reflection both on the process of 'doing' ethnography and also on the subjects of their investigations (James et al. 1997).

Therefore, those adopting ethnography as a research approach in sport-related research became more sensitive to their own identity and the impact that this has on their research findings. De Garis (1999) has gone so far as to suggest that ethnography of sport should be 'sensualised' in order that the participant observer records all aspects of experience of fieldwork that can be articulated. In other words, as well as recording the actions, behaviour and views of individuals and groups within the community under investigation, the ethnographer should record the sights, sounds and smells experienced during fieldwork. In the case of the ethnography of pain and injury, the 'snap' of a tendon, the 'crunch' of a tackle and the 'grimace' of pain can all be recorded in this manner. This approach to ethnographic representation, coupled with other methodologies that are more commonly employed in social investigations of the sport (through interviews and surveys[5]), leads to a more complete understanding of the sporting world and in particular its relationship with pain and injury. The fact that anthropology until recently has been more interested in the colonial 'other' has meant that while medicine has been one of the foci of the anthropological lens, Western constructs such as sports medicine have been missed by the gaze.

By adopting ethnographic methods, and following on from works such as the seminal paper 'Medicine as an Institution of Social Control' (Zola 1972), this book examines how medicine has impacted upon particular sporting environments. The development of fields such as the anthropology of medicine has been devoid of research into the nature of medicine as it pertains to sport. Sports medicine in its modern form is a reasonably new medical sub-discipline, and the anthropological investigation of medical practice has until recently focused on the role of traditional medical systems in non-Western contexts. With the increased interest in an anthropological analysis of Western medical practice, an exploration of sports medicine is timely.

Structure of the book

The book is divided into three parts. Part I is entitled 'The Cultural Nexus: Sports Medicine and the Commercial Body', and sets out the background for the book. Part II, 'Pain, Injury and the Culture of Risk', explores conceptual distinctions and the social importance of central terms. Finally, Part III, 'Theory into Practice', presents the case studies.

Part I is divided into three chapters that should be seen as intertwining threads of the argument that is central to the book. The argument is that the professionalisation of sports medicine is a response to commercial pressures placed upon sports authorities that ultimately have an impact on how elite sporting participants are treated when their bodies are in pain and injured. Part I therefore provides the underpinning argument for the remainder of the book.

Chapter 1 explores the importance of medicine in the context of sport, highlighting particular shifts in social attitudes to issues related to health and illness, and demonstrating their impact on the medical fraternity (and therefore the provisions made available for those who engage in sporting practice). Sports medicine is explored first by examining the discipline's early development and how it was shaped by issues related to health risks such as over-exertion of the heart and an increased understanding of the importance of physical activity. A brief discussion of the forms of sports medicine is followed by a broader examination of the medical anthropological literature. The focus is then turned towards issues related to illicit performance enhancement and how this in turn is acting as a catalyst for the commercialisation of sports-related products.

Chapter 2 explores the importance of the social investigation of the body as it is related to sporting practice, and pain and injury specifically. When the social investigation of sporting culture is broken down to its lowest common denominator there is one tool with which a sportsperson has to work: the body. By exploring the work of the key social theorists Bourdieu and Foucault, this chapter highlights why academic discussions of pain, injury and risk in the context of sport must be contextualised within the literature regarding the body as a social object. The living body is central to much of this exploration (Williams and Bendelow 1998), and throughout this book, paying direct attention to the concept of embodiment of sporting practice is fundamental to the argument. It is my contention that medical provision, commercialisation and the body are all of equal relevance when it comes to exploring pain, injury and risk.

Chapter 3 highlights the shift in attitude that occurs when a sport is transformed from a pastime into a spectacle (Guttmann 1986). The impact of commercialisation upon sports that have traditionally been associated with the ideology of amateurism appears to have some widespread effects, not least in the participants' desire to be rewarded for the sacrifices that they make in terms of undermining their health and well-being – that is, the physical wear and tear on their bodies. These rewards are not always financial. Nevertheless, as commercialism intensifies in newly professionalised sports such as athletics and Paralympic sports, it is clear that there is an increasing desire among athletes that high performance be financially rewarded and compensation be received for the harm and risks to which their bodies are exposed.

Part II of the book deals more specifically with the concepts of 'pain', 'injury' and 'risk'. In Chapter 4 the conceptual distinction between 'pain' and 'injury' is articulated. Specific types of pain are also explored, and a discussion of the treatment of pain and how it may be alleviated follows. Importantly, in this chapter the positive aspect of pain that is foundational in traditional physical training methods – an aspect of the concept of pain that has largely been ignored in the social science literature related to sport – is explained. The chapter closes with a look at the conceptual relations of 'pain' and 'risk', since in the commercial environment of professional sport the concepts are inextricably linked.

Chapter 5 investigates the importance of injury in the commercialised sports world. The discussion begins with an examination of distinctive types of injury and how they are regulated in the context of the ever-changing social environment surrounding sport. This is followed by a consideration of the importance of time in the management and treatment of injury. As pressure on both the sporting participant and the medical treatment staff increases, time away from the field of play due to injury is an important issue and may often be exacerbated by misdiagnosis of injury by treatment staff. Such misdiagnosis can lead to mismanagement of treatment of injuries. The proper (and improper) treatment of injuries can be improved in many cases by the administering of placebos. This has important implications for those for whom limiting the athletes' time away from their sport is essential: the elite sporting participants, the medical treatment team and management of both the club and the sport.

Risk culture, as the product of pain and injury, is the focus of Chapter 6. In particular, this chapter explores issues related to the socialisation that is part and parcel of elite sporting culture, and how this frequently makes the acceptance of risk an inevitable consequence of professional participation in sport. The acceptance of risk and the development of lay knowledge of the function of the body in sport may also be seen to be linked to the quest for a perfect sporting body by both the elite sporting performers and the public. This also has implications for disabled sporting performers who have 'imperfect' sporting bodies. Related to both these populations is the risk of drug use and how this may be linked to the quest for the ideal body.

Part III of the book is devoted to case studies that illustrate how various sports have recently been transformed by their use of sports medicine in the context of professionalism and commercialisation. The cases of rugby union in Wales, distance runners and Paralympic athletes evidence how elite sporting cultures have distinctive ways of dealing with pain and injury. Most notably, while professional rugby players have medical support close at hand during both games and club training sessions, distance runners or Paralympians do not have this facility unless they are at a major competition. This clearly shapes the way in which an elite sporting performer understands and relates to pain and injury in their particular sporting context.

The book closes by articulating a way forward for research into the professionalisation of sports medicine. Through the use of the ethnographic method of participant observation, an increased understanding of the dilemma that faces both elite sporting performers and sports medicine practitioners can be achieved. In a world of commercialised sport, should a serious injury occur, time away from training and competition may mean the loss of wages. Documenting how this time away from the 'field of play' is used may go some way to increasing our understanding of how specific sporting cultures deal with the hardship of pain and injury. By using diachronic case studies, a more complete picture of elite sporting performers' health and livelihood, and the choices they have to make regarding them, can be established.

Part I

The cultural nexus

Sports medicine and the commercial body

Chapter 1

Investigating sports medicine
Medical anthropology in context

The structure and organisation of medicine as it relates to sport has a profound impact on the manner in which elite sporting performers are treated when they become injured. This chapter will start by exploring the foundation of modern sports medicine in order to establish a background for understanding the medical treatment of injury today. It has long been assumed that the heart is the most important organ in the body, and by focusing on the athlete's heart and elementary understandings of it in relation to physical activity, this chapter will enable readers to ground their understanding in the history of sports medicine. After this discussion the chapter turns to explore the relationship between medical anthropology, sport and performance-enhancing substances.

Research into the social significance of sports medicine has increased in recent years (Berryman and Park 1992; Hoberman 1992; Waddington 1996, 2000). This trend highlights the fact that the 'social' is an important consideration in the treatment of injury in spite of the fact that medical practitioners are concerned with treating the physical side of injury that often follows participation in sport (Park 1992a). Today the concerns of medical professionals are still seldom of a social nature, yet there is greater understanding that participation in sport is not always good for one's health (Waddington 2000), and as a participant gets more competitive, the risk of their getting injured also increases. In the light of this, the World Medical Association (WMA) has since 1981 produced guidelines for medical professionals who work with sporting performers (Grayson 1999) – the first guidelines on a global scale for the ethical practice of sports medicine, signalling the importance of the medical treatment that sporting performers receive in this age of ever-increasing professionalism.

A shift of the focus found in those studies of health and lay knowledge (Nettleton 1995) that emphasised lifestyle is of importance here. In fact, the shift from the pursuit of sporting success to enhanced sporting performance in order to achieve success can be articulated as a change in lifestyle priorities. In an era where professionalism at the elite level is the dominant sporting paradigm, simple sports training will not suffice. A participant must transform both dietary practice and overall fitness regimes in order to be ready to undertake the specific training necessary for the achievement of sporting success. With this more intense preparation comes an increased risk of sustaining an injury (Nixon 1993a), and therefore the tension that exists between the health benefits of sport and the ills that long-term serious participation entails means that sports medicine for practitioners is fraught with difficulties. What advice do you give to the participant who repeatedly returns with the same injury? Are you as a medical professional answerable to your patient (the injured party) or to the club that is paying for your services? These are not easy questions to answer. A study by Roderick *et al.* (2000) highlights the difficulty of managing injury in the world of professional football (soccer), and their data are not dissimilar to those gathered in the cultural context of professional rugby union, elite distance running and Paralympic sports, the case studies included in this volume.

The transformations of the manner in which injury is treated by sports medicine teams involved with elite rugby in South Wales, athletics in Britain and Paralympic sport internationally have had a marked impact on how these activities have developed into professionally and commercially viable sports. The transformation to commercialism may be seen as a result of the symbiotic relationship with sports medicine since the management of injury has an impact on the success and failure of sportsmen and sportswomen in competitive environments. Perhaps more importantly, injury to 'stars' has a long-term effect on the number of spectators drawn to the sporting arena. In this chapter I will address some key historical issues that have shaped the medical world as it relates to sport. These ideas will be contextualised and an attempt will be made to uncover why, until recently, sport has been marginalised in the medical anthropological and sociological literature.

The beginnings of sports medicine

It has been suggested that the origins of sports medicine can be traced back to the ancient Greeks and Romans (Berryman 1992; Ryan 1989). However, for the purpose of this book, the seeds of the foundations of modern sports medicine will be considered to have been sown in Britain and the United States at the beginning of the nineteenth century. Sports medicine, therefore, may be defined as the 'systematic application of the principles of medicine and science to the study of sporting performance and the institutionalisation of this practice in the form of professional associations, research establishments, scientific conferences and journals' (Waddington 1996: 177).

The evolution of a medical sub-discipline takes time, and the brief history of the discipline that follows will show that it has taken almost two centuries to develop into the form that is in existence today. The use of the term 'sports medicine' was a relatively late invention, and Ryan (1989) has suggested that the first use of the term was in 1928. Doctors attending the Second Winter Olympic Games at St Moritz, Switzerland, felt a need to adopt a title to describe their work with sportsmen and -women and the treatments that they provided for them, as well as the research carried out using athletes as the focus. A meeting of physicians was held, and the very fact that many nations had team medical staff implies that sports medicine had existed for some time. At this meeting the first international association was established; today it is called the Fédération Internationale de Médecine Sportive (FIMS). A German publication entitled *Grundriss der Sportsmedizin* by Dr F. Herxheimer, which appeared in 1933, was the first book to use the term in its title. It was almost thirty years before the first book in English used the term, in J.G.P. Williams's 1962 work *Sports Medicine* (Ryan 1989: 4).

However, before a formal structure could be established for the organisation of modern sports medicine, the considerations with respect to the training of sporting participants, including their diets and general understanding, provided the focus for the medical sciences. Early researchers were not interested in issues of how to enhance performance as a goal to be achieved by those who were after sporting success, but simply wished to explore how the human body worked (Hoberman 1992). The examination of the early history of sports medicine is problematic since historical materials are relatively scarce. It should be realised that, like most other developments, the evolution of sports medicine is not a simple evolutionary continuum. Fundamental to this discussion is the fact that the aims and objectives of early sports medicine were different from the goals of sports medicine provision of today. This difference is not simply a result of greater knowledge (Waddington 1996), but lies in the fact that early studies adopted both a practical and a theoretical approach to sport.

One of the foremost historians of the field, Roberta Park, has suggested that Walter Thom's *Pedestrianism*, published in 1813, should be considered the first modern treatise on athletic training (Park 1992a). Much of what was written in the early part of the nineteenth century may have been passed down from one generation to the next. The transmission of experience or lay knowledge was fundamental in the establishment of the discipline of sports medicine. Once this knowledge and experience were passed on to literate men with access to publishing houses, they were able to make the knowledge more public. So the understanding of these principles could be considerably older than their date of publication on account of the fact that most early trainers and athletes were of a working-class background and as a result probably lacked literacy.

Park, commenting on these early training methods, has suggested that their exponents relied on simple physiological similarities when deriving the connection between diet and performance. For example, the diet of the performer was strictly monitored: 'The athlete had particular need to reduce fat and build muscle. Therefore, the Georgian pugilist and pedestrian was advised to eat large quantities of lean, red meat [which most resembled muscle, the flesh it was supposed to build]' (Park 1992a: 61). Most training manuals, furthermore, made a point of advising that beef be served rare or 'undone', seemingly agreeing with the ancient vegetarian charge that carnivorous eating habits created an aggressive carnivorous behaviour. Foods could therefore be classified at this time by trainers as purgative, weakening or strengthening. As a result, it was felt to be ideal to cleanse the whole athlete's body before serious training could begin. This was demonstrated through the act of purging the body:

> [T]he trainer must attend to the state of the athlete's bowels. . . . After the physicking, regular exercise began, gradually increasing in intensity as the athlete progressed toward the day of competition. Regularity was deemed essential since both the mind and the body must be disciplined. The trainer was enjoined to keep a watchful vigil to insure that the athlete did not deviate from the prescribed regimen.
>
> (Park 1992a: 63)

There was an understanding that an athlete's training should be monitored in much the same manner as is considered normative today. It is interesting, however, that at the end of the nineteenth century, as the ideals for the modern Olympic games were being developed, amateurism in sport was considered the ideal (Allison 2001); thus outside influences (such as professional coaching) on the athletes were frowned upon. Yet fifty years earlier, sporting manuals for gentlemen had begun to include details of training regimes.

More popular publications of training schedules coincided with the first athletic matches between Oxford and Cambridge, which were run in 1864. These were established for the participation of gentlemen and were designed to exclude professional sportsmen. A similar situation was evident across the Atlantic: 'Albert G. Spalding became the arbiter of American "amateur" sport, establishing the *Spalding Library of American Sport* in 1885 to provide up-to-date information on training methods, techniques, and "records" – as well as to advertise his expanding business' (Park 1992a: 72). Sport became a pastime for gentlemen, and therefore those involved in sport began to consume goods related to sport. At about this time, particularly in the United States, populations were making the transition from rural to urban environments, and medical practitioners became concerned for the health of those making the transition:

> During the nineteenth century particularly American physicians, worried by the increasing sedentariness of a nation rapidly changing

from a rural to an urban life-style, exhorted the public to counteract the staleness of the counting room with the exhilaration of the field and the gymnasium.

(Whorton 1992a: 109)

The debate that ensued on both sides of the Atlantic over the consequences of athleticism, in terms of the impact on the bodies of participants, played an important role in the evolution of sports medicine as an area of specialisation (Hoberman 1992; Waddington 2000; Whorton 1992a).

Also of importance were issues related to hygiene. Games played outdoors were felt to have greater hygienic value because the fresh air of the natural environment was seen as more beneficial to the organs of the human animal, the product of a long process of biological evolution within nature. In 1859 Darwin's famous book *On the Origin of Species* had a profound effect on the conceptualisation of the human organism. In the light of this new understanding and the resulting implications, the Church developed a new approach to the understanding of the human body. In the 1860s, 'Muscular Christianity' became a kind of social gospel that affirmed the compatibility of the robust physical life with the life of Christian morality and service, which contended that bodily strength built character and righteousness and usefulness for God's (and the nation's) work (Haley 1978). In spite of the good associated with this type of 'physical culture', many early physiologists expressed concern for the well-being of athletes.

Risk: the athlete's heart

Initial concerns about the risks in sport in the nineteenth century centred around the belief that the push for victory might lead people to overextend themselves. The physical exertion imposed on sporting performers was of concern to the medical fraternity. While today even a lay knowledge of exercise will attest to the fact that physical exertion that is appropriately controlled is a health benefit, in the past some physicians worried about the strain on the heart. Perhaps one of the reasons that early amateur sport was not concerned about drawing spectators was that the spectators would whip performers into frenzy, thus increasing their flow of adrenaline and so driving them to exhaustion. While spectator enthusiasm is a desired quality in any modern sporting occasion, the fear for the safety of the competitors was apparent in early writings, where it is suggested by Whorton that

> The heart was the most obviously vital of organs, and the one whose functioning, in the form of accelerated beat, was most clearly affected by exercise. Heart attack victims were often stricken while engaged in exercise or work, and even though athletes completing a game or race

were not experiencing cardiac failure, their appearance of pained breath-lessness and exhaustion aroused an uneasy wonder in the spectators.

(1992a: 116)

During this time of 'elemental' physiological understanding, industrial society as a whole began to shift towards brainpower as an ideal as opposed to brawn; so athletes were seen as physiological profligates riddled with the damages of training for competition. Such damage could range from prob-lems with their sex life and/or marriage, sporting suicide indicative of too great a desire for victory, and increased levels of moral and/or physical stress. In spite of such concerns expressed by the medical community, athletes were seldom willing to put their faith in the medical establishment. On the one hand, the medical experts were sympathetic to the athletes' desire for increased fitness (as in the case of the amateur gentleman), and on the other, they were disparaging (to the working-class professional sportsman). Regardless of their background,

> Athletes would be athletes, and doctors could only warn them of the consequences for later life and hope that gradually they would pay heed. In the meantime, it was imperative to stand vigil over young competi-tors and rescue any showing evidence of immediate injury from athletics by barring them from further participation in sports or any strenuous exercise.
>
> (Whorton 1992a: 121)

In 1867 the respected London doctor F.C. Skey wrote to the editor of *The Times* expressing concern for the health of the rowers in that year's Oxford–Cambridge boat race. This letter stated his opinion that sporting activities were bad for the health of the participants:

> I have the strongest reason for believing that this struggle for pre-eminence is fraught with evil consequences to the competitors to a degree not generally contemplated. . . . The young men enter the boat apparently in the condition of vigorous health. Having accomplished their arduous task, they are thoroughly exhausted . . . they have been on occasions so reduced in strength as to be unable to rise from their seats.
>
> (*The Times*, 10 October 1867)

In the several days following the publication of this letter, rebuttals were published in the letters to the editor of the paper, countering the claims made by Skey. One letter in particular by F. Willan, the president of Oxford University Boat Club, cited his experience as a rower as evidence to negate the doctor's statements about participation in physical activity. Willan

(1867) also suggests that if there were any experimental data to add weight to the doctor's assertions, he most certainly would have quoted them.

The establishment of the modern Olympic Games stimulated considerable debate about the effect of stress on the body arising from sporting activity. Dr Philippe Tissié of France was one of those who was concerned. His views were in direct opposition to those of Pierre de Coubertin (who was later to become known as the father of the modern Olympics), since Tissié felt that over-exertion in the sporting arena was bad for health and could even lead to death. At the conference of the French Association for the Advancement of Science, in 1894, Tissié successfully opposed de Coubertin's appeal for track and field events to be held to demonstrate new scientific principles (Hoberman 1992: 80–84). While this debate continued on both sides of the Atlantic until well into the twentieth century, athletic heart syndrome (Morse 1972) is now seen as a positive factor, and a strong heart established through a healthy lifestyle is paramount to well-being. As ideas related to physical exercise became more acceptable to the educated public, there was a shift in attitudes towards those who were involved in such activities.

Culture and physical activity

Early ideas about exercise came from professional trainers and athletes, but as these ideas filtered through to the establishment, gentlemen became more aware of their body as a physical entity that should not be left to waste. As a result, exercise became as much about social control as it was about hygiene. In Britain the diffusion of games, which were developed at public schools, to the far corners of the empire made for a popular means of exposing the peoples of the colonies to some of the values that the ruling classes in Britain held so dear. Unlike Hargreaves (1986), I do not see this as exposing these people to social control, but rather as a more sympathetic way of enculturating these diverse peoples into some of the fundamental principles of Western philosophy. In Britain itself, the dissemination of upper-middle-class values through the codification of games such as association and rugby football meant that those values took on distinctive meanings in working-class communities that adopted them as pastimes.

Investigations undertaken by experts in sports medicine at the turn of the century suggest that they had no desire to improve the athletic potential of the sportsmen they were researching. Those interested in human physiology, for example, approached sport as any other area of human physical endeavour and as part of a larger collection of interesting scientific data:

> The scientists who turned their attention to athletic physiology during the late nineteenth and early twentieth centuries did so not to produce athletic wonders but to measure and otherwise explore the biological

wonders presented by the high-performance athlete of the era. It was a time when phenomena once considered mere curiosities or freaks of nature called out for scientific investigation.

(Hoberman 1992: 8)

Medical researchers were largely influenced by the desire to discover why certain bodily treatments could lead to healthier individuals, and there was no aspiration to improve performance through any similar investigation:

> The primary interest of these scientists was to discover the natural laws that regulated the functioning of the body. If they did not express an interest in applying science to the boosting of athletic performance it was in part because the scientific mysteries they found in the world of high-performance sport were already exciting enough.
>
> (Hoberman 1992: 10)

Because nation-building was still a priority in the United States, a different view as to how sport could be utilised in expansion of the nation was developed in that country. In the United States, physical educators were very much concerned with how organised sport and recreation could add to society's betterment.

> The 'self-made' man had shaped himself by acting upon the material world and testing himself in the crucible of competition. Perhaps nowhere were the changes more graphically conveyed than in athletic games where the body in action was (and is) spectacularly displayed.
>
> (Park 1992b: 141)

Therefore, sport may have been seen to embody many of the qualities of late-nineteenth-century American maleness as portrayed in the popular images of the cowboy or cavalryman (Cooper 1998; Park 1992b). In this way, in the 1890s the evolution of physical education took on differing roles in the United States and in England. The former was still being built into a nation and the latter considered itself the custodian of an empire.

Also in the 1890s, institutions of higher education, such as Harvard University, began to establish degree programmes in disciplines related to physical education; a particular one focused on anatomy, physiology and physical training (Park 1992b). Some thirty years after the establishment of degree courses in the United States, the Germans opened the world's first college devoted entirely to sport in 1920, whose syllabus included medical components. Whereas work undertaken in the United States was concerned more with the physical culture of the citizens, the Germans appeared to have a greater concern for how the human body functioned physiologically (Hoberman 1992). The programmes at universities varied depending on the training of the director of each course; medical doctors were more clinical than experimental, whereas physiologists were more experimental than clinical. As a result of these academic investigations of sport and exercise, books began to be more frequently published on aspects related to physical education. For example, G.S. Hall's work of 1904 titled *Adolescence, Its Psychology and Its Relations to Physiology, Anthropology, Sociology, Sex, Crime, Religion and Education* is typical of the work that was being produced during this period.

Improvements in medical treatment in the nineteenth century had helped the cause of the study of physical culture. The use of such medicines as anaesthetics began to make physical pain seem abnormal, and so the expectation of comfort was increased. As medicine concerned itself with the details of proof, a popular culture of fads and cure-alls catered to the notion that those in the West had not only a right to pursue physical contentment but a right to be consumers of it as well. This affected how athletes trained for sport, and as a result, sport became linked to personal and public health. It has been suggested that

> the goals of sport altered and increasingly centred on the individual's own satisfaction as the object of one's efforts, [and as a consequence] the scientific impulse was to falter. If the goal of sport became the service of the individual and if the individual was by definition unique, then one could not truly test and verify results nor predictively reproduce them.
>
> (Mrozek 1992: 284)

To justify the care for the individual body by the gain society would reap from its health became less necessary. It was enough that individuals enjoyed the physicality of their bodies, which as a result of societal acceptance allowed them to experience personal well-being. This led to the decline of such 'physical' programmes as the posture movement in the United States, which had medical backing with no real scientific justification. Such movements were based on a belief that good posture led to better physical presence and could be justified on account of the fact that to slouch was felt to be a visible abnormality. Interestingly, chiropractors and osteopaths, who play an important role in spinal realignment today, were until relatively recently seen as quacks.

> The true believer may claim that his 'physical faith,' much like a religious one, is only made to appear false when its tenets are taken out of context. For those faithful to the physical regimen, each tenet can survive rigorous scrutiny by arguing that the value of each specific remedy or routine comes only when practised holistically.
>
> (Mrozek 1992: 291)

As a result of this shift in attitude towards the self and the right to the feeling of well-being on the part of individual sportsmen, individuals began to become interested in how sports medicine could improve their own personal physical performance. Countries began to establish associations to regulate further research in the area.

Since the 1950s, all major Western nations have established sports medicine organisations that practitioners can use to guide their conduct, in keeping with research agendas, with respect to the treatment of injury and ethics. The British Association of Sports Medicine (BASM) was founded in 1953. Development of such formal associations is seen by many as positive; however, it could be argued that they exclude methods of treatment that are of a holistic nature which, as a result of this holism, may be better for treating the ills of athletes.

Sports medicine has developed in such a way that sports clubs of even the poorest standard have acquired ultrasound and interferential machines, and other, similar equipment. In comparison to the standard ice/heat treatment frequently used in the past, these resources help increase the speed of recovery from soft-tissue injury. This new technology has, however, brought a need for a greater understanding of the body's physiology, not so much to operate the machine as to 'sell' the benefits to the injured. In this respect it is believed that this modern technology has a far greater placebo effect.

The technologies that are available in most clubs' treatment rooms have done little to directly increase individuals' 'field' performance. As mentioned earlier, the longer a star player is off the pitch, the more the quality of the squad's play is likely to suffer. This realisation has led to an increase in the use of preventive methods of injury treatment such as the implementation of stretching programmes and massage therapy.

The use of massage continues in the clinics of sports club, and it is my belief that the suppleness that is derived from this regular practice, in addition to stretching regimes, goes a long way towards the elimination of many minor soft-tissue injuries. Although the use of massage has a long history within sports medicine, its use today has taken on greater significance since this method of injury treatment has been reinvented. Massage today is important in the curative phase of rehabilitation as well as for its more traditional role of injury prevention. The incorporation of sports massage and osteopathy into the formal structure of sports medicine clinics has been achieved as a result of athletes having a better understanding of their bodies, and the evolution in contemporary sports medicine may be seen as bearing witness to the emancipation of the athletes.

Forms of sports medicine

As we examine the social relationship between sports injury and the development of professional sporting practice, it should be remembered that there are two forms of sports medicine at work at any one time. The first of these forms is *theoretical*. Much of the research and development that was carried out in sports medicine around the end of the nineteenth century had been initiated as a result of the general quest for knowledge concerning the human body (Hoberman 1992). This in the broadest sense may be termed sports science, since early investigations were undertaken to answer questions that were part of a general scientific inquiry. Areas of research included physiology, psychology and anatomy, which are now considered in various forms as sub-disciplines of modern sports science as well as sports medicine.

Practical sports medicine has two avenues of development: one that has been designed to improve the treatment of injury, and the other that uses new technology to increase performance. The evolution of treatment techniques that form *practical* sports medicine is a result of the scientific advances of *theoretical* sports medicine and takes on two forms: *curative* and *preventive*. Only well tried and tested methods of injury treatment are actually put into practice. This is, of course, partly due to a concern for the health of the athletes but is also a result of many grass-roots practitioners, whether properly qualified doctors or lay people, being slow to adapt to new technologies and techniques of treatment.

It is both the treatment techniques and the performance enhancement facets of the *practical* application of sports medicine with which this book is primarily concerned. Physiotherapists and club doctors (often the local general practitioner (GP)) are the individuals who have 'direct' contact with the players, as they are the link between medicine and health or illness. Consumer-driven practical sports medicine such as dietary supplements and more technically justified workout regimes, which are put into practice by various members of a sports medicine team, are also of interest. It is by examining the evolution of sports medicine at a more theoretical level, however, that a better understanding of the social dissemination of medical knowledge will be established. This will enable the researcher to see why medical staff at sports clubs do what they do, giving a better understanding of how modern practical sports medicine effects the treatment of ills, and what impact this can have on the habits of a sporting environment.

The treatment of injury at the time that it occurs has changed less than it has in the sports medicine clinic, and therefore the initial treatment of injury in sports like rugby and football has changed less than in athletics, for example. One of the major differences in 'sideline' treatment is that more precaution is now taken in treating open wounds 'in the field' as a consequence of the fear of AIDS. For example, a rugby player may be substituted for up to ten minutes while he has the wound stitched and covered, whereas in the past, cuts as a result of the game's combative nature were not as great a concern. However, except for the introduction of 'aerosol ice', which eliminates the pain of hard knocks, not much has changed from the days of the 'magic sponge'.[1]

This may go some distance to explaining why social scientists, while quick to realise the importance of commercialism and the effects of the media on sport, have been rather negligent in examining the evolution of sports medicine. Much of what has been written in regard to the social value of sports medicine is related to its commercial implications. One only has to witness the proliferation of written material that has been produced as a result of a market-driven push for the West's demand for healthy living. By examining the evolution of *theoretical* sports medicine, greater clarity will be achieved in understanding the principles that applied practitioners are using, both in terms of the treatment of injury and in initiating programmes that will ultimately improve performance.

Medical anthropology and sport

There has been a move towards 'a critical epistemology of disease as elements of the moral control of individuals and population' (Turner 1997: ix) within the social sciences of medicine, but little attempt has been made to align this type of thinking to the social context surrounding sport. The fact that sport is often seen as a leisure pursuit or a non-serious pastime may be one of the reasons why medical provision surrounding sport has escaped the social scientist's lens until recently. The work of Zola (1972) highlights the importance of the medicalisation of life since it illuminates the fact that in modern industrial societies medicine is an important tool of social control. Often this process has been seen as hegemonic in nature and yet subtle, allowing for the almost complete medicalising of daily life. The labelling of individuals in society as 'healthy' and 'ill' was an important step in this process, but it was the establishment of these terms relative to the population at large that was key.

It has been argued that 'medical professionals neglect the social experience of patients and the social construction of disease' (Frankenberg 1993: 219). In the case of sport, it is evident from research conducted on participants that treatment teams who look after players in times of injury, particularly from the 'sidelines', see the experience of how an injury occurs as vital to diagnosing the appropriate treatment. As life generally becomes more medicalised, and simple 'complaints' become medical concerns, intervention by medical staff, who are often removed from the context of the injury, can create confusion.

Kleinman (1992: 33) compares medical systems to cultural systems, and in doing so highlights the fact that most of the treatment of ills actually occurs not within professional medical sectors but in the broader social environment which is referred to as 'popular'. The three arenas of the health care system discussed by Kleinman (1992) (the professional, the popular and the folk) enable a useful understanding of the context of the development of sports medicine. It is in the context of the popular and folk arenas that much important sports medicine is carried out. The 'folk', in the context of sports medicine, might bring to mind the 'bucket and sponge' approach to treatment. The 'popular' increasingly suggests the sight of personal negotiation between individuals with respect to their medical treatment – for instance, participants telling professional medical staff that there are issues with respect to their ability to perform when required that may have knock-on consequences for their well-being outside sport.

Here again the work of Zola (1972) can be important, since it highlights four medical issues (ageing, pregnancy, drug addiction and alcoholism) that have now been medicalised. In the not too distant past, the processes of childbirth and ageing would have been considered normal and as a result would have taken place in the popular sphere. Today there are sub-disciplines of medicine that target a patient clientele for each of these physical states. Other associated medical fields, such as psychiatry, have also grown to encompass a larger client base as people become accustomed to an increase in the medical influence on their lives. In many cases, people are concerned about limiting the onset of illness and disease, leading to a growing interest in (and therefore an industry for) preventive medicine.

The development of a preventive paradigm in medicine has led to an increase in medical intervention in an attempt to change lifestyle patterns of individuals. Whether this is geared to diet, exercise or institutional changes in marital relationships, preventive medicine is still largely distributed to patients who have a particular 'concern', and not necessarily to the public. With the ever-increasing influence of the mass media, partially through advertising, such an issue of concern could in fact be implanted in the minds of initially 'unconcerned' consumers. The important thing to note here is that the development of sports medicine has been a slow process, in part because 'health, illness and health-care-related aspects of society are articulated as cultural systems' (Kleinman 1992: 31), and these are slow to transform.

Other scholars (Illich 1975) have argued that the medicalisation of life involves a number of interrelated processes. Where Kleinman (1992) suggests three spheres of context for medical provision, Illich's (1975) work highlights the increased expansion of professional medical provision. This results in situations whereby people who are free of therapy-oriented labels have become the exception. A majority of Western populations are convinced that medical intervention is advisable and have therefore become consumers of medical treatment 'for the simple fact that they are unborn, new-born, infants, in their climacteric, or old' (Illich 1975: 44). Therefore, the medicalisation of life has developed a new dualism in life between those who are patients and those who are not.

The dichotomy of health and illness in the general medicalisation of society has a unique twist where athletes are concerned. While the public consider elite amateurs and professional athletes to be prime examples of fitness, this is, to a large extent, an illusion created by mediated notions of health and fitness. In order to perform regularly on the world's sporting stages, athletes must at some point risk their health. One who does so regularly enough may actually be considered ill[2] as a result of maintaining a level of sporting excellence. It is for this reason that the preventive paradigm has been so important in sports medicine.

Developments in preventive medicine have had a great impact on sports medicine. Some of the processes involved in the medicalisation of sport and this new justification for medical intervention can be seen to combine in sports medicine's ever-expanding literature. In J.P.G. Williams's text *Sports Medicine* (1962) he felt it necessary to establish the legitimacy of sports medicine as a discipline. In the introduction to this text he quotes Sir Arthur Porritt, then the chairman of the British Association for Sport and Medicine, who said, 'those who take part in sport and play games are essentially patients' (Williams 1962: v). Sports medicine has had to be developed since trained athletes are different from other patient populations. What is interesting is that at the time Williams's book was published, the 'fitness boom' was still over a decade away, and yet Williams had realised that physical fitness could have associated medical problems in much the same manner as youth and old age. In spite of this development, much of sports medicine is not administered in the professional realm but in both the popular and the folk environments. Only with the advent of a move to commercial sport has the need for professional sports medicine become clearer.

As sports medicine continues to develop, related disciplines such as exercise physiology, biomechanics and sports psychology have also begun to take off. This is contrary to earlier developments, when in the late nineteenth century the related disciplines were developing towards a larger interest in sport, and medicine was the last to adopt this focus (Park 1992a). This may be seen as an indication of the power of medicine, since it is able to structure how Western society relates to the larger world. Not until medicine focused on sport did related disciplines receive much attention outside the 'academy'. Whereas in the past, athletes often trained in isolation, today's elite have access to a large contingent of advisers, including sports medicine practitioners. These developments have made elite athletes ever more dependent on increasingly sophisticated systems of medical support in their quest to increase performance. Because medicalisation has become so important in the West, there is an underlying belief that coaches and athletes need medical support and innovation to bring about a continual improvement in their level of performance (Sperryn 1983). It is important to remember that unless a sportsperson has a desire to push the performance envelope with the use of illicit substances, it is practical sports medicine that is really at work in this context.

The development of chemical performance-enhancement

Most contemporary volumes on sports medicine contain at least one article or chapter discussing the merits and pitfalls of the use of performance-enhancing drugs. In a collection entitled *Medico-legal Hazards of Rugby Union* (1992), D.W. Payne (the editor) thought the issue so worthy of discussion that he devoted two large chapters to it. One chapter is from the players' perspective, and the other is from the point of view of a medical doctor. Although illicit drug use is not entirely a phenomenon of the late 1980s (Todd 1987, 1992), the issue came to the attention of the larger sporting community in 1988 when Canadian sprinter Ben Johnson, at the Olympic Games in Seoul that year, tested positive for steroids.

Over the years there were rumours that the Eastern-bloc nations had achieved their success in sport at least in part by a regimented training schedule that included the use of steroids. Riordan in his work regarding sport and communism has stated:

> [D]rug taking was organised at the top and involved parts of the sports medicine establishment. . . . At the Olympics of Montreal (1976) and Seoul (1988), it has now been revealed that Soviet team had a hospitality ship used as a medical centre to ensure that Soviet competitors were 'clean' at the last moment.
>
> (1991: 123)

What was unique about the Soviet system was that it was state-organised. Ben Johnson had taken drugs with the help and encouragement of his personal physician, but the governing bodies of sport in his nation did not condone such practices (Dubin 1990). In this respect, then, Soviet sports medicine experts were part of the problem in the 'war' on drugs in the Eastern bloc. In terms of the risk involved in their use, Benjamin (1992) makes a convincing case against the use of steroids, suggesting that they will improve athletic performance but at a cost. Long-term use of steroids can lead to liver dysfunction and an increased susceptibility to cancer and other diseases. For this reason, medical doctors do not advocate their use.

Use of steroids is by no means just confined to the former Eastern bloc (as the Ben Johnson case illustrates); however, the cases of known drug abuse in rugby are few and far between. One Welsh international rugby player tested positive and was banned for two years during the period of my investigation. Paul Jones of Llanelli Rugby Football Club became the second player in five years to test positive for steroids (Clutton 1996b). Random tests take place during training and after matches, and they are done according to Welsh Rugby Union and United Kingdom Sports Council guidelines. Positive tests are not as common in the sport of rugby as they are in track and field, and this may be due to the fact that rugby has developed professionally at a slower pace than athletics. Rugby union has come late to the world of professionalism, and as a result, players are not yet under the same pressures to achieve ever-improving standards. Also, in a team sport there is little need to use illicit means to improve performance if there is not a culture of it at the club, whereas athletics is an individual sport and one cannot hide from good or bad performances. The Paralympic movement is still relatively underdeveloped as a global player, and yet in the movement's finest hour, at the 2000 Paralympics in Sydney, eleven positive tests became public knowledge. While this is not good for the movement in terms of its 'clean, friendly image', it could be seen as constructive in that it means that athletic performances are improving, and as a result, elite performers are looking for an edge. The positive test forced the International Paralympic Committee (IPC) to launch a programme entitled Doping Disables, which was designed to educate sporting participants with impairments against the use of drugs (IPC 2000).

The use of medicine to help in the enhancement of performance is a result of greater rewards being made available to sportspeople who achieve national and international success. If sporting success was not important symbolically to the political agenda of nations, and performers were not rewarded for their success, there would be no reason for the use of such substances. Sporting governing bodies have banned some performance-enhancing substances, while others, such as the food supplement creatine, are approved for use.

Repackaging the steroid: creatine

Owing to the fact that money can now be made from sport as a spectacle, the desire to increase sporting performance has led to the development of legal substances that boost performance in much the same manner as illicit drugs. This is a clear indication that theoretical and practical branches of sports medicine are working together to enhance performance. While ethical issues and the risks associated with steroids do not allow them to be prescribed, the benefits of steroids in enhancing performance can be determined by how levels of play improve in sports such as basketball, in which the National Basketball Association (of the United States) has not banned the use of these substances. These drugs can lead to a massive improvement in both strength and speed. To replicate the benefits of steroids, elite sprinters and rugby players alike have been turning to legal food supplements such as creatine.

Creatine[3] has been shown to be of similar benefit to anabolic steroids in the manner in which it facilitates an increased frequency and intensity of the training undertaken by sportspeople (Welsby 1995). This product was being used by some athletes at the Barcelona Olympics before it was considered by the IOC's Medical Commission. Widespread use of the supplement has been quick to develop, to the point that an estimated 75 per cent of the First Division Welsh rugby players (during the 1995/6 season) were taking the substance in one of its many forms. In recent years, use of the supplement has declined both in rugby circles and in athletics as many former users have suggested that the onset of heavy cramping while on the substance detracted from their performances. While the IOC has now declared the use of the substance legal, many questions still remain to be answered. If the results of the use of this substance mirror the results of anabolic steroids, then are there any side effects similar to those of the banned substances? To date there have been no studies published on the long-term use of creatine that might illuminate the long-term health implications of heavy use. While it is my belief that such studies are probably being undertaken, one can only wonder whether we are heading up the same avenue that was taken when research began on blood doping.

Blood doping, according to Waddington, 'does not involve the administration of drugs but is a technique involving the removal from an athlete of some blood, which is stored and later reinfused into the athlete' (1996: 189). Blood is removed from the body to allow the body to produce more red blood cells, which are of prime importance in the transportation of oxygen within the body. After the body has replaced the red blood cells (in much the same manner as would occur with anyone who acts as a blood donor), the red blood cells that had been removed months before can be replaced prior to competition to provide the athlete with a greater ability to absorb oxygen, thus enhancing performance.

Waddington (1996, 2000) has suggested that research into the use of blood doping as a means of enhancing performance was initially carried out by qualified medical researchers. Research in the 1970s was not carried out by

> 'quacks' working on the illegitimate fringes of sports medicine and rejected by their more reputable colleagues; they were in fact highly reputable sports physicians working within the mainstream of sports medicine, and their research was published, not in underground publications that circulated illicitly, but in the mainstream journals in sports medicine.
>
> (Waddington 1996: 190)

Blood doping was not in fact made illegal until after the Los Angeles Olympics in 1984, in which the USA's cycling team dominated their event (Waddington 2000). It is also of interest that at the 1984 Olympiad a Finnish distance runner who had taken the silver in the 10,000 m before being disqualified for the use of anabolic steroids admitted that his system was tainted because he had removed blood for the purpose of doping while he was taking illicit steroids.

Waddington (1996, 2000) has commented on the shift in attitude of sports authorities in the area of blood doping and its 'illicit' status since 1984. The transformation was unusually fast. In attempting to enhance sports performance, to where does the sports medicine team now turn? What is legal today may go against the ever-changing rules and regulations tomorrow. It is clear, however, that these rules should not be retrospective. It has been commonly debated in athletics circles whether or not the great Finnish distance running star of the 1970s Lasse Viren employed the technique of blood doping (something he has always denied) to beat the world's best. Even if Viren had used this technique, he would not have acted illicitly and should not be vilified as a result. It should be considered that the Finns were using science to enhance performance, and scientists around the world were using the public forum of journals to try to do the same.

What makes the case of blood doping of interest is that blood is natural in the human body. Unlike the highly publicised issues surrounding the use of anabolic steroids, which are foreign to the human body, blood is not an additive. Recently, with the advent of tests for erythropoietin (EPO), it has been suggested that blood doping may once again be on the increase (Gains 2002). It is clear to see how confusion could exist: after all, are we not allowed to have control over what is clearly ours? While blood doping remains illegal, advances in sports medicine, while not eradicating the use of anabolic steroids, have led to the development of legal supplements, such as creatine, which provide similar results to those produced by the banned substances but are not considered a health risk.

Like blood, creatine is a natural substance that occurs readily in the body's muscle tissue. Creatine is involved in muscle anabolism and the metabolism of exercise. The average human body contains 120 grams: 98 per cent in the muscles, 1.5 per cent in nerve tissue and 0.5 per cent in other organs. The body's stores are maintained by the intake of meat or fish, which contains 3–5 grams of creatine per kilogram (Welsby 1995: 1). Creatine is a vital component of the energy-producing system within the cells, particularly those in which the demand for energy may vary greatly over a short period of time. In its phosphorylated form, creatine functions in the maintenance of cellular adenosine triphosphate (ATP) homeostasis. It serves as a reservoir of high-energy phosphoryl groups for the rapid regeneration of ATP from adenosine diphosphate (ADP) in muscle tissue.

Loading the muscle tissue with creatine makes the muscles better suited to recover after intensive use. Therefore training is enhanced. But what is the difference between this and blood doping? It could be argued that both are forms of doping and therefore should be made illegal. Each human body is blessed with only so much creatine; therefore, to supplement the body's supply could be seen as unethical. One of the reasons given for making the practice of blood doping illicit was the problems associated with transfusion; however, today when such practices are carried out on a regular basis the

risk has been almost completely eliminated. It is my belief, then, that legal-
ising the use of creatine, with only a limited amount of research having
been conducted into the supplement, involves a conspiracy to avoid the
illicit use of anabolic steroids. The health of the individual is being ignored
in order that sporting performance can continue to improve. By finding
substances that are naturally produced in the body and that also enhance
performance, such as creatine, sports sciences are engaged in a battle, the
ultimate aim of which is to win sporting events legally. By encouraging the
use of food supplements, those making decisions about what is legal and
what is not are effectively attempting to direct elite sporting performers
towards better performances. Of course, as recent cases surrounding the
detection of metabolites of nandrolone in some over-the-counter food
supplements show, the fine line between legal and illicit substances is a mine-
field (Ferstle 1999; Ward 1999). This is an issue that can spill over, having
an impact on the public's use of sports supplements.

Public use of sports medicine

A distinctive transformation that has occurred in the area of sports medicine is the increase in access that the public has to specialist clinics. As the
number of people participating in some form of exercise on a regular basis
increases, there will also be a proportional increase in the number of sports-
related injuries (Gwyther 1995). In addition to the number of injuries rising,
the severity of each case could also increase, as the individuals who have
moved into an active lifestyle will tend not to be as biomechanically sound
as sportspeople from whom the ideal type has been derived. Sports medicine
has in the past been available as a simple curative orthodox practice;
however, with society placing emphasis on a healthy body, the focus has
shifted very much in favour of preventive medicine. This shift in attitude
has had a profound effect on the consumer as the flow of commodities to
clients expands and therefore enables elite athletes, who are used in
marketing the products, to benefit as well. 'Given the emphasis on leisure,
individual expressivity and consumption, the body emerges as a field of
hedonistic practices and a desire in a culture, which recognises that the body
is a project' (Turner 1996: 4). This in turn leads to what might be called
lay knowledge in so far as participants in sporting activities gain some understanding of how to eliminate minor pain and injuries through their own
experiences.

As financial reward becomes greater in elite sport, athletes begin to push
themselves to limits where even being structured in a more physiologically sound manner does not guarantee freedom from injury. Since injuries
to the elite are becoming more commonplace, the use of star athletes to
promote products deemed necessary for prevention also becomes an important factor. Therefore, advertising seeks to make the public recognise that

a product is fundamental to achieving the aim of looking like their favourite sports star.

Because there is now a desire for the public as consumers to 'buy' a healthy lifestyle, when injury occurs they seek help by employing the services of the sports medicine clinic. Similarly, professional rugby clubs also employ a treatment team to look after their players. It could be suggested that in future, because the sports medicine team is employed both by clubs and by the public, the health and interests of the players themselves may become less important than in the past. Domhnall Macauley, editor of the *British Journal of Sports Medicine*, recently considered this question and suggested that 'In this highly competitive sporting market doctors may find their professional independence threatened by pressures to treat, rehabilitate, inject, or operate in a manner that they find unacceptable' (1997a: 1). Even so, the very best performers, those who are believed by the coaching staff to be irreplaceable, will still be treated in their own best interests as the best treatment is also for the good of the club or nation. Professionals on short-term contracts who may be easily replaced, however, may be forced to return to action before they are fit, thus putting their health at risk.

Summary

In this short discussion it can be seen that sports medicine is not immune to the social influences that surround humankind on a daily basis. It may be seen that the development of sports medicine has been associated with two major processes of social change, one within the world of medicine and the other within the world of sport. The medicalising of life, coupled with the increased desire for winning on the world's playing fields (which often leads to winning financially off it), has brought great changes to sports medicine. Because the elite sporting performers in this study are clients of sports medicine practitioners and are of importance as symbols within their communities, the impact of sports medicine on these individuals is even more profound.

Chapter 2

Amateur pastime to professional spectacle

Until the early 1960s, sport in the United Kingdom was dominated by amateur ideals. However, from this time onwards, sport began to be transformed from an amateur pastime to a 'professional spectacle' as increasing numbers of businesses began to see the potential of sport as a tool for marketing their products (Allison 2001). Professional sports such as association football have also changed dramatically since that time. While amateurism was the dominant sporting model in the British Isles and the Commonwealth, not all parts of the globe were under the same amateur spell. Certainly the United States of America, while adopting many English Victorian sports, had transformed them into commercial enterprises by the turn of the twentieth century. Television coverage of sporting events has increased since the 1960s at a staggering rate (Rowe 1999), and as a result, companies realise that there is commercial benefit to be gained by their involvement in sport. Commercialism in this context should be seen as an influx of money that initially was channelled into those sporting federations and/or clubs that allowed themselves to be associated with certain products. This enabled these clubs and federations to collect advertising revenues. It is commercialism, and the money that has accompanied it, that has provided the catalyst for the transformation from amateur to professional sporting concerns (Howe 1999), since sporting participants wished to share the money that was ultimately the fruit of their labour.

This chapter discusses the transformation of sport from pastime to spectacle that has occurred in Britain over the past forty years.[1] It will highlight how, through the implementation of the tools of professionalism, commercialism has become a dominant force in the formation of contemporary sporting praxis to the point where it has even impacted upon sport at 'grassroots' level (Allison 2001). The debate will be illustrated primarily by examining the development of professional rugby union in Wales, and more particularly at Valley RFC. The role of television and sponsorship will also be explored. In order to do this, the semantic distinction between the amateur and the professional will be articulated, before a brief discussion of the split that occurred in the philosophy and structure of the game of rugby. This split led to the establishment of the two distinct codes of rugby: union and league.[2]

Amateur versus professional

The debate concerning amateur and professionalism has a long history within the context of sport (Allison 2001; Smith and Porter 2000). By examining the debate surrounding what seems to be an irreversible trend towards professionalism this chapter will articulate the importance of professionalism as a vehicle for the improvement in sports medicine provision that is highlighted in Chapter 1. For the elite sporting performer, professionalisation can be a mixed blessing, particularly in the context of pain and injury (Chapters 4 and 5).

The argument between amateurism and professionalism has long been rooted in the principle of equality. 'An amateur was expected to participate for the love of the game, whereas a professional received some form of remuneration' (Porter and Smith 2000: viii). This has had two effects on the games that were a product of Victorian ideals of fairness. As long as the game is played by individuals who are in the same circumstances with regard to the work/training time ratio, teams and competitions of near-equality will generate 'fair' matches that are exciting and entertaining. This principle is at the root of the establishment of leagues and divisions that typifies British sport today. Ideally, this structure allows teams of near-equal resources and abilities to play together.[3] To have a team that has professionals in its membership in an amateur league creates inequalities. This has a number of implications: it reduces the excitement that uncertain results can provide, as well as upsetting the betting on a given match. As there become clear favourites to win matches, more spectators may take a chance on the 'underdog' at the betting shop, and thus the nature of an entertaining match may be altered so that your main interest is to see whether your side can beat the point spread on which you wagered. The ability of sport to draw spectators may be seen as a catalyst for the shift from sport as an amateur pastime to a professional spectacle. Commercial interest will be drawn to the game because the spectators will give companies that wish to invest in sporting clubs a market to sell their goods (Polley 1998). Therefore, the shift from amateur to professional, which has led to inequality, may also be seen to play a part in the shift from pastime to spectacle. For example, when the game of rugby union became professional in August 1995 (Fitzsimons 1996; Howe 1999; Smith 2000), some clubs had the financing to contract players' services and others did not. As a result, there are at present only half a dozen teams that are realistically in contention for league championships and cup victories in Wales, because these clubs will attract the best players. It is possible to envisage that eventually the degree of

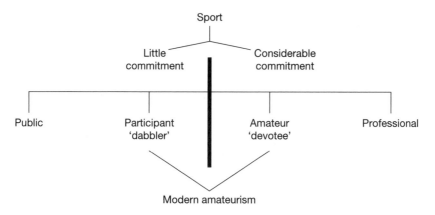

Figure 2.1 Continuum of sporting involvement. (Adapted from Stebbins 1992.)

inequality will be minimised as clubs find the level at which they can compete 'equally', perhaps rendering the divisional system into a talent and financial filter.

Before any systematic social analysis may be undertaken effectively, it is important to distinguish what is meant by the terms 'amateur' and 'professional' in the sporting context. The *Shorter Oxford Dictionary* describes an amateur as an individual who cultivates anything as a pastime, whereas, in direct opposition, 'professional' may be seen as applied to one who follows by way of profession what is generally followed as a pastime. While these definitions adequately address common-sense notions of the amateurs and professionals of the contemporary sporting world, it could be suggested that all that separates these individuals is the payment for performing services. Stebbins refers to this as modern amateurism, and it has been developing in connection with some leisure activities in which some participants are now able to make a substantial living from their chosen activity and as a result are able to devote themselves to it as a vocation rather than an avocation (1992: 8). The continuum shown in Figure 2.1 illustrates how closely related the modern amateur is to their contemporary professional counterpart.

This continuum is used to illustrate how an individual may change the focus of the activities in their life. As life situations change, so does the level of commitment that can be given to a leisure pursuit. If the individual's endeavour is more serious and thus more work-like, then their activities will occur closer to the right side of the continuum. It is suggested that modern amateurs can be subdivided into '*devotees*' and '*dabblers*', depending on their attitude. Stebbins (1992) suggests five attitudes that can be used to distinguish between the two types of amateur – confidence, perseverance, continuance commitment, preparedness and self-conception – and placed on a relative continuum. Overall, a *devoted* amateur will go to greater lengths to duplicate a professional's attitude than will an individual who *dabbles* in the pastime. The strength in degree of these attitudes is what separates the amateur from the professional. Allison (2001: 154–155) suggests that

> Professionalism is about careers. Thus professionals, when they have important decisions to make, have too much at stake to make them well. That whole bundle of status, self-esteem and personal financial management which we call a career is a lot to have to put on the table. Professionals in any field are likely to err in the directions of caution, conformity and self-interest when compared to the amateur.

Many amateur sportsmen and -women want to gain advantage over their fellow competitors and therefore, while they are employed to do work other than their sport, they will make sacrifices to achieve better performance. For example, they may limit social outings (parties, nights at the pub, etc.) in order to commit more time to adopting the physical habitus required for their sport. This type of sacrifice may lead to increased levels of performance, and therefore their approach to the sport may begin to equal that of the professionals. Both amateurs and professionals, therefore, may be seen to have created an identity within their sporting activity and club with which they are involved. The complete understanding of club habitus may be lacking in some members of an amateur club, since they spend less time developing it than do professionals' clubs and their members; however, for those amateur *devotees* involved, the habitus is often just as important.

From time to time, an elite amateur whose habitus closely resembles that of a professional in the same activity may face the dilemma of whether or not to make their living from their chosen leisure activity, especially if they wish to continue improving their skills. Such decisions are difficult to make and may depend on the age of the individual, lifestyle requirements and the enjoyment found in current employment. Until August 1995 this was a decision that rugby union players did not have to make, as professionalism was illegal, but since that time the elite amateurs (*devotees*) have had to consider their future within the sport.

Professionalism and Welsh rugby

The history of rugby union and Valley Rugby Football Club (RFC) in particular may be seen as comprising a transformation from a club structured for and by players and committee-men (ex-players) to a spectacle that is now managed as a business (Howe 1999). It has been suggested (Donnelly 1993; Dunning and Sheard 1979) that the advent of the Sports Council in Britain during the late 1960s and early 1970s provided the impetus for a massive transformation in the game of rugby union as well as other amateur sports.

The use of government funds meant that success on the playing fields was expected. This led to

> the further democratisation of the game to the lower middle class, which resulted in an additional loss of the old elite values and a greater emphasis on winning; and the shift from a player-centred to a spectator-centred game, which resulted in further financial dependence and commercialisation and the motivation to produce a quality (spectator) product.
>
> (Donnelly 1993: 130)

Pressure on sporting authorities at national and club level to draw spectators as well as to win sporting contests therefore was greatly increased in the later part of the twentieth century. The net effect of this was that sports such as rugby union and athletics, which were clinging to the principle of amateurism, were under pressure to adopt a more commercially oriented approach to their sports.

The debate as to whether rugby football, at the elite level, should be played by amateurs or professionals has been developing since some point in time before the two rugby codes of union and league formed separate ruling authorities, over a hundred years ago. The split in the game that resulted from this debate appears, from a distance, to have occurred simply as a result of money. A detailed historical account of what became known as the *great split* has been written by Collins (1998), so here only the bare bones of the argument will be outlined. Briefly, clubs in the north of England, primarily Yorkshire and Lancashire, believed that players should be rewarded financially for the efforts that they put into the game. The game in this part of the country had developed differently from how it developed in the rest of the country. Yorkshire and Lancashire had a large industrial middle class which was eager to exploit the business potential of the game and as a result initiated an earlier and more distinct transformation from pastime to sporting spectacle than occurred in the rest of Britain. The individuals who controlled the game in the conservative environment throughout the rest of Britain believed that the game should remain a pastime and that deriving income from this sort of activity was unethical. Because of these differing ideologies the two codes of the game, union and league, became separate organisations after October 1895.

Wales at this juncture was in a unique position, since the cultural values within Welsh society had considerably more in common with those of the north of England than they did with those of the south (Smith and Williams 1980; Williams 1991). However, owing to a small but powerful middle-class influence in the form of, among others, key members of the Welsh Rugby Union (WRU), the professional league game was never successfully established in Wales. Because of this, and the sometimes desperate state of the

Welsh economy, the northern professional game may be seen as a safety valve used, throughout the past hundred years, to maintain the amateur ideal. Welsh rugby players who wished to turn professional could, if they were good enough, move to a rugby league club in the north of England (Williams 1994). While it is important to establish the economic as well as the cultural context of the club being used as the illustration of the transformation in sporting practice it is important first to examine what is meant by the terms 'amateur' and 'professional' in the context of sport.

Professional identity

The players at Valley RFC share an embodied habitus, which helps in establishing a collective identity. In the past, one of the major influences in their identity was their place of work. Often, players were employees at the local mine, and this, as well as their rugby, gave them great affinity with one another. Over the past two decades at the club there has been much less continuity provided by shared work experience. However, with the advent of professionalism, the opportunity for increased commonality of habitus is present for at least the first twenty-one players (First XV plus substitutes) contracted to the club, since more training is done together as a squad. The coaches and players at Valley RFC have, over the past ten years, been increasing the fitness level required by a player in the squad. As the players become determined to perform at a more elite level, they begin to mimic professionals in their approaches to fitness, and also begin to establish a desire to be rewarded accordingly. With this shift in the habitus of the player, the league and divisional structure, which, as mentioned earlier, was designed to ensure equality of performance between clubs, now may be seen as a pyramid or ladder: the higher your club climbs, the greater the financial reward for the players, and the transformation from pastime to spectacle and from amateur to professional becomes more complete.

Therefore, within the serious sporting community, amateurs and professionals coexist. While only professionals make their livelihood from sport, devoted amateurs adopt the attitudes of the professionals to the best of their ability. Eventually some devotee players wish to be rewarded for their commitment to the game, and this could lead to commercialism before it develops into professionalism. In some sporting contexts there may be seen to exist pre-professional sportspeople (Stebbins 1992), such as young association footballers who have apprenticeships with Premiership squads throughout Britain. If these young players do not develop into elite professionals, they may have a career with a lower-division club or may leave the sport entirely. Such a system does not currently exist in Welsh rugby, although it is possible that in time it could be seen to be advantageous, since it would give the larger clubs a future talent pool on which to draw. The situation is not much different in rugby, where devoted amateurs who do not have the skills to play professional rugby will often play in lower divisions as long as they derive continued enjoyment of the training and social environment around their club as time passes, their approach to the game is likely to shift from that of the devotee to that of the dabbler. Time management at work as well as injury (see Chapters 4 and 5) and age may also be factors that will determine whether a player continues to play the game.

Shamateurism

Until the game of rugby union was declared professional, there were often claims by one national union that others were not playing the game according to the amateur rules. It was generally felt that the nations from the Southern Hemisphere were taking more liberties with rules regarding payment for performance than those from the North. However, whether this was the case is uncertain (though some are rather certain on this point (Allison 2001)). During my time in the field, informants often talked frequently of how other clubs were 'avoiding' the rules regarding payment for performing, but I could never get them to expound on the extent to which their own club was doing the same. In this respect, discussion of money for performance on the pitch was a taboo subject. On a micro level, discussion often concerned Valley's local rival, which, it has been alleged, had attracted so many new faces to its squad in the mid-1990s, as a result of heavy financial incentives, that many of its supporters did not recognise the team. This situation is not dissimilar to that in well-established professional sports such as football in England and continental Europe, and the big four professional sports in North America (American football, (ice) hockey, basketball and baseball). In these situations superstars are transferred from one club to another, leaving the supporter with the impression that these players are only available to the club with the largest budget.

It has been acknowledged (Fitzsimons 1996; Wyatt 1995) that some nations were not as strict about payment of players as others. If players could train more often as a result of being paid for it, the end result would be an improved national squad. The outrage over illegal payment was perhaps a result of the British Isles' loss of superiority in international rugby. After all, it is a game that had been their invention. Today, in the new professional age, teams are legally allowed to pay players, and therefore this has eliminated the scope for complaints about illegal payments to players. This is not to say that financial incentives are equal to all who play the game, but is rather to say that performance on the pitch and the financial stability of the club played for are the determining factors in the amount a player is paid. In this respect rugby is not unlike other sports. Success on the sports field often determines a player's relative value. Today, financial matters for players are openly discussed, as they clearly have been within the playing fraternity for some time, and a 'reflection' of these discussions may be seen in newspapers and topical magazines. What has been made clear from observations during fieldwork, prior to the 'legal' professionalisation of the game, is that money was an influence in the game of rugby union, and now that the game is more open, it should not be overlooked as a force in its social change.

The Welsh have come under more criticism than the other 'home' nations (Allison 2001) for turning a blind eye to the rule regarding earnings from the game. While history may one day justify such rumours that the Welsh did breach financial rules with far greater frequency than the other unions, the Welsh certainly suffered the most at the hands of professionalism. This suffering took the form of players heading to the north of England to exploit their talent in the legally professional code of rugby league. A far greater number of players of Welsh origin went north to play rugby league than did Scottish or English players (Williams 1994). It can also be argued that the difference in class structure of the home nations is an important influence in determining which players switch rugby codes. Throughout periods of Welsh rugby success, because the Welsh game's foundations were strongly working class and had strong similarities with those in the counties that were playing the professional game, the WRU was often accused by the more conservative English and Scottish unions of allowing illegal payment to players. With the radical policy changes in late August 1995, the once 'amateur' game of rugby union has become openly professional, leading many to wonder whether a new hybrid form of the game will come into existence. More than being the dawn of a new era, the International Rugby Football Board's (IRFB) establishment of an openly professional game has ended a hundred years of ever-increasing hypocrisy within the sport. The time is now ripe for an in-depth social examination of the evolution of an amateur game into a professional concern.

Cup to commercialism

That which occurred from the time of the acknowledgement of professionalism and the official announcement of the International Rugby Football Board in August 1995 was a profound change in the structure of the game. Two books of a journalistic nature with illuminating titles, *Rugby War* (Fitzsimons 1996) and *Rugby Disunion* (Wyatt 1995), discuss issues that are related to the professionalisation of the game. Professionalism, from my observations, is about changing the attitudes of club officials in regard to the players, who have the desire to be financially rewarded for their time commitment to training since the clubs are benefiting at their expense. Commercialism, on the other hand, may be seen to be concerned with the transformation of club habitus so that these shifts in attitude can be financed.

What is of prime importance, therefore, is the influence of money from the Union, the club and their sponsors and how it has impacted on the players and their supporting community (Howe 1999).

The influence of multinational media groups has had a profound impact on changes that have occurred in the game (Fitzsimons 1996; Hargreaves 1986; Smith 2000). This influence has in part resulted in the media (and hence the public) having labelled the game since its 'opening', with the abolishing of monetary restrictions, as 'professional'. This I believe to be a somewhat inaccurate representation. While the media have been quick to highlight the changes that have occurred in the game, I would suggest that the main change has not been so much a shift from amateurism to professionalism, as a transformation from co-operative organisation to a commercial enterprise. This shift has occurred on two levels – first, at the level of the game's administration, and second, at the level of the individual clubs – and by examining these structures the role of financial capital in the game will be established. Because of the recent arrival of professionalism and the consequential development of commercialism, rugby union has used the media to great effect. For most clubs at this stage, the tools of commercialism are focused to allow their organisation to operate at cost. In other words, profit margins are not the issue, but having the finances to pay the bills is fundamental, and therefore clubs such as Valley RFC may be seen as in a transitional stage at present between being a co-operative institution and becoming a business enterprise. Larger clubs such as Cardiff RFC have targeted business success as a goal, and as a result, Cardiff has become a public limited company (PLC) (Rees 1996). The question remains: how have these clubs at the elite level in Welsh rugby (the new PLCs and the smaller community clubs) restructured themselves?

A struggle for hegemony

Since the early years of the game, power in the administration of the affairs of the national squad as well as the overall management of clubs has rested with the WRU. The Rugby Football Union (RFU) was established in 1880 in order that former pupils of Rugby School and other public schools that had adopted the game could play matches of 'their' game throughout the country, and therefore a degree of uniformity was imposed.[4] As the game became more popular throughout the British Isles, each region was encouraged to establish its own administrative committees, and thus the WRU was born. The WRU set down rules in accordance with the specifications of the RFU, and later the International Rugby Football Board (IRFB), as to how the clubs should be organised to comply with the amateur ethos upon which the game was originally established. Each club was given a vote on the general council of the WRU. Therefore, the WRU may be seen as very much a co-operative organisation, with each club having a vote in electing union officials. All the Welsh clubs were involved on Union committees. At the current time, however, there is a push from leading clubs competing in the top division of the Welsh Rugby Union to secure a greater say in how the game is administered. As the game has become open, leading clubs felt that they must have more control over their destiny. Money, through corporate sponsors, has begun to be made available to the WRU, and the clubs (especially those in the top flight) feel that if their relationship with the WRU is allowed to continue in the same manner as before, they will not get what they deserve. The top clubs have founded their own commercial committee, an action taken to force the WRU to listen. This sub-section will examine the impact of the establishment of the new commercial arm of the leading clubs known as First Division Rugby Limited (FDRL).

The development of league rugby is important as it may be regarded as the start of commercialism in the sport. Rugby union has been getting more competitive since the 1920s with the advent of unofficial league structures such as the merit table (Dunning and Sheard 1979). It was at this time that the results over a season became important. In the past, winning was considered important within the context of each match, but there was little measure of how one team compared to others. Each club established its own fixture list, and therefore it might not play the same opposition as the neighbouring club. While Valley RFC was involved, from the 1930s, in the Glamorgan League, playing many local clubs, the advent of the merit table altered the focus from a local level to a national level. The merit table was a very loosely structured league in which all the larger clubs throughout Wales were involved. Each club was in charge of its own fixture list and the results of these matches were recorded so that the club with the best record won the league. It was unofficial because not all the teams always played each other in home and away matches. Despite the discontinuity in terms of fixtures from one club to the next, even at the top flight of the merit table, this development of the merit table can be seen as an embryonic form of the commercialised game. What really initiated commercial interests was the re-establishment of the WRU Challenge Cup. The Cup, for its winner, was the first indication of national superiority, since without winning each match a club cannot progress to the next round. The WRU Challenge Cup was initiated in 1971, and up until this time there was an attitude that participation in rugby made you fit. With the advent of the Cup, however, there has been a marked shift in ideology whereby you must be fit to play rugby.[5] It was then that the level of time commitment to the sport greatly increased.

The establishment of the cup competition by the WRU has seen an increase in the emphasis placed upon the importance of winning. While a point-scoring system was developed in the early days of the game, and therefore winning was of importance, the establishment of a knock-out competition that offered a cup as the prize meant that winning had begun to take on an even greater significance. Success in such a competition also did a great deal to draw spectators to the grounds. The word 'spectator' is used deliberately in order to keep it distinct from 'supporter'; 'spectators' may be drawn to the club by its success, whereas a 'supporter' will be in the stands through good and bad times. 'Followers' of a club are midway between the two, in that they support the club when it is convenient for them to do so or offer support from a distance. In the current climate, spectators of the game have become fundamentally important as they are transformed from having a role of simply observing matches to one that includes the consuming of the products that may be associated with the club or the Union. As a result of this new-found access to consumers, local businessmen increasingly wished to contribute to their successful club. Their hope has been to gain exposure for their enterprise within the community. One of the Valley supporters commented, 'While the ads in the programmes detract from the available space for stories and commentary on the club, when I am on the high street I will take my custom to the businesses that support our club' (Notebook 1: 20).

Until recently, increased exposure, as a result of association with a club, was limited to advertising in the programme and around the club ground. The late 1980s saw the addition of sponsors' names on the club kit, much in the same manner as the practice that has been pursued in association football for some time. With the advent of 'official' league rugby in 1990/1, rugby continued to head towards an era of commercial enterprises rather than co-operative clubs. A major brewery, Heineken, was the league's sponsor until the end of the 1995/6 season. The gimmicks that have been used for the league's promotion (and therefore by association the promotion of the products themselves) are varied. When the Wales and British Lions outside half Neil Jenkins became the first player to score 1,000 points in league competition, one can of lager was presented to him for every point he had scored. Heineken has since pulled out of Welsh domestic rugby and is sponsoring the European Rugby Cup instead. The WRU has been unable to attract a long-term sponsor since the 1996/7 season, which is perhaps an indication of the future direction that commercialism will take the game. Partly because of the loss of the league's main sponsor, First Division Rugby Limited (FDRL) was founded to monitor the business actions of the WRU, and it has played a role in negotiating all the major sponsorship contracts that may have an impact on club rugby in Wales. The struggle between the WRU and FDRL may be seen as a hegemonic battle for the long-term control of the game, but as the game continues to grow and the importance of European rugby takes centre stage, the role of FDRL in voicing the collective concerns of the elite clubs in Wales has been of paramount importance.

A European focus

During the 1995/6 season the first European Cup competition was played and selection for entry into the tournament was based on league performance. Therefore, the first two teams in the first division as well as the winner of the WRU Cup took part in the inaugural event. Because this new international competition brings more money to the clubs involved, success in the cup once again takes on a very important role. As of the 2001/2 season there was a Welsh/Scottish league consisting of nine clubs from Wales and two regional teams from Scotland (Glasgow and Edinburgh). In addition to this, the WRU is currently in talks with the other home nations (minus England) to develop a Celtic League, which could mean that some clubs, at the highest level, will lose their identity. The consequences could be disastrous for the clubs concerned. Club sponsors will not be as eager to be associated with teams seen as second-rate and therefore, as a result of receiving less exposure for their product, may decide to support a club that will remain in the most elite league. In this manner, the top clubs, which will get more media exposure as a result of being involved in European competition, will attract more financial support from sponsors, thus leading to the game becoming less egalitarian.

The teams that stay in the Premiership (the old First Division) will benefit from increased exposure as well as a smaller domestic fixture list. A mixture of league and European fixtures scattered throughout the season means that clubs that are not involved in playing European rugby will have time to rest key players (if they can afford to keep hold of their 'stars'). Importantly, players will be afforded the time to do more training as well as resting minor injuries, whereas in the past a player with a minor injury would have been requested to continue playing as a result of the congested fixture list. However, the price for this is less money coming in to keep the club financially viable. This situation is made worse by the struggle with the Union for financial control of the game in Wales (Clutton 1996a) as well as in England (Smith 2000). The uncertainty that exists in professional rugby is not good for medium-sized clubs such as Valley RFC.

The problems that now exist in the restructuring of rugby in Wales are occurring in other nations (Smith 2000); however, restructuring is perhaps more important in Wales as the game is a national obsession (Smith and Williams 1980). The balance of power within rugby in Wales has yet to be determined completely, but it is clear that the top clubs are eager to be given their fair share of the money that the WRU receives from any television agreements. Commenting on the relationship between FDRL and the WRU, the chair of FDRL, Eddie Jones, commented, 'I am a rugby man with a wealth of experience in the game. We [FDRL and WRU] are in this together and Welsh rugby will get nowhere unless we work together as one' (Rees 1997).

With clubs such as Cardiff becoming PLCs in their own right (Rees 1996), the end of the co-operative era in rugby is close at hand. In the future the power of the WRU may be limited to running the national squad.

The power that has existed within the WRU is derived from its control of the money that has come into the sport. By distributing the funds that have been secured through sponsorship, as well as rights for television and gate receipts for international matches, the Union has been in a position to dictate how the game should be structured.[6] With the establishment of an open game, the WRU's position as 'banker' for the Union is under threat. The clubs feel that owing to the increased media exposure, which is in part a result of their more entertaining play, they should receive more of the money generated by the game. The clubs' financial teething problems are not unexpected, since the changes to the game have been rapid (Howe 1999; Smith 2000).

Improved fitness at Valley RFC: a by-product of commercialism

Ever since the advent of official league rugby within Wales during the 1991/2 season, players in the upper divisions have begun to adopt a more focused approach to the fitness training needed to succeed in the game. This attitude could be seen as professional, because the level of time commitment that the players devote to achieving an enhanced performance mirrors that of professional athletes. This commitment includes simple things like attending all club training sessions, personal fitness training, as well as monitoring of dietary intake of both food and liquid. Such commitments may appear to some as minor; but for the family who miss spending leisure time with their husband or father, they can put a great deal of strain on social relationships. The players pursue certain activities in order to improve their performance, and pursuit of these is generated by their desire. It is the presence of this that largely distinguishes devoted amateurs from participants, and therefore its presence gives them much more in common with professional sportsmen who make a living through sport on account of their levels of commitment.

This commitment to fitness and the success of the club extends to other areas of the game as well. The players' representative on the committee at Valley RFC also liaised with the company that produces the uniforms for the players. He acts as a middleman between the manufacturer and both the local shops that stock the replica jerseys and the club's own supporters' shop. Diet supplements too are important to elite rugby squads, and this player was also the local contact for this component of the professional sphere. The players are therefore able to increase their value to the organisation by controlling these areas of off-field enterprise. Such involvement also has taken pressure off members of the administrative committee, as all these individuals at the club were unpaid volunteers. As the professional era develops, whether a player (a contracted employee) will have control of vital links in the club remains to be seen. It is still early in the professional era of rugby union. It is likely that difficulties surrounding the game, as a result of monetary influences, will increase until the players entering the elite ranks have previous players to act as role models, to emulate in terms of contracts etc., in much the same way that association football has operated for some time. The financing of construction projects and individual players contracts is an important issue that needs greater care and consideration at Valley RFC than it would require at a profitable association football club such as Manchester United. This is because clubs like Valley RFC are also in a process of transforming themselves into business enterprises.

Success every week is the key if a club is going to stay at the elite level, and this increasingly means playing rugby in Europe. Therefore, defeating the opposition on match day is no longer sufficient in itself. While much drama is still associated with the WRU Cup competition, and certainly a club generates great kudos from being successful in this competition, a club's survival in the elite ranks of Welsh rugby is more important than winning the Cup, as it is this that impacts upon the club's ability to attract sponsorship and quality players. Valley RFC has a great history as an elite club; however, until 1996, the side's inability to win the cup represented a blemish on its otherwise good reputation. Valley has now been in the finals three times and is the only club to have made it to two consecutive appearances (1995 and 1996). In spite of cup success in 1996, resurgent form in the 2001/2 season and several cup final appearances, the club is still relatively unfashionable. Even after the decline of heavy industry, the town in which Valley RFC is located is still not a fashionable place to live. Yet the club has always produced quality players who have had to go, on a regular basis, to other clubs, such as Cardiff or Swansea, to gain a place in the Welsh squad. It has been suggested that this is a result of two factors: first, the stereotypical beliefs about society in the valleys and the rough-and-tumble way in which the valley sides have traditionally played rugby; and second, the fact that the club has failed to win the league.

Off the pitch, the commercialisation of the habitus may be seen to manifest itself in the way a rugby clubhouse is structured. All the other clubs in the Premiership appear to be less egalitarian in the physical structure of their facilities: after matches, the players, the committee and the supporters all have separate bars in which to drink and socialise. Players do not appear to be encouraged to mix with the supporters. In this manner the players are given elevated status, yet the end result is a reduction in the supporters' sense of community. At Valley RFC, however, although separate bars do exist, the players first have a post-match meal and a drink. After this they gravitate to the clubhouse bar. Throughout my study, all the players appeared to enjoy fraternising with the supporters. Even when Valley RFC travelled to the larger clubs, the players would join the supporters for a drink. The sense of community among the players is very strong and there is a clear realisation that their rugby would not be as enjoyable, or for that matter as financially rewarding, if it were not for the support of the community.

Because of the changes taking place in the modern game, it is of vital importance that clubs, as a whole, become more forward-thinking. In the spring of 2002 a proposal was put to the WRU that only the top six clubs in Wales should maintain a professional status. While all the member clubs of the WRU rejected this proposal, this initial proposal may have been a response to the difficult time that the leading clubs are having with the pressures of the professional game. Even as full-time professionals, players are contracted employees whose successful employment is based on their physical skill and fitness. Each player is therefore answerable to his club for the level of physical fitness he must maintain, as well as to the Union if he is a contracted member of the national squad.

Television and the commercialisation of sport

Anyone who has watched contemporary sporting events on television will be aware that companies unrelated to sport advertise their products during sporting events. The day when producers at the BBC became the first to turn television cameras on a live sporting event, the annual Oxford–Cambridge boat race, was 2 April 1938. From these simple beginnings the televising of sport has become a multi-billion-dollar business. The impact on sport that is televised is immense. As well as the match or event that is broadcast, the events become enmeshed in diplomacy, public policy and other far-reaching influences. Everyone is aware of the intrusion of politics into sports arenas around the world. Although television was not present at the Berlin Olympics in 1936, the film clips that are now shown on television of those games are accompanied by post-period commentary. This is done to leave no question in the mind of the viewer that it was politically embarrassing that Jesse Owens, a black American, made the 'master race' lose its 'superiority' so publicly on the athletics track. These problems are still very apparent, especially in Olympic coverage, which has the greatest worldwide audience. Examples such as Mexico City in 1968 with the Black Power displays, the boycotts by West and East of the 1980 and 1984 games respectively and the student riots in Seoul demonstrate how groups not primarily interested in the sport are able to use the positioning of cameras to their benefit.

According to Klatell and Marcus (1988), the catalyst that began to greatly increase audiences was the 1972 Munich Olympic kidnapping and massacre of Israeli athletes. Like all forms of media, television benefits greatly from coverage that is indirectly related to the event. Viewers who would otherwise be uninterested may be compelled to watch the Olympics because of the political event brought to their attention by other forms of media. The nationalistic pride created by events such as the Olympics or, in rugby, the World Cup or the Six Nations Championship (the six nations being England, France, Ireland, Scotland, Wales and, now, Italy) serves as a bond between individuals and society. Six Nations Championship rugby is currently broadcast by the BBC and BSkyB, and in spite of the limited commercial advertising during broadcasting (there are no advertising breaks), sponsors are able to promote their products on boards around the ground and now even on the kit of the national squads who are competing on the pitch.

Television often features contrasting heroic personalities. Before certain Five Nations clashes between Wales and England (those of 1993–5), BBC Wales built the event up as a clash of opposing outside-half positions, between the public school- and Cambridge-educated Rob Andrew and the working-class lad Neil Jenkins. Such publicity in the Principality led to the vilification of Andrew in spite of his obvious talent. The television companies benefited from this contrived struggle. Free advertising is also initiated by the printed media, which comment on matches that may be attended by only a limited number of spectators. Such pre-match analysis certainly swells television audiences and hence increases benefits to sponsors, and in turn will increase the price Welsh rugby can hope to receive the next time its television contract is negotiated. Coverage of key matches may be so extensive that for the avid sports fan the distinction between events personally attended and those viewed on television may be blurred.

Rob Andrew has now retired from rugby, but he and Jenkins were the most prolific kickers in Five Nations rugby in the 1990s, and as a result of their different backgrounds, such a confrontation made for 'good' television. As the game became open, Andrew left his club (Wasps RFC) and became director of rugby for Sir John Hall at Newcastle RFC. As the mystique in English rugby circles surrounding Andrew is great, his inclusion as player-manager will attract more spectators and will continue the revitalising of rugby in the north-east of England. Andrew since his retirement has become the mentor of current star English outside-half Jonny Wilkinson. With an injection of several million pounds it was hoped, by those holding the money, that Andrew's flair on the pitch would be mirrored in the boardroom. Because of this capital, Newcastle became over a short period of time a symbol of the new era in the game of rugby, though this was short-lived as the principal financial backers pulled the plug on the club in the late 1990s (Smith 2000).

As media presence at major events on the rugby calendar has increased, now including most Premiership matches (both in the Celtic league and in England), winning a match has become so important that the game has begun to stagnate. As previously discussed, finishing high in the league table can mean promotion to the next division and therefore entails more exposure for the club, which in turn should lead to more sponsorship. However, if the game is boring, television networks and other media will soon become uninterested. If and when such a situation arises, action will need to be taken. Because of the importance of attracting spectators, the IRFB has begun to alter the rules of the game at an increasing rate over the past two decades. For example, the IRFB increased the value of a try to five points, believing that by making it worth two more points than a penalty, teams would be encouraged to run the ball more frequently. This in turn would lead to a more attractive style of rugby, thus drawing more spectators, and would bring more money to the clubs and ultimately the Union.

Spectators did become drawn to the game; however, these rule changes became only a short-term solution, as the necessity for a win, in both league and cup matches, led to a new form of 'conservative' play in which the penalty became the primary method of scoring. Clubs in the First Division, which by 1994/5 were competing for a place in the European Club Championships, were determined to win at any cost. Therefore players began to break the rules deliberately by being off-side or 'killing the ball', preferring to give away a chance at a penalty goal as a result of their poor play rather than allow a try to be scored. Clubs with good goal kickers soon began to dominate, as this unprincipled desire to stop a try often worked against the offenders when a successful penalty goal was kicked.

An attempt was made at the beginning of the 1995/6 season to return the game to a more spectator-friendly running style, by giving clubs in the Welsh leagues (and later throughout the British Isles) the chance to gain bonus points for positive play. If a team scores three or four tries in a match, it receives one extra point. For five or six tries it will receive two bonus points, and seven or more tries will give it three bonus points. Therefore, a win with seven tries is worth five points, whereas a win when less than three tries are scored is worth just two. For the 1996/7 season the bonus point system was altered again to make it more difficult to obtain bonus points on top of the two points available for a win. Though this system has been altered in recent years, the bonus point system for 'positive' play is part of the modern game as played in the Celtic League at the time of writing. In this manner the game has been forced to become more fluid and thus more entertaining, increasing the amount of media coverage and rekindling Welsh 'myths' of fluid rugby and outside halves 'who were like gods'. This has also meant that teams that win most consistently may not do well in the league if they do not score tries. However, this system has no effect on cup matches, which means that a team may play in a different manner depending on whether a cup or league match is being played, which makes the coach's job more difficult. The key consideration, however, is that the television camera stays focused on the game. This gives sponsors a shop window for their goods and services. Therefore, rule changes have been designed to enhance the relationship between the game and the media.

It is of interest to note that on arrival in Valley RFC I was unable to appreciate rugby not played in a fluid, running style. However, over the period of my stay in the community I gained an understanding and respect for the rucking and mauling involved in the game. It was not until I had gained this understanding of the importance that scrummaging played in the game that I considered myself to have become a supporter of the game. Therefore, a bonus point system may initially make the game more spectator-friendly, as a better understanding of the game's subtleties takes time. I would suggest that in order to avoid such a transformation at the European level the marketing of the game must be altered to focus on the traditional qualities of the game. Attracting an audience of consumers in this manner should mean that their support is long term. Therefore, allowing the audience to embody rugby habitus rather than altering it to suit them will have long-term benefits. Of course, the public, the players, club committees and administrators all have a distinctive habitus, but they are interconnected and, as a result they all play a role in the transformation of the sport. It is my contention that selling rugby to consumers as a package will enable them actively and constructively to take part in the game's transformation. However, officials of the game of rugby wish to market and transform the game, and the key in the professional era is to maintain the interest of the spectators and the television viewers. Only when this is achieved will rugby be a sustainable professional product.

Why sponsors want sport

Mass participation in sporting activities over the past two decades has created a more health-conscious society (Kew 1997). The timing of the move to a more health-oriented society has, not surprisingly, coincided with the ageing of the populations in Europe and the United States. Therefore, companies wish to commercially target this segment of society and have their products perceived as paramount to health and well-being. The idea that sport is health-promoting and even life-enhancing is one that is frequently stressed by sporting federations that are out to attract sponsorship. If commercial sponsorship is attracted to a sport, elite performers will eventually expect to be financially rewarded for their performances, with the sports organisation benefiting financially as well. Though the ideology linking sport and health is a powerful one, and a message that is widely consumed, an examination of certain aspects of the organisation of sport casts some doubt on the assumed closeness of the relationship between sport and the promotion of a healthy lifestyle. Sponsorship of sporting events and the widespread use of legal drugs to manage the bodies of sports participants are two areas that often test the direct relationship between sport and health.[7] However, to the public the message is quite simple: involvement in physical activity equals a healthy, happy, long life.

Sponsorship of sporting events is big business. One of the industries that has heavily invested its marketing capital in sporting events is tobacco. While tobacco producers have taken the opportunity to exploit large multi-media-generated audiences, and no doubt incurred financial gain as a result of this association, it is interesting how, by association with healthy athletes, a drug such as tobacco can be seen as in vogue by some sectors of society. Damon Hill was sponsored by Rothmans when he won the 1996 Formula One Championship; therefore this sponsor hopes to share in the reflected glory of this success, so that when a Formula One supporter who smokes, goes to purchase cigarettes, they may choose to try one of Rothmans' many brands. It can be observed how sport and advertising are interrelated since, when we watch a match on television, it often appears that the match is used as a link to connect the adverts rather than the other way around. In the case of major television sporting events such as American football's Super Bowl, corporations pay millions of dollars to run new advertising campaigns during the game (Whannel 1992). In this sense, then, sport is big business, as its relationship with corporate giants is symbiotic. Allowing the promotion of harmful (if pleasurable) products at sporting venues, and thus allowing the public to draw the connection between the sponsor and the sport, brings great financial benefits to the sporting community.

Financial rewards, in the form of contracts, can now be made to the players as a result of the infusion of money; in the past, sponsors could only offer employment. In the 1980s a cigarette paper company, Rizla, became the main sponsor of Valley RFC. This manufacturer has a big factory near to the town and gave several players jobs while it was the club sponsor, feeling that the association with the club would improve its sales. Many people who smoke 'roll-up' cigarettes are 'unfashionable', and at the time so too was Valley as a club, so the association was well constructed. This is partly a result of sport being risky, as is the use of tobacco and alcohol products, but the enjoyment that can be gained from all three makes the association plausible. There is also the influence of machismo in this association since tobacco and alcohol smell 'male' (as does the sweat of a sportsman).

Money from a large brewery (Heineken) has helped move Welsh rugby into the open era. Whether supporters make the connection with the product of the sponsor is of no real concern to the clubs, as each club negotiates clubhouse beer contracts individually. What is clear is that the audience for sporting events is much more diverse than just a simple collection of those individuals directly involved in sport. Since this is the case, an athlete's 'healthy' lifestyle can be seen to have real impact on the marketing of alcohol, and tobacco consumers draw a parallel between the success of the athlete and the product the athlete 'must' be using to achieve success. Between 1991 and 1996 the rugby union campaign in Wales was commonly referred to as the Heineken-National League, and in spite of the withdrawal of the sponsorship, many supporters still refer to the league as such. This means that the brewery is no doubt benefiting from its association with Welsh rugby although it is no longer investing in it. The shift to a European focus on rugby for the brewing group will continue to keep its product in the view of Welsh rugby supporters, while exposing the beer to a much greater audience throughout the rest of rugby-playing Europe.

Athletes have been known to take it upon themselves to reject sponsors whom they perceive as negative while they have the world stage and media spotlight. In the 1986 Commonwealth Games in Edinburgh, the Guinness Brewery was one of the key sponsors and its name was spread across the numbers worn by competitors in athletics. One of Britain's best-known athletic personalities, Daley Thompson (twice Olympic decathlon champion), removed the advertising from around the number on his vest. This initially upset the sponsor, but the surrounding debate, which highlighted the sponsor and its products, might alternatively be seen as good if the axiom 'all publicity is good publicity' is true. After the dust had settled, two (one official) reasons were given for this behaviour. The official reason was that the number was too large and that it had to be trimmed down or it would hinder the athlete's performance. The alternative explanation suggested was that Thompson thought the sponsor was inappropriate, owing to the fact that alcohol use by athletes can lead to impaired performance. Interestingly, it is currently illegal to alter the shape and form of a competitive number, according to the International Association of Athletic Federation rules, which now gives the authorities control over this advertising space. Some have suggested that Guinness is high in iron and therefore could, in small quantities, be good for women. In spite of such suggestions, the overriding implication is that alcohol is not compatible with good sports performances. While this type of negative exposure may seem harmful to firms, increased exposure in the media where the company has not paid to advertise (i.e. the tabloids) can only benefit these industries. This manufacturing sector continues to invest heavily in sporting events to the point where some sports could not do without this revenue source.

Summary

Professionalism has changed the nature of the elite player. No longer is the club just an environment in which to spend leisure time, for 'too many players were enjoying executive responsibility within the private sector not to appreciate international rugby's commercial potential and to recognise that they were marketable assets in their own right' (Smith 2000: 148). Because elite clubs such as Valley RFC 'house' international players between matches, their attitudes towards professionalism are important as well. Sport is cheap programming for television companies. As a result of the link between advertisers and television, more money is able to be brought into the game, though the rules of the game may be changed to increase the size of the viewing audience as well as to attract more spectators to a match.

Because of the close link between commercial success and winning, it is my contention that spectators collectively control the sporting world. As Guttmann (1986: 184) suggests,

> Fame and fortune beyond the dreams of nineteenth-century athletes are now the prize for the physically gifted, but the fame is prior to the fortune. It is because millions of ordinary, and extraordinary, men and women feel themselves personally represented by sports heroes and heroines that they buy millions of tickets and turn on hundreds of millions of television sets. No fame, no fortune.

Valley RFC stood at the nexus between amateurism and professionalism in the late 1990s. This is the point where success on the pitch and success in the commercial world meet. In this commercial age, whether or not Valley RFC is destined to be an important player in debates surrounding professionalism in Wales will depend largely on how successful the club remains on the pitch. It is worth remembering that many sports clubs are facing the same uncertain future as Valley RFC and that rugby, and this club in particular, should be seen as an illustration of the transformations taking place in elite amateur sport. It is of importance, therefore, to explore fully how the habitus of a sporting environment can be determined by more closely examining the sports participant's only tool – the body. In the next chapter the focus of our attention will be the role that social theories can play in enhancing our understanding about the body in a professional sporting environment.

Chapter 3

Sporting bodies
Mortal engines

This chapter will build on the understanding of the importance of sports medicine as a distinctive cultural environment in which the body can be managed, as was illuminated in Chapter 1. In relation to medicine, the body can be conceptualised as an engine with a mortal quality, to borrow from the work of Hoberman (1992). The body is the one tool with which a sportsperson ultimately has to work (Howe 2001). Because humans are embodied actors within society, the social investigation of the body is problematic since it is from our vantage-point within a body that we view the social world. The social world that the body occupied therefore can be observed from many distinct points of view. For example, a body that is seen as the focus of biomedical investigation may be seen as completely distinct from the same body explored from a symbolic perspective. This 'stratified' body (Maguire 1993) suggests that it might be difficult to articulate the importance of the body from one moment to the next. The stratification of the body highlights the flexibility that may be employed to understand the body's importance in the cultural world of sport. This flexibility in the interpretation of the body's importance can be combined with Hoberman's (1992) notion of mortality, which is related to how the body may be altered through various methods of performance enhancement that are a by-product of the push for commercial success discussed in the previous chapter. This current chapter will focus upon an exploration of the key conceptualisations of the body as they relate to sporting culture and in doing so it will lay the foundation upon which pain, injury and risk are explored in subsequent chapters.

The body and social theory

Since the beginning of the 1980s there has been a proliferation of social scientific research into the importance of the body in society (see Turner 1996; Falk 1994; Shilling 1993; Featherstone *et al.* 1991). In the discipline of anthropology, for example, the focus on the body was rarely made explicit, since the very nature of the ethnographic enterprise meant that communities under investigation were explored from an embodied perspective

(Lock 1993). This traditionally has been articulated through the senses of the participant observer who is a long-term resident within the community. Because much of the research into pain and injury does not adopt an embodied approach, this chapter signals the importance of the body in the investigation of pain, injury and risk. As a result of embodied practices being of central importance to high-performance athletes, the body is central throughout the discourse of this book.

Sport has, to a limited extent, become a focus of body research (for an accessible overview, see Blake 1996) within the works of social theorists such as Bourdieu (1977, 1984, 1990), Foucault (1979) and Merleau-Ponty (1962, 1965). These are the materials employed by those in sports studies to explore the importance of the body. I believe sporting culture to be somatic, or pertaining to the body in a corporeal sense, in much the same way that Turner (1992, 1996) uses the term to relate to a society in which political and personal problems are both developed and expressed through the body. In this way, the study of sporting bodies is rather an investigation of embodiment where the body becomes a social space that is transformed through its involvement in sporting practice. In this chapter it is my contention that all research into the social significance of sport should consider issues of embodiment since, as has already been pointed out, the body is the primary tool with which elite sporting participants have to work in order to enhance their performance. In other words, sporting participants may use multiple training methods to improve their body but ultimately it is the body that performs in the sporting arena.

Habits will be explored in this chapter as a vehicle for understanding how the body can be trained and manipulated to serve the elite sporting performer. Adoption of habitual training of the body can be seen to be central to much of the work, past and present, that examines the body in the social world (Bourdieu 1977, 1984, 1992; Leder 1990; Merleau-Ponty 1962, 1965; Shilling 1993). The examination of habit illuminates the concept of agency as important to a practical and embodied praxis. In other words, the physical manifestation of culture through embodied action is fundamental to exploring the importance of the social theory of the body in the context of sport. The concept of discipline, which has a central place in the work of Foucault (1979), can be seen as habit that is created as a result of the power that is exerted upon various actors in the sporting environment. Before examining the concepts of habit and discipline more closely, I will briefly turn to the early understanding of the body as a mechanical object which is central to the work of René Descartes (1978).

Mechanics and meat

The work of Descartes (1978; first published 1637) has been of enormous importance in drawing the world's attention to the body, and while at times there has been criticism of Descartes's legacy of dualism (Crossley 2001; Turner 1996), it is important to remember that Descartes was writing in a world where a mechanical understanding of science was fashionable among academic elites. Every author is a product of the times in which they write and therefore it is important to contextualise the work of Descartes as one would that of any great thinker of the past. In fact, it could be argued that the development of sports medicine that is explored in Chapter 1 presupposes a mechanical body, as the goal of performance enhancement is best achieved by understanding the body as a machine. The body in the context of sports medicine is an object that can be controlled and manipulated, and thus may be understood as a complex mechanical machine.

Ryle (1949) refers to Descartes's construction of the dualism of mind/body as 'the ghost in the machine', which may be a helpful way of understanding the sporting body. Leder (1990, 1998), on the other hand, sees Descartes's conceptualisation of the body as a corpse or piece of meat, which, interestingly, is what Turner placed upon the front cover of the second edition of his classic work *The Body and Society* (1996). This analogy of the body as meat will be of importance when the context of professional sport is more fully examined later in this book. At this point, however, it is important to acknowledge that in some sporting environments, bodies when in a state of injury are no more than unwanted meat (Howe 2001). An injured body to those who control professional sport may not be treated as if it were of value, because while most cultures value human well-being, some sporting cultures limit concern to those individuals who are able to perform on the day of competition.

Some social theorists have suggested that the work of Descartes is useful because the social scientist is searching for an understanding of the nexus between the mind and the body (Crossley 2001). All social actors are at once both mindful and embodied, and as a result, the distinction that Descartes makes needs to be more closely examined. Ryle (1949) suggests that the dualism of Descartes should be questioned, owing to the fact that there are physical acts that are also mental. An example of this is the act of talking to oneself. Speech requires physical action from the body but an agent can also internalise a response within the mind. For example, a social norm that many parents try to teach their children is to 'think before you speak'. As adults, some of us forget this valuable piece of advice, but what occurs when we do remember it is that we effectively talk to ourselves, albeit internally. From the 'training' that we receive from our parents, the act of thinking before we speak becomes habitual. It is to physical acts or auto-responses of the mind and body that I shall now turn, acts that are triggered in a specific social context such as the environment of sporting performance either in training or in competition.

Habits

Habitual responses can take the form of emotions, which are a form of natural language and, like all languages, must be learned. For example, pain, which will be discussed later in the book, takes on a representation that is public when the behaviour that accompanies it becomes apparent (Williams and Bendelow 1998). Children can be socialised in how to express pain because parents are able to see the signs or gestures that are part and parcel of the body's reaction to being in pain. In this way, a child is taught the gender-appropriate behaviour to pain, a behaviour that social scientists of sport have been interested in exploring (Nixon 1989; White et al. 1995; Young 1993). Whether a physical movement associated with the onset of pain is a conscious act or not, this is an important issue that can be addressed by the work of phenomenologists. It has been suggested that

> [c]onsciousness, the phenomenologists argue, is always 'conscious of' something other than it. It always 'intends' objects. The importance of this 'intentional' definition of perceptual consciousness is that it chal-lenges the Cartesian notion of the 'inner theatre of the mind' and constitutes a first important step towards a critique of introspection.
>
> (Crossley 2001: 46)

Physical action that becomes embodied in certain situations may be seen as habitual, and such habitual acts are often drilled into an actor through countless repetition that lacks imagination. This can take the form of kicking drills in football or sprinting drills in track and field, for example. Habitual acts that are further developed by improvisation can be considered dispositions (Ryle 1949). A disposition is an underlying tendency or pro-pensity to act in a certain way and is therefore more flexible than a habit established through rudimentary drills, but is still achieved without conscious thought before the action. The disposition to fight is fundamental for a boxer, and requires more than technical skill and physical fitness. The dis-position is the embodied ability to put the habitual training together in such a way that it can be quickly adapted to suit any fight situation. Given a social situation, our disposition will suggest that we are likely to act in a certain way. This distinction between habit and disposition is useful in that it explores the notion of human intervention in the sporting environ-ment. What can be confusing, however, is that both Merleau-Ponty (1962, 1965) and Bourdieu (1984, 1992) use the terms 'habit', 'habitus' and 'disposition' interchangeably.

Merleau-Ponty (1962) understands that the relationship between an agent and the environment cannot be explored independently of the idea that the environment at some level is subjective to the agent. Perception of the environment is then seen as an embodied activity. The agent who perceives can be seen to be an effect of the perception rather than its cause. In other words, it is the social meaning attached to the environment around a social interaction that has a fundamental influence upon our behaviour or disposition. Merleau-Ponty acknowledges that there may be issues of innate understanding in relation to perception, but his primary concern is the role played by habitual schemas of perception, which have social value.

Focusing on football (soccer), Merleau-Ponty in *The Structure of Behaviour* reflects upon perception and action of players (agents) on the field of play:

> For the player in action the football field is not an 'object', that is, the ideal term which can give rise to an indefinite multiplicity of perspectival views and remain equivalent under its apparent transformation. It is pervaded with lines of force (the 'yard lines'; those which demarcate the 'penalty area') and articulated in sectors (for example, the 'openings' between adversaries) which call for a certain mode of action and which initiate and guide the action as if the player were unaware of it.
>
> (1965: 168)

The footballer is engaged in the action that takes place on the field and is controlled by the constraints upon action that are part of the game. For example, an agent who has a disposition for football will see openings on the field where someone without such a disposition would not see the openings. Even the spectator who has an understanding of, if not a disposition for, the game will see the game differently from the player on the field, and the speed with which a player embraces reflective action will often be directly related to the success of the habitual drills that have been carried out on the training field. If the player is proficient, action will be spontaneous, and in team sports (where there are many different skill levels) players' abilities will often be on a par with those of the other players in the same game (though star performers stand out, generally skills across a league are similar). Most of all, players find the game a 'normal environment' in part because of the training they undertake before they play. In a sense, the game can be a 'virtual reality of human construction' (Crossley 2001: 76). While a game is being played, the well-trained player has minimal time for reflection upon the actions of other players, as the game happens in the spaces between players. In a game such as rugby, where physical contact is part of a match, a good player still needs the ability to 'read' space regardless of how limited the space may be. Physical contact such as tackling limits space at one point on the pitch but opens up space elsewhere. Therefore, how the players perceive and act at the same time is shaped by the game and reflects its structure.

Every action of a player embodies a structure and logic that is distinctive to the game and level at which it is played. Accordingly, the work of Merleau-Ponty (1965) and that of Bourdieu (1984, 1988, 1993) are useful as allies to aid explanation. For Bourdieu, an agent's habitus is the embodied sediment of every encounter they have had with the social world. It can be used, in the present, to mould perception, thought and action to the extent that it gains an important role that influences the decisions that an agent might make in future encounters. In this sense, actors can be seen not simply to follow rules but also to bend them much in the same way as is propounded in the work of Merleau-Ponty (1962, 1965), which highlights improvisation as being fundamental to an individual's disposition. Dispositions, or more generally forms of social competence, may be seen as a product of well-established social environments. In other words, while society may be seen as shaping agents, it needs the improvisations of the individual from time to time if it is going to evolve. Therefore, in the post-industrial society in which we live, it is important to see the body as much a product of the self as it is of society. It is the self that provides improvisation by drawing upon the sediment of previous social encounters. This is evident when a sporting contest is observed. While the game is played within a set of rules (any transgressors are ideally penalised), a sporting performance is full of improvisation,[1] much like good jazz.

> Both sports and jazz share this element of moving, of improvisation, an element which pulls against the rationalised and bureaucratised view of aesthetics which has dominated the criticism of the arts as well as sport, in the West since the Renaissance.
>
> (Blake 1996: 201)

To Shilling (1993), the self-project of the body is an area where self-expression is the norm and where economic individualism is allowed to flourish. At the heart of this view is consumer culture, which, as well as having a great impact on the evolution of professional sporting practice (see Chapter 2), has altered the social body. Fundamental to consumerism is the body, and since the body is the central focus of most sports, it is important that the understanding of the relationship between the body and the outside influences that regulate it (such as consumerism) is examined more closely.

Long before those involved with the administration of the game had taken any steps to utilise the commercial opportunities derivative from the players, the players themselves, of games such as rugby union, were aware of the consumer potential of their own bodies. As we have seen in Chapter 2, sports authorities are fully aware of the potential in the game as a whole and are eager to exploit this by securing large television contracts which will in turn lead to better marketing of the game. Whether or not the sports administrators are aware of the value of the players' bodies as a platform for increasing consumer interest in the game is rather unclear. However, the hegemonic nature of sporting governing committees (Gruneau 1983; Hargreaves 1986) suggests that if they were aware of this potential, they would attempt to take advantage of the situation, with little concern for the participants. Because the elite sporting participants do not live in isolation, they will be aware that the body in society may also be seen as the focal point of contemporary consumer culture (although they may not articulate this fact in this manner).

> The body is clearly an object of crucial importance in consumer culture and its supply industries: and sports, together with fashion, . . . dieting, keep-fit therapy, . . . advertising imagery, . . . are deployed in a constantly elaborating programme whose objective is the production of the new 'normalised' individual.
>
> (Hargreaves 1986: 14)

The elite sporting performers will begin to see themselves as objects that can be marketed. A rise in the number of elite sporting participants who have agents to look after their sporting and non-sporting interests highlights how they are becoming more aware of their potential commercially.

Sporting bodies may therefore be seen as being influenced by a number of factors (Figure 3.1). The increased use of technology in sports medicine, the notion of discipline in the works of Foucault and Bourdieu, the commodification of the body (Featherstone 1991; Hargreaves 1986), in addition to the symbolic body, have all influenced the construction of the 'body' as a theoretical object worthy of investigation.

Therefore, the sporting body is conceived as being in a state of flux among these representative bodies. However, on the level of practical performance, the elite sporting participant's body, while the participant is fit, may be considered as focused on a disciplined body, where habit is also of influence, but in times of injury this focus shifts towards a biomedical body. Increasingly, commodified bodies may be seen to operate at this level as well. This can occur when a player is contracted to wear a certain product (e.g. shoes) and their sport's national governing body (or increasingly club) has signed a contract that requires its players to wear a specific (different) brand. The danger with the examination of the social impact of any object is that by trying to focus on its importance, the researcher may forget that the object (in this case the body) is malleable. 'Sporting bodies and bodies of sportspeople need to be examined as "figurations in flux", not as uni-dimensional or compartmentalised social units or individuals subject to "single factor" causal influence' (Maguire 1993: 47). While I do not advocate widespread use of figurational sociology, it is important that the sporting body should be seen as a flexible entity. In this regard, the work of Foucault, on the notion of discipline, delivers an explanation of great importance as to how the elite sporting performer reacts to the training drills in an environment where power relations between coach and performer are often unequal.

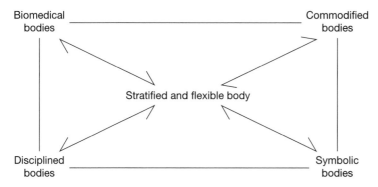

Figure 3.1 The flexible sporting body. (Adapted from Maguire 1993: 46.)

Foucault's discipline

Foucault's conceptualisation of discipline portrayed in *Discipline and Punish* (1979) has given me an understanding of my corporeality as an athlete and my mindset as an anthropologist. This conceptualisation of the socially disciplined body has also been, for generations, in one form or another, and perhaps unconsciously, a focus of good coaches' training procedures. One of the main concerns of this book is how and why sporting bodies are disciplined and how their discipline has changed within the context of professionalism. Featherstone has commented that physical activity is often undertaken for the simple pleasures that it brings to those who enjoy it and not the utilitarian values that are often associated with it: 'The notion of running for running's sake, purposiveness without a purpose, a sensuous experience in harmony with embodied physical nature, is completely submerged amidst the welter of benefits called up by the markets and health experts' (1991 [1982]: 185–186).

While participation in leisure activities may initially be a result of the enjoyment had by the person involved, often individuals are unconscious of the other changes that are occurring, because what is happening in and to the body, owing to the physical requirements of participation, may be more apparent. In the process of partaking in physical exercise the individual unconsciously objectifies the values of society that are appropriate to such activities and thus the individual's mind becomes the caretaker of its socially disciplined body.

According to the work of Foucault (1975, 1979), power is focused upon the body, which as a result may be seen as a formation or product of hegemonic interaction. In this sense the body may be seen as an object that is transformed through power relationships:

Foucault regards medical science as the crucial kink at the level of knowledge between the discipline of individual bodies by professional groups (of psychiatrists, dietitians, social workers and others) and the regulation of populations by panopticism (in the form of asylums, factories, schools and hospitals).[2]

(Turner 1996: 63)

In the context of sport, the body can be disciplined through the creation of habit by the repetitive rudimentary drills that are set down by coaches to enhance players' performance. This is the sort of environment in the sporting context where a 'system of expansive discipline and surveillance [that] produces normal persons by making each individual as visible as possible to each other, and by meticulous work on persons' bodies at the instigation of subjects themselves' (Hargreaves 1987: 151).

The social environment that is a product of a collection of individuals with the same disposition means that Foucault's work on discipline marries well with that of Bourdieu's concept of *habitus*. Bourdieu's concept of habitus may be seen to be related to Foucault's concept of discipline, since 'the body is used (walks, carries itself) differently by different social groups, and sport is one of the most important ways that the body's *habitus* is learned' (Blake 1996: 23).

Bourdieu's habitus

Habitus to Bourdieu informs action in the same way as grammar structures a language. This can allow for multiple forms of expression through the body, whether it is how the body moves or how it is covered (Bourdieu 1984). Social agents are players in a game actively working towards achieving a goal with acquired skills and competence but doing so within an established structure of rules, which are only gradually transformed over time. Habitus predisposes action by agents but does not reduce them to a position of complete subservience. In *Outline of a Theory of Practice* (1977), Bourdieu 'shows that the methods of gymnastics and by extension, those of sports or other codified physical activities, are cultural products shaped by those who practice them. These products embody the fundamental particularities of the group to which they belong' (Clément 1995: 148).

The theory of practice developed by Bourdieu (1977, 1984, 1992) identifies the nexus between the body and the social environment surrounding it. Bourdieu (1984: 101) sees the relationship as a mathematical equation:

[(habitus) (capital)] + field = practice

In this formulation, habitus is a combination of various habitual schemas and dispositions, multiplied by capital of an appropriate form (i.e. cultural or economic) in addition to social conditions that have over time been structured to develop in a particularly specific manner.

In a sporting context, then, the games metaphor that is employed by Bourdieu in both the non-sporting and the sporting contexts (1984, 1988, 1990, 1993) highlights the nexus between capital and field. The multiplication of a player's disposition, their competence (habitus) and the resources at their disposal (capital), in relation to the social environment, highlights the social actors' position in the world. In the particular environment of elite sport it is the embodied disposition or doxa that enables a social exploration of the distinctive character of sporting practice and body hexis (the performative aspect of habitus). In a sense, embodied sporting practice is made up of the habitual disposition established through the training drills that might be part of a traditional training regime and the actual desire to play the game. Sporting practice is therefore structured at a number of levels, with improvisation grounded in sediments of previous sporting activities. For the elite sporting performer there is the structuring of personal training regimes. If the individual is also a member of a team, training for the team as a squad will also be of importance. Structure is also imposed in the form of rules and regulations that have been codified by the sporting federation. All three levels of structure determine the nature of the game but these still allow room for improvisation on the part of the player. Fields therefore allow the social scientist to see beyond the body as object and allow for an appropriate conceptualisation within the sporting environment. Capital on the other hand allows for the exploration of those issues to which a disposition in a particular social field may be subject that are associated with assets, both economic and cultural.

An example from the work of Bourdieu may be appropriate here:

> The habitus as the feel for the game is the social game embodied and turned into a second nature. Nothing is simultaneously freer and more constrained than the action of a good player. He quite naturally materialises at just the place the ball is about to fall, as if the ball were in command of him – but by that very fact, he is in command of the ball. The habitus, as society written into the body, into the biological individual, enables the infinite number of acts of the game – written into the game as possibilities and objective demands – to be produced; the constraints and demands of the game, although they are not restricted to a code of rules, *impose themselves* on those people – and those people alone – who, because they have a feel for the game, a feel, that is, for the immanent necessity of the game, are prepared to perceive them and carry them out.
>
> (1990: 63)

This account of habitus highlights the transformational nature of habitus and how practices are incorporated in the body and continually embodied in the hexis of new recruits to that particular sporting practice over time.

The physical action of players in a game is strategic, and the better the strategy is, the more embodied cultural capital or physical capital a player possesses (Shilling 1993; Wacquant 1995). Qualities that are associated with sporting bodies such as strength, stamina and fitness are all part of a continuum of performance. When an athlete has a high level of achievement in any or all of these categories, they will possess physical capital in the sporting environment (field) where those qualities are revered. During a game, however, players do not have the time to reflect upon their actions if they are to perform to the highest level. Moments of indecision on the pitch, which may be frequently observed in matches by sporting spectators, might, to a player, be moments of reflection, but, if that player is to do their job well, such moments should be eliminated. The arbitrariness of a given game can be reflected upon after a match or by a social scientist interested in the construction of sporting dispositions and/or habitus. It is for books such as this one to address the importance of embodied pastimes and spectacles.

The physical act of training that is required to perform (hexis) in a game means that the structure of the game is a fundamental component of a player's habitus. This enables a player to perform during a match in an unreflective manner that allows for access to sediments of past games to form the roots of new improvisations. A new member of a given sporting community may also see the importance of acquiring good skills as part and parcel of the social environment surrounding the game.

Mead (1967) explores the dualism of the self that is bounded in the grammatical distinction between 'I' and 'me'. The distinction between 'I' and 'me' is that 'I' provides a sensuous understanding of the social world around a given actor whereas 'me' is the socialised form of the self. The social actors' understanding of their 'me' enables them to see themselves as an embodied agent and it acts as a reflection of what the agent is in the social world. Therefore 'me' is a representation of the self, similar in nature to that of a mirror image, whereas 'I' is everything that an individual is. The relationship between 'I' and 'me' is clearly temporal and reflexive and it is akin to the social actor following or being followed by their own shadow.

This has great importance when exploring the role of the body in sport because it is useful in helping to decipher how the informants involved in the research process engage with and understand their bodies. The 'I' through habitual acts becomes embodied, whereas 'me' is a product of narrative discourse, which is an image that is developed through reflection. The interpretative project that the social anthropologist must pursue can be seen on two levels. One of these is the body that may be observed in the form of habitus and sediment, which ground improvisation. The other is through the exploration of narrative representations of the self that are evident in a thorough review of transcripts. This distinction becomes more confused when it is understood that as an embodied social actor the anthropologist must filter this material through their own sense of self, which obviously possesses the same two levels of understanding as the social actors under investigation. In this way the objectification of the distinctive understanding of social actors in the sporting environment in question (or any other social environment for that matter) can be both time-consuming and problematic. Debates such as this have been the focus of many publications (see Clifford 1987; Clifford and Marcus 1986; Marcus and Fischer 1986), but the debate was phrased in such a way that the struggle was about trying to determine whether an objective truth was possible in anthropological investigation. While I would not claim that such a truth is available to me or to any other social scientist, the act of attempting to find an objective understanding in the sporting world should not be abandoned. The empirical work that is the foundation for the case studies (Chapters 7–9) has been done with a personal understanding of the primary components of elite sporting habitus. To borrow from Laberge and Sankoff (1988), my access to the communities into which I have researched has been eased as a result of overlapping habitus.

While some have suggested that Bourdieu's work illuminates the importance of creativity, it fails to highlight how social fields transform (Jenkins 1992). It could be argued that his emphasis on reproduction (i.e. Bourdieu 1977, 1984) is another way of articulating the same point. Bourdieu has explored the concept of habitus before that of agency. This is very much in line with Merleau-Ponty's (1962) assertion that habits are but leftover sediment from previous action, and as such, the nexus between the two social theorists is unmistakable. It could be argued that the approach adopted by Bourdieu is rather like the proverbial discussion about the chicken and the egg. Does there need to be an agent before there is habitual behaviour or does habitual behaviour predispose how the agent will act without the sediment of past acts to inform the agent's habitus? It is best described as a co-evolution.

Merleau-Ponty's (1962) concept of corporeal schema nicely articulates the embodied agency of a player both as an individual and as a member of the social environment that surrounds sporting contests. The corporeal schema comprises the skills required for the performance and the practical understanding of the game, and these skills may be transformed depending on the action of other players. A good player reads a game without thinking. In other words, they explore the relationship between different levels of structure that constrict movement at a subconscious level.

Commenting on the work of Merleau-Ponty, Crossley suggests:

> Habit involves a modification and enlargement of the corporeal schema, an incorporation of new 'principles' of action and know-how, which

permit new ways of acting and understanding. It is a sediment of past activity which remains alive in the present in the form of the structures of corporeal schema; shaping perception, conception, deliberation, emotion and action.

(Crossley 2001: 125)

In fact, the emphasis on innovation (Merleau-Ponty 1962) gives the player the raw material to turn into habit. As a result, innovative habits that are a product of creative praxis result in a diachronic shift in the social world.

Thus far, the body has been discussed as disciplined and habitually trained as part of sporting praxis. The next step, then, is to explore how the social theory of the body can help to illuminate an understanding of the body when it is confronted by pain.

Pain and the body

From the work of Merleau-Ponty (1962) and Leder (1990), we can see the human body as a vehicle for living in the world, but unless it is brought to our attention by an outside influence, such as pain for example, it is not an object of our understanding. That is to say, the physical requirement to move our bodies in daily life, which appears to be getting easier with the advent of cyborg technologies (Cole 1998; Haraway 1991; Shogan 1999) and the like, has made it easy for us to go about daily routines without having to think about how physically to manage our bodies. This is assuming, of course, that there is no physical impairment that may draw your attention to your body, as is highlighted by Murphy (1987). Clearly the act of moving one's body is distinct from that of moving an external object. For the social world, however, where interaction is fundamental, the enactment of social rituals is embodied. Importantly, action, in a social context, is both embodied and also full of thought, at least at one level. Certainly, ritualised social action is gradually transformed, eventually becoming habitual and therefore embodied.

Traditional medical approaches are a result of social action targeted at alleviating pain. Yet in spite of a long history, the medical fraternity is unable to claim complete expertise over the relief of suffering – something that may in large part stem from the failure to transcend the Cartesian mind/body dualism upon which Western medicine is premised. Traditionally in the West, the body was the concern of the medical profession and the mind was the focus of clergymen. However, it has been argued by Turner (1992) that the medicalisation of the body has led to rationalisation, which has had a profound effect on the secularisation of culture. It is important to remember, however, when considering the literature on embodiment that relates to pain, that while it can offer useful insights for the understanding of pain, there are limitations in the material, not least in that it is often assumed that the body is undifferentiated, presumably white, male, and unaffected by disability. This book attempts to avoid part of this research lacuna by exploring Paralympic athletes' understanding of pain and injury in Chapter 9. Less explicitly than in Chapter 9, age and disability do enter the book in Chapter 7, since many of my informants into pain and injury in rugby were ex-players who had had their careers ended by an injury, often one that led to disability, yet were still active members of the club. Interviews with many of the club committee members have proved that chronic pain may be a feature of this life-after-rugby.

The elevation of sensation over emotion in traditional medical and psychological approaches to pain results in the lack of attention to subjectivity, which in turn leads to a limited approach towards suffering and a neglect of broader cultural and sociological components of pain. In other words, a far more sophisticated model of pain is needed – one that locates individuals within their social and cultural contexts and that allows for the inclusion of feelings and emotions. Therefore, I hope that by examining injury in the elite sporting cultures of rugby players, track and field athletics and Paralympic sport, I can establish a better understanding of the social role of pain.

Turner (1992) has suggested that Merleau-Ponty's early discussions about embodiment are of great importance. Merleau-Ponty's work suggests that a better understanding of pain can be readily accessed since it is in the lived human body that pain, both emotional and physical, occurs: 'It is not possible to talk about human perception of the world without a theory of embodiment as the "perspective" from which observation occurs. Our perception of everyday reality depends on a lived body' (Turner 1992: 43). Despite the implication of this insight, Leder goes further to suggest that without pain our bodies are 'taken for granted'. In his view, our bodies are normally phenomenologically absent from view:

> While in one sense the body is the most abiding and inescapable presence in our lives, it is also characterized by absence. That is, one's own body is rarely the thematic object of experience. . . . I may be engaged in a fierce sport, muscles flexed and responsive to the slightest movements of my opponent. Yet it is precisely upon this opponent, this game, that my attention dwells, not on my own embodiment
>
> (1990: 1)

Yet as Leder also points out, this normal bodily state of being 'taken for granted' tends to be profoundly disrupted in the context of factors such as pain, disease and death. Here the body becomes a central aspect of experience, albeit in an alien and dysfunctional manner. In other words, in contrast to the 'disappearances' that characterise ordinary functioning, in the context of pain, suffering and death the body dys-appears. That is to say, 'The body appears as a thematic focus for [attention], but precisely in a *dys* state – *dys* is from the Greek prefix signifying "bad", "hard" or "ill", and is found in English words such as "dysfunctional"' (Leder 1990: 84). Therefore, the apparent effortless performances of highly trained athletes that spectators see as the embodiment of perfection is not 'felt' by the athlete at all. It is the grace and simplistic artistry of sport that seems to captures most spectators' imaginations. We all at some time have tried to master what appear to be the simplest of leisure activities, only to feel dysfunctional within our own bodies. Yet in the performance, with ease, of daily tasks that we have mastered, the body seems to be absent. Individuals who have set world records in athletics or ice-skating, for example, or have achieved Olympic gold, have often had difficulty recalling their specific bodily actions. An athlete with a disability such as cerebral palsy would, on the other hand, regardless of the intensity of training, be constantly aware of the body, as the neuromuscular deficiencies would not allow trained responses to become automatic.

The 'automatic' kicking action of a rugby player who takes penalties is a case in point. He rehearses these actions to the point where they become instinctive. It is only from watching the video of his performance after the match that the kicker is able to relive the magic.

> I train real hard at my kicking. . . . In school I was a natural kicker but at the international level you can't afford to mess up . . . everyone wants my spot so I must practise so that the techniques I use once again become natural.
>
> (Notebook 3: 2)

The same is true for a scrum-half, who often trains with a weighted ball to increase the strength of his pass from the base of the scrum. My informant stated:

> My ambition is to be the Welsh number one and in order to do that my actions at the base must be effortless and yet unpredictable [to the opposition]. Sometimes the pain in my hands and wrists is so bad that I wonder whether it is all worth it.
>
> (Notebook 2: 15)

With the advent of technology such as virtual reality, it is possible to create the same 'perfect' performance environment without having to endure the endless training regimes – which often lead to the pain of overuse injuries – that even the most gifted bodies (sporting participants) must undertake to achieve perfection at the elite level in sport. Through virtual reality simulation, even individuals with 'imperfect' bodies are able to, without much bodily strain, climb Mount Everest, scuba-dive the Great Barrier Reef, or even partner Michael Owen for Liverpool FC. The development and use of this technology is a clear signal that the mind and body are inseparable, since it is primarily the mind rather than the body that is exercised by their use. The term 'virtual' to describe this new technology is rather fitting, since

> Whereas in day-to-day events we are our body without hesitation, suddenly pain renders the body disharmonious with the self. Such times, along with those of hunger, exhaustion, disability and approaching death, can be seen as experimental antecedents to dualism.
>
> (Leder 1984–5: 262)

Here the painful body emerges as 'thing-like'; it betrays us and we may feel alienated and estranged from it as a consequence. Thus while at an analytical level the study of pain may demand a transcendence of dualistic thinking, at the phenomenological or experiential level it may perpetuate the Cartesian dualism (Loland 1992).

The fact that mind and body are fully one while pain is present also points to another fundamental issue: namely, that physical experience is inseparable from its cognitive and emotional significance. It is for this reason that pain can be used to describe not only physical agony but emotional turmoil and spiritual suffering. As Scheper-Hughes and Lock (1987) argue, emotions affect the way in which the body experiences illness and pain, and these are projected in images of well and poorly functioning social body and body politic.[3] In this respect, exploration of sickness, madness, pain, disability and death are investigations of human events that are full of emotion. On an emotional level, therefore, there is no difference between the pain of a 'broken heart' that develops with the loss of a loved one and the gut-churning, nauseating experience that controls a runner before an important race or a rugby player before a vital match. These events are shared cross-culturally, and much of the current research in medical anthropology continues to suggest this:

> There are fundamental aspects of human experience which are transcultural or universalistic and which point to a shared ontology. The discussion of theodicy and morality in religious doctrine points to these fundamental human experiences of which pain and suffering seem to me primary illustrations.
>
> (Turner 1992: 252)

This will be illustrated through the case studies that provide the exemplars for much of the theoretical underpinning of the book.

Summary

The conceptualisation of the sporting body that has been highlighted here is heavily influenced by the work of Merleau-Ponty, Foucault, Bourdieu and Leder. The body may be seen to be disciplined on a personal level through the training, for example, that sporting participants undertake in order to have the fitness to perform at club training and on match day. Another type of training with their clubmates sees the body disciplined on a level where a specific social code is followed; the rules of the game of rugby union are an example of this. In these two distinct environments, *habitus* of the body is established, where exercises and drills are repeated until they become automatic. In a sense, then, the body, in the discipline and *habitus* of training, become what could be called an '*autobody*' – which, importantly, does not appear until the body is confronted by pain and injury.

Part II

Pain, injury and the culture of risk

Chapter 4

Pain and injury

Signal and response

The previous three chapters should be seen as comprising the cultural back-drop for what follows in the next three chapters. This chapter, with its focus upon pain and injury, should be understood in relation to the cultural environment surrounding sports medicine, the transformation from amateur to professional sport, and the roles that the body of sporting participants plays in both. The body is, of course, of prime importance here because it is quite literally the only tool with which a sporting participant has to work.[1] Pain and injury have a fundamental impact on the body of individuals involved in sporting practice because, when they occur, they limit partici-pation. The lack of ability to participate due to pain and injury becomes particularly crucial in an environment where sport is a professional concern, and the health of performers may be sacrificed for the betterment of the sporting organisation that supports them. This places pressure not only on the body of the participant but also upon the sports medicine team, which is confronted with the ethical dilemma of which customer to serve: the sporting participant, the team management or the sport's governing body.

Since the early 1990s there has been an increased interest in pain and injury and its social importance, particularly from the discipline of sport sociology (Nixon 1992, 1993a; White et al. 1995; Young 1993), and this has focused on the personal experience of this phenomenon through the medium of interviews. This book presents an analysis of pain and injury based upon ethnographic research. Ethnography is an approach that enables a diachronic understanding of these concepts, as the participant observer is present at the point where injury occurs, and also allows observation of the medical treat-ment of injury and the associated pain. This method helps to illuminate the relationship between the injured player and the expectations of their sporting environment. This chapter will begin by discussing the concept of pain and then focuses upon medical practice and the nature of pain. Following this, the related issues concerning the importance of alleviating pain from the world of the sporting participants will lead to a discussion about pain as it relates to risk. It might be surprising that injury has not been specifically mentioned in the chapter overview. This is a result of the manner in which the relationship between pain and injury exists in the context of professional sport. Pain as it is articulated in what follows is a marker for injury, and as a result this chapter is primarily concerned with the nature of pain in relation to injury.

The concept of pain

Although closely related, pain and injury are physically and conceptually distinct. Pain is a highly subjective phenomenon, and this has led to its exclusion from much discussion of injury, which may be seen as more objective. Adopting the same conceptual distinctions as are outlined in previous work (Howe 1997, 2001), injury can be understood as a breakdown in the structure of the body, a breakdown that may affect its function. Pain is the marker of an injury and is an unpleasant sensory and emotional experience associated with actual or potential tissue damage. It may be divided into acute and chronic components. Acute pain is a short, sharp sensation that is experienced at the point when injury occurs and for a limited period thereafter. Chronic pain is often associated with a pathological[2] process that causes continuous pain, or pain that recurs at intervals for months and, in some cases, years after injury. If pain is still present even after a cure should have been achieved, it must be considered chronic.

Unpleasant sensory, perceptual and emotional experiences distinguish chronic pain from acute pain, and hence chronic pain may be associated with psychological, emotional and behavioural responses. Although psychological factors have a profound influence on the experience of acute pain, with rare exceptions acute pain is not due primarily to psychopathology[3] or environmental influences. This is in contrast to chronic pain, in which psychopathology and/or environmental factors play a prominent role. With some injuries, acute pain imposes limitations on further activity, thus preventing additional damage. Chronic pain, on the other hand, is a pain that persists for a time beyond the course of an acute injury's healing schedule.[4]

With the onset of chronic pain and injury, greater emphasis is placed on psychopathology or environmental factors. In its chronic persistent form, pain never has a biological function, but is a negative force that often imposes severe emotional, physical, economic and social stresses on the patient and their social group. Throughout the research that informs this book, both types of pain were reported. However, the large majority of injuries that were observed were accompanied by acute pain. In the distinctive environment surrounding elite sporting practice, however, the role of acute pain takes on the qualities of chronic pain as it is seen to the outside world. This is because the performance of the body is of much greater importance to an elite sporting participant than it is to the general public. The physical contact from sports such as rugby football or the wear and tear a body is exposed to as a result of overuse in training/participating in elite athletics (track and field) is not normal in modern society. Therefore, in spite of the fact that participants train as part of their preparation for elite performance, the body does break down. As a result of the body's value during such contests, the psychopathology of pain becomes of fundamental importance.

The causative agent of injury and the catalyst for pain is the concept of hurt. Hurt triggers pain that is preliminary to injury in the case of positive pain, discussed later in this chapter. Because of the constant uncertainty surrounding when and if injury will arise, elite sporting participants, while playing, are not, it seems, consciously aware of injury and only consider the necessity of maintaining their bodies in an injury-free state once pain surfaces (Leder 1990). For the most part, therefore, most professional sporting performers, often at the expense of maintaining a sound physical structure, undertake training on a daily basis in the hope of enhanced physical performance. The physical habitus of natural sporting movement makes the body 'invisible' and therefore is one of the problems involved when persuading players to use preventive medicine such as massage therapy and stretching regimes, which are known to control injury to some degree. It is only after the onset of pain that the body 'appears' and alterations in training routines are attempted to limit the severity of injury.

Whether the injury is structural or functional in nature, it is always accompanied initially by acute pain. In the case of a structural injury, pain could be immediate (e.g. a broken leg), whereas the onset of pain and hence diagnosis of injury could take longer in the case of a functional injury (e.g. various overuse syndromes). Risk as it relates to sports injury, on the other hand, is the consequence of ignoring both physical and psychological pain. In other words, risk is noticing a danger but carrying on despite it. This act may cause injury and is therefore not the contemplation of the odds of being hurt. That is not to say that there cannot be a risk present without injury that is marked by pain, but in the context of this current study, of paramount concern is why athletes take risks (see Chapter 6) – risks that are highlighted by pain as a result of injury.

Reactions to pain are not simply involuntary and instinctual, but are determined in part by the social context in which pain occurs. Another social distinction of the type of pain experienced can be derived in a sporting context, namely playable and unplayable pain. The effect of these types of pain is self-evident, but sporting participants in different sports may experience them differently. For example, a pain in the shoulder may not stop a distance runner from performing, but the same pain may force a rugby player to examine more carefully the consequences of playing. Cultural groups, including sporting subcultures, display distinctive responses to pain. For example, the experience of pain may be normalised within some groups and problematised in others (Curry and Strauss, 1994; Nixon 1992, 1993a, b; Young 1993). Meanwhile, the manner in which a player copes with pain may reflect a particular social construction of gender identity (White *et al.*, 1995). Furthermore, stoicism may be valued in the face of pain (e.g. Kotarba, 1983). The ability to function with (sometimes intense levels of) pain may therefore be seen as a litmus test for acceptance into sporting subcultures.

White *et al.* (1995) have suggested that within these subcultures it is important to identify the 'location of discourse' of pain. Here a distinction between private and public pain can be made (Helman, 1990). Public acute pain, and its associated injury, is witnessed by spectators, officials as well as the other players and squad members when it occurs during a match. Private pain can be subdivided into personal experience, where it is not revealed to others at all, and 'shared private' experience, where only individuals close to the sporting performer (e.g. immediate family, medical doctor) are aware of the pain the participant is in. During this experience, individuals draw upon personal understandings of their own bodies, and these shape both their interpretation of and their response to pain (Kotarba 1983). Keeping pain private, or expressing it publicly, may or may not be desirable within the context of a particular group's belief and value system. All three levels of pain can exist at any one time and all were evident within the communities of sporting participants that form the case studies in this book.

Some pains are visible to society at large and others are kept private; the sufferer either does not tell a soul or limits this knowledge to a number of individuals. The shared private pain that might be articulated to a sports physician puts this individual in a difficult position. When pain is acute, those surrounding the sporting participant are aware that the injured individual should not play, but when the situation becomes chronic there is room for a distortion of the problem. The sporting performer may say they are fit because they may be afraid of losing their place on the team, or, with the advent of professionalism, may need the match fee which they will be paid for playing. On the other hand, the coaching staff may try to manipulate the sports medicine team into convincing the participant that the pain does not exist and that therefore they should play. Both situations are full of risk, which is prevalent in the social environment surrounding a sport.

This is a problem that has confronted sports medicine teams that work for professional American football clubs. One doctor stated:

> I was very curious whether I was in line for a share of the Super Bowl bounty . . . it seemed blatantly unethical for a team doctor to have a financial stake in whether the team won or lost. There could be a lot of questioning of motives if particular players were allowed to play despite injuries, or were given painkilling shots to play despite injuries.
>
> (Huizenga 1994: 70)

This dilemma is faced by medical practitioners who are responsible for the health and well-being of elite participants in other professional sports. Because being a professional in sport is seen by many as an occupation, this chapter will now address the concept of pain from an occupational perspective.

Occupational pain

The work of Kotarba (1983) is of interest in that he has contextually situated pain through an analysis of how pain is managed in different occupations, including professional athletics. He contrasts professional athletes with manual workers since in both occupations physical capabilities are paramount and pain constitutes a major threat. As Kotarba shows, an 'average' level of pain can be expected and as such is seldom disclosed.

> The pain-afflicted person may decide to conceal the experience of pain from potentially critical audiences if the social and emotional costs resulting from the disclosure outweigh the perceived benefits. The benefits of pain disclosure include access to health care, sympathy to one's suffering and help in adjusting to the contingencies affected by the pain. But the cost of pain disclosure, as learned through experience, can be perceived as overwhelming. Certain reactions of critical audiences may elicit feelings of shame and guilt.
>
> (1983: 134–135)

The decision to conceal or, alternatively, openly express pain may be seen as distinct to the subculture that an individual belongs to. This may ultimately determine whether an elite sporting performer stays actively involved in the sport, owing to their ability to deal with pain in a manner that is seen as appropriate to others within their particular subculture.

In contrast to a sportsperson, a manual worker at first sight may have less reason to conceal pain, especially if the union of which he is a member has real power in the workplace. However, as Kotarba (1983) points out, the rewards for disclosure may be less relevant than the symbolic costs involved in doing so, such as the threat to self-image and identity, fitness for work, and capabilities as a breadwinner. Kotarba suggests that workers, in contrast to athletes, find the resources for handling such situations in what he terms the 'tavern culture' – which include the circulation of information about treatments, the folk prescription of alcoholic beverages as painkillers, etc. For both athletes and manual workers, pain is a familiar feature of their normal everyday lives: athletes risk injury in training or competition, while manual workers risk the perennial threat of job-related accidents or back-ache. In other words, these two occupational subcultures regard pain as a 'normal' dimension of life – one which, according to Kotarba, gives rise to a 'chronic pain sub-culture'.

In spite of the importance of such studies in drawing attention to the socio-cultural dimensions and the shaping of pain, many have been criticised for crudely reinforcing ethnic stereotypes. Perhaps more importantly, accepting that these studies took place in a particular time and context, Bates (1987: 48) points out that research has tended to be rather collectivist and deterministic in orientation; portraying the individual as a passive entity who simply responds to social cultural forces. Kotarba's (1983) study is a far more interpretative approach to these issues. This work, while recognising the crucially important role that social and cultural factors play, accords a far more active, critical and reflective role to the individual, who draws upon their own lay knowledge and beliefs in shaping both their interpretation and their response to pain.

Kotarba's (1983) work has clear implications concerning this current volume, since all the case studies (Welsh rugby, athletics and Paralympic sports) have until relatively recently been amateur concerns. This means that these sports are at the nexus between the values of the amateur ideology on the one hand and professionalism on the other, perhaps in a liminal state akin to 'serious leisure' (Stebbins 1992). As government agencies try to encourage individuals to become more committed to physical betterment, injury and therefore pain will from time to time become part of their lives. Therefore, although Kotarba's work with sportspeople focuses on the professional performer, it is equally relevant to the ever-increasing numbers of eager amateurs.

The notion of the 'uneducated' athlete (uneducated in terms of knowledge about practical human physiology) has led many to suggest that the athletes have little choice about accepting the pain and injury that have become part of sporting tradition (Curry and Strauss 1994; Nixon 1992, 1993a, b). It could be argued that only the most committed elite athletes seem to ignore a standard level of pain. In part because the proliferation of popular sports literature, where advice is given on all matters concerning the well-being of individuals involved in a given activity, much more self-education is available today. Therefore, those involved in sport on a recreational level are better able to avoid the pain and injury that may in the past have curtailed mass involvement.

Any investigation of pain is problematic since it is a subjective cultural construct. Since levels of pain cannot be accurately determined from one injured sporting performer to the next, it is difficult to distinguish whether or not pain's only function is that of a marker for injury. This chapter will now turn to an examination of medical practice and the nature of pain. The focus then shifts to a general discussion of how pain is alleviated in sport. I will then suggest that sports medicine teams use placebos to great effect, and seek to establish how the use of such a method of treatment may take on even greater importance in professional sport. The manner in which pain, injury and risk are interrelated is of paramount importance, and this current discussion of pain will conclude with an exploration of how pain and risk are related in the context of sport.

Medical practice and the nature of pain

The Challenge of Pain (Melzack and Wall 1982) is an appropriate title for a book that deals with the subjective nature of pain. The book addresses issues concerning pain that exist at the nexus between nature and culture along similar lines to the work of Turner (1992) but with more reliance upon work that highlights the body's physiological response to pain. It is an important work partly because, as Good (1994) has highlighted, treatment of pain often tends to be liminal to Western medicine. In this work Melzack and Wall (1982) discuss what they call the gate control theory of pain. This theory suggests that psychological variables and social cultural embodied practice have a fundamentally important role with regard to human physiological processes that are the by-product of pain. Their understanding is that there exists a mechanical 'switch' as part of the nervous system that is near to the dorsal horns area of the spine. The social environment surrounding the individual who is in pain in part controls the switch that meters this flow of nerve impulses. This influence of the social environment may be seen in the light of the work of Foucault, which emphasised how medicine has become transformed from a unidimensional corporeal environment based upon the science of physiology to a two-dimensional environment that incorporates components of a psychosocial subjectivity (Nettleton 1992). However, seeing pain as embodied is fundamental to exploring pain as a social psychological dimension (Turner 1992).

While this acceptance of the new 'enlightened' medical paradigm may in some circles be seen as positive, it can create new problems, particularly as it relates to the treatment of pain. Pain, as a result of its psychosocial component, can now be interpreted as an issue that can be controlled by a strong-willed individual. For a sports participant who is in pain it can become an issue of mind over matter. In other words, if there is no observable damage to the individual (either structural or physiological), pain may not be taken seriously by those in a social environment where personal management of pain is highly valued. The presence of pain can also, interestingly, act as a way of reinforcing the traditional notion of the mind–body dualism that has been evident in Western medicine since the time of Descartes. The central tenet of Western medicine that objective knowledge of the body and disease are possible apart from subjective experience is brought into question in the environment surrounding chronic pain (Good 1994). In other words, 'Pain makes us believe that we can cut ourself off from the body. Through rationalizing pain . . . "I" and my body become two separate entities. Thus pain can be depicted as the experience of psychophysical dualism' (Vrancken 1989: 442). The body in pain can be seen, therefore, to reinforce the dualistic notion of the body that has traditionally impaired social scientific explorations of the body (highlighted in Chapter 3).

Traditional Western medicine has reinforced rather than healed the dualism between the mind and the body. Through the use of tried and tested medical regimes the individual in pain and injured may describe their body through technical medical language. This allows for the prioritisation of cure of disease over its prevention, which in turn increases the separation between the body and the mind. It could be argued, however, that embodiment is fundamental to a better understanding of the way in which pain influences sporting culture. Increased corporeal awareness on the part of the chronically ill or, in the case of elite sport, those participants who suffer from acute pain and as a result injury, as well as over-training syndrome (O'Toole 1998), has had an impact on sporting culture. Sporting participants, like all human beings, are at once part of nature and culture (Turner 1996). In this regard, then, the physical experience of pain is linked with the cognitive experience: 'The fact that mind, body and self are thoroughly interfused in pain, albeit in a problematic way, also points to another fundamental issue . . . namely, that physical experience is inseparable from its cognitive and emotional significance' (Williams and Bendelow 1998: 161).

Because of the structure of Western medicine, in which treatment of the mind and treatment of the body are separated, the alleviation of pain becomes difficult. However, the environment that surrounds professional sports and the desire to have the performer fit at a moment's notice require a new way of dealing with pain. It has been argued by Kleinman (1988) that culture should be interpreted as a filler of existential space between the embodiment of disease (as a physiological process) and its human experience. If this is the case, it is imperative that research should continue to explore sporting culture in such a way that it may illuminate this relationship. As I have suggested elsewhere (Howe 2001), a sound ethnographic approach could be seen to be a distinct advantage. The ethnographic tool of participant observation gives the researcher a good avenue with which to explore sporting culture and see its ability to link injury to the responses of the community.

As mentioned earlier, in the context of an elite sporting environment acute pain can be seen to manifest itself as chronic, in part owing to the importance of being 'active' in this elite context. It has been suggested that loss of self is what occurs when pain becomes chronic (Kleinman 1988; Murphy 1987), and this influences the individual's social world. While the work of Kotarba (1983) can be seen as a set of occupational stereotypes (Williams and Bendelow 1998), the behaviour exhibited by both the professional sportsmen and the manual workers in the force of chronic pain illuminates this distinction nicely. My concern is not the issue of stereotypes but rather a need for this quality work to be updated to give it a more inter-pretative understanding. I feel that contemporary work in this area should explore pain response as 'action' rather than 'behaviour', much in the manner that has been suggested by Williams and Calnan (1996). The action of prime importance could be seen to be the alleviation of pain.

Alleviating pain

The desire to alleviate pain has brought about the continual evolution of medical practices. Though pain has a central role in medicine and associ-ated disciplines such as psychiatry, it is exceedingly difficult to analyse. In the West, medical practice has long revolved around the alleviating of bodily suffering, to the point where pain as the indicator of ailments has often been ignored in discussions, being simply placed to one side as a by-product of structural and functional inadequacy. Pain is of cultural as well as physical importance, however, and through the examination of bodily performance, as seen in elite sport, the role of pain in cultural evolution may be deter-mined. It is pain's subjective nature that has led to its exclusion from most discussions of injury. As Western cultures are increasingly centred on objec-tive fact, concepts such as pain that are more subjective in nature are deemed irrelevant. This has even occurred in the social sciences, which often forget their roots and adopt the foundations of physical science. Pain helps to construct an environment through which its reactions can be acceptably interpreted. The lack of objectivity[5] in the measurement of pain has posed a large problem for research into the social role of pain. Levels of pain are difficult to distinguish, as the severity of each individual's pain will always be relative.

> The core conflicts between pain patients and health professionals involve many factors – frustration on both sides over the inadequacy of therapeutic intervention, distrust over the assessment of pain and its implications for disability determinations, and disagreement over the influence of voluntary control over symptoms and the question of accountability.
>
> (Good et al. 1992: 8)

When an athlete is injured, a physiotherapist will often poke, pitch and twist in the region of the injury, in order to determine the extent of physical damage. Therefore, the treatment team increases the level of pain in the short term in order to get a better understanding of the injury and thus speed up pain relief in the long term. Once the nature of an injury has been deter-mined, painkillers may be administered to offset the discomfort of an injury.

The use of drugs to control pain has a long history. Opium has been used to control pain for two thousand years, and morphine, a chemical derivative of this substance, has been used medically since 1898 (Welchew 1995). In the case of injury in rugby union and athletics (see Chapters 7 and 8), participants are often prescribed anti-inflammatory drugs such as ibuprofen which help to reduce swelling around an injury and, as a result, speed recovery. This does present a degree of risk, however, since the swelling in the area of injury is effectively designed to limit mobility, which encourages disuse of the injured body. As a result of reduced inflammation, a sportsperson may feel compelled to return to action before the injury has had time to heal. The taking of anti-inflammatory drugs does reduce pain (McLatchie 1993), which can be caused by inflammation. On several occasions a player was given an injection of anti-inflammatory drugs directly into his sore abdominal muscles as this was felt to give greater relief than the constant use of the same drug taken on an oral prescription. Many players have suffered negative side effects from prolonged use of oral anti-inflammatory drugs. Stomach upset and gastrointestinal function problems are the most common inconveniences with the use of such drugs. The risk highlighted here is important, and it is almost impossible to separate the components of pain, injury and risk in the process of investigating the social impact of sports injury in culturally specific communities.

Because pain is both a physical and an emotional signal of distress to an individual, it has been suggested that pain exists at the intersection between biology and culture (Turner 1992; Bendelow and Williams 1995). It is for this reason that the social environment surrounding sport, as collectively outlined in the first part of this book, is of fundamental importance to the exploration of both pain and injury. While medical expertise is important in determining the level and severity of a given injury, it is also important to be aware of the role of the social environment surrounding the injured party, in providing the individual with cultural norms with which to give pain and injury intrinsic value. A doctor may tell an individual that they have a broken leg, which could mean inconvenience in commuting to work and simple tasks like taking a shower as a result of the associated plaster cast. However, if the individual is also an elite sporting participant who will be out of competition for some time, the physical pain may be minimal in the long term but the psychological pain could increase through the period of injury. One area of pain treatment where science and culture collide is in the administration of substances that have a placebo effect:

> Even the 'placebo', normally dismissed as an 'irritating' or 'confounding' variable in (medical) science, offers doctors a powerful illustration of how minds and cultures, emotions and beliefs, shape the meaning and experience of pain, as well as responses to treatment.
>
> (Williams and Bendelow 1998: 158)

Placebos

The rapid return of sportsmen to the performance arena is the goal of injury treatment in sport. With many injuries pain may be the only guide that a medical practitioner has to enable them to establish a diagnosis of what is wrong with the patient-athlete. Because of pain's subjective nature, the treatment of it is problematic; however, research has shown that placebos may be used to enhance the treatment of pain (Turner 1994). Therefore, the sports medicine team, who are eager for their patients to return to fitness because time on the sideline for a sporting participant may mean the loss of income, may incorporate the use of placebos into treatment regimes. Recently, Hróbjartsson defined the placebo effect in simple terms by suggesting that

> the placebo effect [is] the therapeutic change in a patient's condition that is causally connected to the patient's awareness of being in a clinical situation . . . a placebo [is] a medical procedure that has no direct physicochemical effect on the condition in question.
>
> (1996: 345)

Therefore, the sports medicine team who are involved with elite sporting participants may use methods of treatment, such as ultrasound, that some have argued have no therapeutic value (Dyson 1985), to convince both the patient and the medical staff that alleviation of pain (and therefore injury) is actually occurring, and as a result the placebo effect is initiated and the body responds by healing itself.

Because of its mysterious nature, the placebo has been an enigma in medicine for many years (Pearce 1995; Turner et al. 1994), but until the mid-nineteenth century the use of placebos was commonplace for medical practitioners since placebos were believed to be useful in establishing healing at the mind–body interface (Benson and Friedman 1996). With the advent of scientific medicine (identifying specific causes for a given disease and the subsequent treatment of it with a focused remedy) and its success in treating disease, the use of non-specific therapies declined. Recently the placebo effect has once again come to the attention of medical research; it has been found that three conditions are needed for the effect to work. These conditions, according to Benson and Friedman (1996: 195), are:

(a) positive beliefs and expectations on the part of the patient;
(b) positive beliefs and expectations on the part of the physician or health care professional;
(c) a good relationship between the two parties.

Placebos appear to work in the treatment of about 30 per cent of cases of pain (Turner et al. 1994), and therefore in the current environment of the evolving professional sports (rugby union, athletics and Paralympics) with which this book is particularly interested, there appears to be no reason to reduce their use. The increased commercialisation of sport has encouraged the consumer explosion of the use of sports placebos, such as sports drinks and other nutritional supplements, in the field of sports medicine.

Placebos may take the form of attention given to the injured sporting performer by treatment staff at a personal level as well as the employment of various technologies that are believed to speed recovery from injury. Treatment of injury in professional rugby union was observed to be very unsystematic during my time as a participant-observer (Howe 2001), yet players were regularly leaving the treatment room cured. Unless the injury was a common occurrence, such as a sprained ankle, the players appeared to be given different treatments until one of the methods tried began to relieve the pain. As players came into the treatment room they would be given the next available modality machine (ultrasound or interferential) regardless of the injury sustained. In spite of this unscientific approach to the treatment of injury, the players would return to fitness within reasonable time.

Obviously, the time required for an injury to heal so that it is playable will depend upon the location and severity of the injury. A broken arm will take longer to heal than a sprained ankle. To a degree, this hit-and-miss treatment method was not as frequent when the sports medicine team had acquired the services of a qualified physiotherapist but it was still apparent (for more detail, see Chapter 7). What is of importance is that the players believe, and expect to be healed by, the treatment staff.

The acquiring of the services of a qualified sports medicine team, which brought better scientific medicine to professional rugby union, also brought different personnel who were able to create an altered treatment environment that was still distinctive of the club habitus, giving another productive avenue for the placebo effect to help speed recovery. Therefore, the personality of treatment staff may act as a placebo because in part a good personal relationship between treatment team and patient is important in increasing the speed of recovery from injury (Benson and Friedman 1996). Alternative medicine such as osteopathy may also provide an environment in which placebos can work effectively.

Although there are no statistical data as to whether certain placebos perform better than others (Turner *et al.* 1994), most of the literature concedes that a positive response is individualised, and there does appear to be a case for changing the name of the concept. All too often, if the phrase 'placebo effect' is mentioned, it is given a negative reception along the lines of 'placebos are just mind over matter'. It is of course much more complex than that, although they remain difficult to explain. Benson and Friedman have suggested that the phrase 'remembered wellness' replace placebo effect, since the evocation of the placebo effect depends on central nervous system events that result in feelings of well-being. Remembered wellness has always been one of the physician's most potent therapeutic assets and its remarkable potency should not be ridiculed or disregarded. Unlike most forms of therapy, remembered wellness has withstood the test of time and continues to be safe and inexpensive.

(1996: 198)

While this term is more debatable as a concept than 'placebo' it could be more appropriate for use in a sports medicine clinic, since an elite sporting performer's desire to compete again and make their body 'disappear', as a result of well-being (or a return to fitness), is remembered.

Because the success rate for placebos is, on average, 30 per cent (Turner et al. 1994), their use may eliminate the acute pain of less serious injuries such as sprains and strains but be less successful on more serious injuries where there is heavy structural damage. This may be a result of mis-diagnosis in the case of serious injury, but time is an important factor, as more serious injuries take longer to heal. Therefore if ultrasound is applied to a sprain, for example, the sprain may heal not as a result of the treatment but purely through the passage of time. While some evidence has suggested that ultrasound may not cure injuries (Dyson 1985), it is possible that as a placebo it can cure pain. Anti-inflammatory drugs may be used as a placebo and in some cases to a negative effect. As previously mentioned, they reduce swelling around an injury to promote healing, but in some cases the reduction in swelling may entirely eliminate the pain that marks the injury. Therefore, the sportsperson and the medical staff may be given the false impression that the injury has healed, thus increasing the risk of more serious injury when, and if, participation resumes prematurely. It is important to remember, therefore, that placebos are in use (known and unknown) by the sports medicine team in the hope of improving the speed with which injured sporting participants become fit to perform.

The use of placebos in some sporting contexts takes on mythical qualities. For example, the 'magic sponge' that was traditionally used on the sidelines of many team sports was the precursor, in many instances, of the current level of medical provision found in many professional sporting environments. Placebos and their use are generally seen as positive, although they are brought into use as a consequence of pain and injury that are seen as negatives. I will now briefly explore the positive side of pain as it relates to the training that elite sporting participants undertake in order to enhance performance.

Positive pain and training

Positive pain is a term used to describe the fatigue that an elite sporting participant goes through in the course of trying to enhance performance.

It is believed that all properly structured training schedules should be developed to maximise this component of pain. Exposing sporting participants to pain, while they are injury-free, in the process of training is believed to increase their pain threshold, thus allowing for the potential of improvement in performance during competition. Carmichael's (1988) notion that pain must be confronted may be seen as related to the ideal of positive pain.

Examples from elite rugby union and athletics highlight how positive pain may be used to enhance performance. The training week for players in elite rugby union often consists of squad training sessions on Tuesday and Thursday evenings as well as a game on Saturday (and, occasionally, mid-week). Ideally, this competitive-season regime is supplemented by two weight-training sessions and a circuit routine. Circuit routines are used to bridge the gap between the lifting of weights and the technical side of rugby, which is the reason for the squad sessions on weekday evenings. A vast majority of the circuits that are used by rugby clubs are done using body mass drills (sit-ups, push-ups, pull-ups, stride jumps, etc.) and light aerobic activity (jogging) between sets. During the off-season, mid-May to early August, the players did not meet as a squad (unless they were going on tour). It is currently part of most club contracts that the players have to maintain a degree of fitness during the off-season. If a player is fortunate enough to be selected for the national squad's summer tour, then realistically competitive training continues through to mid-July. At this time of year there is really only a fortnight before club squad training sessions begin. These quality players most often rest over that two-week period; not much fitness will be lost, and the rest could be of therapeutic value.

Pain plays a part in both the off-season training and the training that is done between matches. It is hoped by the players and coaches, however, that this evaluation of pain remains positive. According to elite rugby union coaches, players should be worked really hard on the Tuesday evening session, during which the forwards do a lot of scrummaging and the backs concentrate on ball handling and sprinting. Pain will often be felt as a burning ache all over the body during and after the session. On a Thursday the practice is set up to go through the detailed skills that are needed to beat the opponents of Saturday's match. Therefore, one coach suggested that in an ideal situation

> The boys should work hard every Tuesday at improving their skills, which can be painful because the emphasis is on working the body. ... Thursday's session is more about mind and getting the game plan finalised. ... It is important also not to risk the chance of a last minute injury.
>
> (Notebook 2: 13)

Therefore, the training structure can be seen to emphasise positive physical pain on Tuesday, with a less stressful session on the Thursday so that no unnecessary energy is wasted before Saturday's match. This training regime may be contrasted with the structure of training that an elite middle-distance runner has undertaken over the course of a decade.

The structure of training for the elite distance runner is established to maximise the use of positive pain.[6] Throughout the year, an elite runner's schedule is constructed on the basis of a three-day micro-cycle in which the perceived effort of training is easy on the first day, steady on the second and hard on the third. During the competitive season (May to August) the quantity of training is decreased proportionately, with an increase in quality,[7] and a rest day is implemented at the end of every three micro-cycles, which allows for the body to recover from the stress that it has been put under while the quality of training is high. This form of training is commonly referred to as periodisation (Coe 1996; Martin and Coe 1991). Ideally, positive pain is non-existent on an easy day, marginal on a medium-effort day and tremendous on a hard-effort day, and in this manner the body increases its threshold for pain. When it comes to a race, two easy days are placed in the training schedule to allow for plenty of energy to be stored for maximal physical effort in the race.

Elite middle- and long-distance runners use this type of training regime with a degree of variation to reproduce positive or 'fatigue' pain that is associated with regular training regimes, and this is indicative of every athlete's programme to achieve their best. A highly respected distance runner from Wales suggested:

> On my long road sessions I may run ten times one mile at race pace
> ... by halfway through I can really feel it ... the pain is incredible. For
> the last year I have been suffering from a hernia problem. .... I am told
> I push myself too hard in training, but you've got to.
>
> (Notebook 3: 23)

Pain is constructive only when it is limited to periods of intense training that are followed by no negative side effects. In this case, positive and negative pain have come into collision. If there are negative side effects from training and/or involvement in competition, then this is termed negative pain, which could be associated with injury and risk. The fine line between these two types of pain in the distinctive habitus that surrounds much of professional sport is what is encompassed by risk culture.

Pain in relation to risk

Traditionally, many individuals in the sporting community derived great kudos as a result of the myth that playing a game while injured brings out positive qualities in one's character. Since playing with pain and injury can cause irreparable structural damage to the body, it could be argued that today, with the advent of 'professional' sports medicine practitioners, the number of athletes who take such risks has been reduced. However, there has not been a reduction in the number of athletes who talk of hardship, because of the positive images associated with going 'through the pain barrier'. In view of the significant implications of the physical risks and costs of sport participation, it seems important to understand how and why elite sporting participants accept these risks and costs. Welsh rugby players accept the hardship of injury, at least in part, because the game itself is so embedded in nationalism. In his intriguing study of literature, in order to determine whether pain is a human universal, Morris (1991: 182) has noted the pervasive and peculiar acceptance of pain in sport, which is manifested in varied ways – for example, in nicknames such as 'House of Pain', which fans of one professional American football team gave their stadium, and slogans such as 'No Pain, No Gain, No Spain', which one company used to advertise its product prior to the Barcelona Olympics. These particular expressions are a by-product of North American sporting culture's interpretation of pain, but as sport becomes a global phenomenon (Maguire 1999; Miller et al. 2001), such expressions may begin to have international appeal. However, while it may be considered acceptable, in the eyes of their supporters, for elite sporting performers to go through the pain, injury and risk, it is important to remember that this dilemma is not so simple.

Even star performers are not above condemnation for avoiding risks with pain and injury. This can be seen in the attitudes of many of the supporters at Valley RFC when a player of quality is out with an injury for a considerable length of time. The player's commitment to the team is often questioned: 'All he is concerned about is playing for Wales; he's afraid to get injured before the international. Ever since he has become a superstar he has been afraid to take it on the swede [head] for Valley' (Notebook 2: 24). The player concerned has been a star in international rugby.

Summary

Elite sporting participants and supporters frequently discuss pain and its function in determining the time required by an individual to return to activity after an acute injury. The use of placebos has been shown to have a positive effect in about 30 per cent of cases. The extent to which this practice will continue in the environment surrounding sports that are transforming themselves from amateur to more professional concerns, however, can only be a matter for speculation, but the likelihood is that with the increase in consumer-based sports medicine there will be an increase in the use of placebos. Because of pain's subjective nature, levels of pain cannot be measured accurately and therefore this makes study of such a concept difficult, but the adoption of ethnographic methods (Howe 2001) will go some way to strengthening the more purely interview-based research (Nixon 1992, 1993a; White *et al.* 1995; Young 1993). Realising that pain is the signifier of injury may help establish some explanations of the concept's cultural importance. In a sporting environment where 'perfect' performance is the objective, acute pain often develops chronic traits as the desire for success is increased. As the need for success increases, so too does the risk involved in achieving ever more difficult goals.

It is important to remember that when an elite sporting participant is in pain after suffering an injury, their response to pain and injury will depend on the particular sporting environment to which they belong. It has been suggested that 'a reified sense of the body and disease may be the unhappy consequence of people's dealings with modern medicine at times that are already highly charged with physical suffering and emotional distress' (Williams and Bendelow 1998: 162), and this is clearly the case in the realm of professional sport. In the case of chronic pain, the effect becomes worse as it transforms the social world (which is counter to ordinary human experience (Scarry 1985)), particularly in the case of elite sporting performers, where acute injury often manifests itself in this form. Since pain by its nature is invisible, whether it has the ability to shape individual and cultural world-views is difficult to determine.

Chapter 5

The importance of injury in the commercialised world of sport

This volume began by exploring how the relationship between sports medicine, professionalism and the role of the body in the sporting environment could impact upon a reconfiguration of the sporting ethos that has emerged from the twentieth century. Injury is an important component of this rubric, and this chapter will explore how injury is treated in a commercialised world as well as exploring the legacy of political battles that were fought in the name of international sport and the role injury and sports medicine played in these. The discussion will begin by exploring the nature of injury in relation to the context of the previous chapters and the impact that a more commercial sporting world has had upon the often disposable human bodies that perform in sporting arenas.

As we have seen, sports medicine has evolved to such an extent that medical provisions for securing health and fitness after injury are becoming increasingly expensive. This chapter will examine the role played by injury in sports that are particularly physical, such as rugby union and soccer. This is not to say that people who do not perform in such sports do not sustain injury. Rather more research in the world of sports medicine has been conducted on the nature of injury in contact sports such as soccer and rugby (Hawkins *et al.* 2001; Lee *et al.* 1997; Muir *et al.* 1997; Sharp *et al.* 2001).

Those involved in the social investigation of a sporting practice and how medicine is used should not lose sight of the fact that the participants who get injured from time to time are all embodied and that all injury occurs to the body. While it is clear that psychological injury can occur, with no apparent physical side effects in the sporting environment other than perhaps impaired performance, this component of injury is of limited importance here. The work of Heil (1993) and Pargman (1999) should not be ignored, however, as psychological components of injury can have a profound impact on the rate of recovery from injury. However, to explore the psychological imperatives associated with the commercialisation of the sporting environment would require an entire new volume. The habitus of the sporting body as well as the club for which it performs can have an impact upon how injury is treated. For this reason, injury could be described as a structural, functional or an otherwise indescribable limitation that keeps sporting participants away from the arena. An injury can develop as a result of competition or training, and, as mentioned in Chapter 4, it can be clearly articulated and/or brought to the attention of the sporting participant by the presence of pain. This chapter will now briefly explore two types of injury followed by discussions of how they might be regulated and managed in the context of the commercial environment that surrounds much of sporting practice today.

Two types of injury

Injury is damage to the body caused by mechanical stress to which it cannot adapt in time or space. When confronted by such a stress, the body attempts to adapt by avoidance or transmission. By transmission I mean that, although a part of the body may not be functioning as it should, injury may not appear until a less robust body part cannot handle the reformulated stress. This site then becomes an area of injury, and in order to heal it, the original functional abnormality must be addressed. At times, when none of these mechanical actions is possible, either because the intensity of the stress is too great or because the duration is too prolonged, structural damage occurs. The nature of the primary damage is dependent on the type of stress applied. The body is able to distinguish between different mechanisms of stress (for example, a direct blow as opposed to a sudden stretch), and this is reflected in the consequent tissue damage. However, the body is unable to differentiate between the different situations in which such a stress may be imposed, for example in an automobile accident, a domestic accident or on the rugby pitch.

The type of activity in which an individual is engaged at the time of the injury will, however, largely influence secondary features of the pathological response. For example, in the case of a fracture of the tibia and fibula, haemorrhage will be far greater in a rugby player who sustains their injury in the middle of an active game than in the case of a sedentary passenger similarly injured in an automobile accident. Therefore, the level of fitness of an individual not only influences the secondary effects of injury but also significantly affects the recovery process. A haematoma may be very much larger in an athlete with high blood flow through exercising limbs, but the very process of training prepares the limb for the rapid re-absorption of extravasted fluid, and therefore haematomas are more rapidly absorbed in fit, athletic individuals than in sedentary people. The essential similarity, in terms of tissue damage, of the effects of similar stresses is particularly true in cases of instantaneous injury where relatively great external forces are applied, causing well-recognised damage patterns.

Injuries occurring in a sport as a result of participation can be distinguished as either primary or secondary. The primary injuries are the direct result of a specific stress or overload on a given region of the body. Secondary injury on the other hand is where the pathological condition has been itself provoked by some previous injury. An example of the impact of a secondary injury may be seen in the injury case below, which is an extract taken from a field notebook.

An international rugby player was suffering from a sore hamstring for an extended period of time. As it turned out this ailment was actually secondary, because the 'major' problem existed in the misalignment of his pelvis, which was causing lower back pain and in turn was making the hamstring too tight. The pain gradually worsened, spreading down the back of his thigh and it was deemed that the player was probably suffering a pulled muscle. However, as a muscle tear occurs instantaneously, producing immediate pain at the time of injury, this was an unlikely diagnosis. Gradual onset of pain in the back of the thigh during exercise is almost always sciatica due to lumbar nerve root irritation. While I was not aware of the relationship between lumbar nerve root irritation and thigh pain at the time, I have since been able to find this information in widely used sports medicine texts. Too often, practitioners are not made fully aware of the symptoms a player feels and as a result misdiagnosis can occur. In this case, the player missed taking part in crucial matches, perhaps as a direct result of treatment being focussed on the hamstring area rather than the lumbar region. This player's problems were eventually correctly diagnosed and successfully treated by an osteopath. In cases of inappropriate diagnosis, players may be subjected to long but sporadic lay off periods because ineffective treatment is directed to the wrong body part. The primary site of injury can remain undetected and untreated because the physician and player are not effectively communicating.

It is in this manner that many of the most serious injuries may in effect be masked by a minor injury. Therefore, when a player takes a bad hit on the rugby pitch, while nothing serious may result through the initial incident, in time this contact may result in serious injury. King (1983) has used the expression 'second injury' to refer to a situation where a minor injury is sustained yet the athlete continues to perform, thereby increasing the risk of developing what may be a more serious injury. In this manner, minor injuries can 'build' into serious ailments. Problems exist in getting players to leave a match because of minor 'knocks' (bruises, strains, cuts, etc.), and they may ignore the risk surrounding such events because of the surrounding culture of risk (see Chapter 6).

Every athlete suffers from various forms of aches and pains from time to time while striving to improve performance. While a diligent warm-up and warm-down regime before and after exercise may limit the onset of injury, distinguishing between what is a serious ache or pain and something trivial is problematic. The practice of a proper warm-up and warm-down was largely ignored by many elite sporting participants. This task was formerly often left up to the individual, whether or not they play for a team. But as the financial burden of injury has become an issue, sporting teams have developed tighter control over how participants prepare for games (Howe 2001). This may be seen as an example of how the fear of injury has led to improved provision for players' well-being, at least until injury strikes.

The other form of injury that is important here is primary in nature. Primary injuries are often a result of the environments in which we live, work and play. These injuries can be referred to as extrinsic, as they take place outside the control of the body. Internal primary injuries may be called intrinsic. Because the human body is designed to restrict the severity of the injury, the damage caused by an extrinsic injury will most often be greater in the sporting context than that resulting from intrinsic injury. When considering soccer or rugby, the most common cause of extrinsic injury is heavy contact as a result of the compulsory tackling in the game (Hawkins et al. 2001; Lees et al. 1997). Reality suggests that unless humankind confines itself to the 'bedroom of life', extrinsic injuries are always going to occur, regardless of the level or amount of sports participation. The way in which the sport medicine team and the governing bodies of sport can be the most effective in minimising risks is to change the laws regarding how games like rugby union are to be played. On 1 September 1996, for example (see Appendix I), the WRU made it legal for players to wear padding on their shoulders and other areas of contact, thus allowing for players to attempt to eliminate some of the risks of extrinsic injuries. Two months later (see Appendix II), teams were allowed to legally replace players during a match, thus allowing for the opportunity to strategically remove a player who may have taken a bad knock and thereby reduce the risk of 'second injury'. While in principle this change in the laws may be seen as a risk-controlling measure, the prevalence of risk culture will regard replacement predominantly as a strategic alternative in the playing structure of the game. Intrinsic injuries are much harder to monitor and may often be considered as 'overuse' injuries. Achilles tendinitis is an example and is a common occurrence in athletes who do not properly monitor their stretching routines. Intrinsic injury therefore largely develops in sporting participants during the individual drills and training between matches; however, this type of injury may become a 'second injury' as a result of an earlier knock in a match.

Regulating sports injury

There are recognised patterns of injury in specific sports, and Weightman and Browne (1974) have suggested that this is due to the structure in which each sport is played. Therefore, by changing the rules this structure may be altered. In rugby union, changes in the laws regarding the scrum have greatly reduced the number of cervical (neck) injuries (Burry and Calcinai 1988). Further changes to the laws of the scrum could bring about another probable reduction of the risks of such injuries (see Appendix III). In the professional world of sports such as rugby union and soccer, participants are playing for their pay cheques as well as enjoyment, and as a result, the contact injuries are on the increase as the level of performance becomes linked to livelihood. For example, Davies and Gibson (1978) have suggested that 30 per cent of injuries in rugby union occur as a direct result of foul play. This research was conducted when rugby union was amateur, and there is every reason to assume that as the sport gets more 'serious', the injuries related to foul play are likely to be on the increase. In an attempt to reduce foul play, however, the four home unions (England, Ireland, Wales and Scotland) introduced a law at senior and international level that linesmen were able to bring infractions of the law to the attention of the referee (Davies 1992). A study by Sharp et al. (2001) highlights that the records used by referees are a useful way of determining which players are most often replaced, thus allowing teams to select players for the replacement's bench accordingly. It is assumed that this sort of material could also give researchers an insight into foul play, since the reports would also include details of players who had been penalised or sent to the sin bin.[1] Which actions are foul is often rather ambiguous and open to the discretion of the referee. However, there remains scope to further reduce the incidence of injuries during play by alterations to the rules so as to avoid dangerous situations. An example of this is the 'front-row replacement' rule. This has recently been implemented by the WRU and states that if a player in the front row is thrown out of a match, there must be a properly trained individual on the bench to take his place. If not, he stays on the pitch and another player is removed. Of course, the player in question who was banned initially will still be suspended after the match. This rule was implemented to improve safety, as head and neck injuries are widespread in players who are substituted into the scrum never having been properly trained in scrummaging techniques. Thus steps are currently being taken to limit the high-risk situations that currently exist in the game and contribute to injury (see Appendix III).

Mismanagement and misdiagnosis

Owing to the nature of professional sport, there is in sports medicine a pressure to eliminate pain and injury that is not commonplace in other medical sub-disciplines. Treatment staff who work for a particular sporting club or organisation, on training nights and during competition, no doubt feel the pressure more overtly than those who are farther removed from the action in sports medicine clinics. It is the fact that sporting spectacles are seldom scripted, and hence the immediacy of sport and the push for victory at all costs that is endemic in the contemporary sporting world, that has increased the pressure on sports medicine practitioners. This pressure is a result of the sporting communities' desire to have injured athletes back on the pitch as soon as possible. During an elite-level sporting contest the risks taken by medical practitioners may be quite great, partly because of the expectations from which this pressure develops. However, if the immediacy of the match situation is eliminated, there is not necessarily a corresponding elimination of risk, only a reduction of it. Therefore, risk in a clinical setting is reduced in part because the environment is more conducive to making the appropriate decision about the method of treatment. It is important to realise that what exists surrounding injury is a risk culture (see Chapter 6) that is linked closely to the treatment of injury.

Injuries can be mismanaged on a personal level since elite sporting performers are often over-eager to return too soon after injury. Fitness levels of elite performers are an important factor when considering a return to high-performance training. For example, a performer who seems super-fit might succumb to injuries to the immune system, in which case patience is a definite virtue. Athletes who are highly trained suppress their immune system and therefore take more time to recover from flu than the average individual, for example. It is important to realise that ultimate fitness is seldom equated to health in medical terms, although the two are often considered synonymous in the popular press.

> Most athletes may in fact be too physically fit for their own good. Recent scientific work has suggested that constant training for the peak of fitness can leave the body more open to viral infections leading to collapse during competition, or at worst to early retirement from sporting competition: this is especially a problem for young players whose bodies are overstressed before their physical peak is possible.
>
> (Blake 1996: 153)

Because of the importance of the body to athletes, when functional damage does occur, the impact on the athlete's psychology may be far greater than any structural limitation, in part because of the pressure from coaches, administrators, supporters and sometimes even their families. It is well documented that long-term injury that leads to long absence from the competitive arena has a strong correlation with a lack of self-belief within an athlete (Heil 1993; Pargman 1999). This reduction in confidence is, in turn, reflected in the outlook of the supporters towards coming matches and to their lives in general.

One of the many problems with sports injuries is that medical practitioners often compartmentalise injuries as being related to a specific sport. While this may be a short cut in analysis, it may also lead to a problem in diagnosis. For example, there are a lot of rugby injuries in countries where the game is still developing. Croatia, for example, has twice the injury rate of developed rugby nations such as Scotland (Babić et al. 2001b), as the game is not often played in schools and therefore adults who take up the game lack many of the skills required to avoid injury. Since doctors, as a whole, are not familiar with the game, it is important that they have a clear understanding of the mechanics of the body, as it may be inappropriate to assume all contact injuries to be closely related to soccer injuries, since the body can (as previously mentioned) be layered in injury. This means that the body can have several injuries at one time, and therefore the knock-on effect of structural imbalance may mean that the presence of several injuries causes more serious injury to develop (as in the case of 'second injury'). To some extent this is also the case in an overuse injury, and a clear description of the patient's training programme will often give a strong clue as to what is going wrong. It is therefore very important to keep records of training schedules as well as records concerning treatment of injury. In the more amateur sporting environment in which rugby has existed until recently, the keeping of records for each individual player was often seen as unnecessary (Howe 1999, 2001). As the game became more professional, the new importance given to the management of injury in the game has made the keeping of medical records important.

Because continuity of treatment is an important component in helping to minimise injury, an effective medical treatment team must therefore have a sound understanding of fundamental anatomy and biomechanics required for the proper interpretation of case histories of injured athletes, as well as an understanding of the nature of the sport concerned. Knowledge of the sport is important, as many instances of injury occur as a result of faulty technique, particularly in highly technical sports, and correction of poor technique becomes an essential component of patient-athlete management. This is particularly so in a situation where as a result of injury the athlete is left with bad habits. It is not necessarily every practitioner of sports medicine who is in a position to advise and coach patients out of their technical faults, but it is important that the athlete corrects their shortcomings in order to eliminate recurrence of the injury. Misuse injuries are often a problem for sporting performers who desire to increase their level of play/performance while not having the requisite skills (Maran 1998), which can lead to an unending cycle of injury until premature retirement is reached.

A practical difficulty that is of paramount importance for the practitioner relates to the return of the patient-athlete to training and competition.

It is often the case that the patient-athlete wants to be better – yesterday. Many athletes, particularly the 'elite' ones, are often under severe pressure to return too soon from injury. This desire is even written into the rules of some sports. Rugby union football now allows substitutes (see Appendix II); therefore, there may begin to be a tendency to play players who are not fully fit, thus putting them at risk of perhaps more serious long-term injury. This is of course the negative side of the law, which may have positive consequences too for players' health. Playing a player who is far from fully fit, because the player in question has considerable crowd-pulling power or performs at a level superior to that of his replacement, and thus increasing the club's profits, is often done, but goes against medical ethics (Huizenga 1994). For the medical practitioners asked to advise in this situation, a dilemma may arise. The relationship between treatment staff and the player becomes more tenuous (Macauley 1997a), as the club may today employ the services of a sports medicine team. The fulfilment of the doctor's duties towards the club therefore may conflict with the best interest of the patient-athlete:

> The sports physician is therefore likely to be confronted relatively frequently with patients who demand greater autonomy with regard to treatment decisions and furthermore is quite likely to be providing a service where he may have a responsibility to a third party, such as a governing body or team management.
>
> (Payne 1992: 4)

In the context of commercialised sport, a fourth party, namely sponsors, may also have an influence on whether there is added pressure put on sports medicine physicians. In countries such as the United Kingdom it is only the elite who receive specialist treatment for their injuries (Boyce and Quigley 2001), and funding for the private elite clinics could also be seen as an important factor that could unduly affect the quality of treatment. Of course, there are numerous other factors such as the culture of litigation, which is also on the increase as a result of the money that haemorrhages from commercial sporting practice (Macauley 1998).

Time

In sport, time is one of the defining factors. In the case of team sports, every match is defined by the amount of time allowed for it to take place. In the professional era, time is also influential in the treatment of injury. This has led to direct changes in the rules regarding injury treatment in rugby:

> Since 1988 changes in the Rugby Football Union (RFU) regulations allow an injured player to receive attention on the field of play whilst

the game continues. This places added responsibility on the physiotherapist who now has to be tactically aware as well as medically aware.

(Murphy 1992: 31)

As well as time 'limits' set for on- and off-the-field treatment there exists
the threat of negligence (Dougherty et al. 1994; Gallup 1995; Macauley
1998), which no doubt makes the job more stressful. At times in the
frenzy surrounding an injury, especially in the middle of a match, when attention may be drawn elsewhere, it is important that the sports physician
remembers that

Doctors who associate themselves with sports medicine have a duty not
only to treat patients who appear with injuries, but also to endeavour
to reduce the incidence of injury by collecting and analysing information in order that patterns of damage may be identified.

(Payne 1992: 8)

While all doctors may have this as their goal in developed sports such as
professional football (soccer), there appears to be no codified practice that
is used to select medical teams that work within elite clubs (Waddington
et al. 2001). Within sports where there is less contact with officials and
administrators, such as track and field, participants are either forced to
receive private treatment or seek help from their general practitioner (GP)
(Boyce and Quigley 2001).

It has only been in the past fifty years that sport as a human activity has
not been viewed as irrelevant by most medical practitioners. Patient-athletes
who become injured in such activities thus often receive scant attention or
sympathy from GPs or emergency room staff. Such an uncaring attitude
invariably prejudices correct history-taking and a proper and careful examination. In the past, infection and 'minor' tumours, which may have been
first noticed as pain in sport and left undiagnosed for too long because of
negative attitude to active treatment by the practitioner concerned, were a
common problem, especially to the non-elite athlete who may not have had
direct access to a proper sports medicine clinic (Boyce and Quigley 2001).
In the world of elite sport these minor injuries are taken seriously if brought
to the physiotherapist's attention. Partly as a result of the habitus surrounding sports medicine clinics at the nexus of commercialism and amateur
ideology, such as at Valley RFC, the players' health was never knowingly
risked by members of the sports medicine team (Howe 2001). The team
physiotherapist even suggested that knocks and bruises taken by the players
at the club, if mentioned to him outside the treatment room, would be
noted in his medical records, thus giving him a more detailed history on
which to base any future treatments. In this way it is believed that 'The

physiotherapist forms a special relationship with the injured player in their lowest and most painful moments and may gain considerable professional satisfaction from seeing that player return to full activity in the shortest time possible' (Murphy 1992: 37).

One major difficulty facing the sports medicine treatment team is the plethora of anecdotal and otherwise unreliable material disseminated in both printed and verbal form to the concerned patient-athlete. While much of this information is correct and published in the best interest of the athletes, some claims, mainly on behalf of product manufacturers, may be misleading and therefore put the athlete-consumer at risk. This media attention has led inevitably to the encouragement and practice of ideas and treatment measures which do not always work under close examination. Among these may be included the use of steroid injections (not those used for performance enhancement), the use of therapeutic ultrasound and even the use of ice for treatment. All these modalities of treatment are popular in the management of sports injuries, and all carry a significant element of risk. One of the depressing features of sports medical practice is the frequency with which patients have the severity of their injury increased by the use of these and other forms of treatment.

The advent of these injury treatment modalities has occurred in the past twenty-five years, and in spite of their widespread use, the benefits they are said to possess have been disproved by research. Dyson (1985), for example, suggests that the use of ultrasound as a therapeutic tool on soft-tissue injuries, such as Achilles tendinitis, may do more harm than good. It appears that there is no method for accurately regulating the dose of sound waves in the injured area. While others (Binder et al. 1985) have promoted the use of ultrasound on soft tissue, the debate still continues. During the 1988 Paralympics in Seoul, Korea, I was exposed to ultrasound treatment for the first time. Because I did not know what to expect, I believed that the burning of my skin was part of the treatment, much like sunburn in the injured area. Not until much later did I find out that the physiotherapist had used the modality incorrectly.

The most common form of modality for the treatment of injury over the past half-century has been the bucket and sponge. In the past decade its use has been decreasing, since there are risks involved in its use, brought to the attention of practitioners as a result of the concern for the spread of HIV.

> The 'bucket and sponge' communally used to 'treat' injuries in a variety of team sports must now be viewed as a mode of transmission of the virus, especially where bleeding has occurred. Sensible medical advice must therefore discourage the use of this traditional item of equipment and ban it completely in [geographic] areas of high risk.
>
> (Loveday 1992: 137)

In its place, however, ice and aerosol ice can be as harmful as clean cold water, as cold treatments suppress the action of nerves and therefore help mask pain. While pain is something that not many athletes enjoy, it is a signal that the body is structurally imbalanced to some degree, which in turn suggests that an injury is present and needs to be treated.

The use of these treatment modalities has been hallowed, perhaps incorrectly, by years of practice without critical reappraisal. It is likely that such modalities are in fact placebos (see Chapter 4), and therefore their only value is in the belief that a cure is being initiated in the mind of the players. The sporting public's heightened expectations with respect to proper medical management may in future prove to be the catalyst to proper critical appraisal of methods of treatment currently in vogue which are popular without being rational. What is key here is that the use of pain-relief applicators on or near the field of play might have a negative impact on the health and well-being of players. In a sense, this treatment of players has been a result of the desire by the management of sports clubs and teams to get the most out of the individuals in whom they invest so heavily (Howe 2001). Regardless of how much planning is put in place to eliminate injury, and therefore time away from competition, there will always be unseen circumstances in which sporting participants are absent from competition owing to illness that is not necessarily directly related to the negative physical results of sports participation.

Absence from participation due to 'illness'

An illness in the context of this heading, as well as referring to the usual ailments that are associated with the term, is a non-contact injury that it is possible to eliminate by means of the appropriate management. As previously illustrated in cases of hyper-fitness, a sporting performer can become more susceptible to infection. This is a result of extremely high levels of training, which have been shown to suppress the body's immune system (Shephard and Shek 1994) and therefore may be a risk that elite sporting participants face. Elite sporting performers are becoming more aware that their bodies are close to breaking point. If a performer is in a peak state of physical fitness and yet becomes ill with a cold, in the United Kingdom their first port of call is often the general practitioner (GP). GPs are still the front line of defence in the treatment of sport-related injuries and illness (Macauley 1997b), but their lack of understanding of sport as anything more than a pastime could be seen as a hindrance to the well-being of participants. All too often when an elite sports participant goes to the GP they are told to rest, which no doubt is often sound advice, but in the habitus surrounding elite sport, where the cultural importance of activity is paramount, this advice is not necessarily the most sound. Taking time off for injury or illness is the last thing on a sporting participant's mind when they visit a GP. They are most often seeking a quick return to pain- and injury-free performance.

As well as minor illness, the elite sports performer may suffer from a wide variety of ailments that are not commonplace within the general population. A kind of injury that is a result of participation in certain sports, such as long-distance running, and as part of the fitness conditioning in professional sports such as rugby union, is the overuse syndrome (Corrigan 1968). This is a result of internal stresses generated chronically during training and is therefore relatively uncommon outside the elite sporting community, although it may be observed in the enthusiastic individual who suddenly engages in unaccustomed activity. Overuse syndrome also occurs in some areas of industry involving people who take up new jobs requiring unaccustomed repetitive activity, such as working on an assembly line. Occupations where physical performance is of importance, for example the military, also show an increased rate of overuse syndrome, since the development of a high level of physical fitness is required. Until recently, the aetiology, pathology and incidence of overuse injury were relatively uncertain, but there has been wide documentation of such injury in recent years (Helal *et al.* 1986; O'Donoghue 1984).

In addition to specific injuries, patient-athletes may have clinical problems, due less to specific stress overload than to a secondary condition, that are usually constitutional. These may lead to biomechanical inadequacies for the activity performed, thus enhancing and multiplying the effect of what, for a normal person, would be acceptable stress levels. Examples include long-distance runners and joggers who have torsion of the tibia and excessively pronating feet, which on a day-to-day basis may cause no problems. Under stresses of running or jogging, however, the faulty biomechanics makes the absorption of otherwise reasonable stress levels impossible, and breakdown occurs.

An important factor when examining injury in sport, as a form of illness, is that frequently symptoms and signs may be vague because presentation occurs in early stages of the condition. In trained, high-performance participants, whether in sport or in any other physical activity, a relatively minor problem in clinical terms can cause a significant loss in ability to continue with the activity for short, or sometimes long, periods of time. Most patients in ordinary, mildly active or sedentary lives can cope readily with injuries, whether of the impact or overuse type, injuries that would significantly and adversely affect the performance of an active sportsman or -woman of elite class. Therefore, although symptoms and signs of presentation may be relatively diffuse and difficult to interpret, they must not be taken lightly. It is important, then, for athletes to 'listen' to their bodies, because the frequency with which significant and serious injuries first come to their attention as discomfort of a vague and initially mild nature is rather alarming.

Early attention to stiff and sore muscles, for example, may lead to complete elimination of the need for a rest due to injury. This is because the vast majority of injuries in sport do not require any form of specialised medical knowledge or treatment. Even among those attending specialist sports injury clinics, it has been shown that more than 60 per cent of the cases could have been dealt with perfectly well by the patient's family doctor or by a podiatrist or similarly qualified individual (Sperryn and Williams 1975). Across the population of sportspeople as a whole, the percentage of patients requiring highly specialised sports medicine treatment is lower among those athletes who take the time to stretch and, more generally, warm up and down. However, some have suggested that a knowledge and understanding of the mechanics of injury in sport and its specialist management can only be acquired by formal study (J.G.P. Williams 1990). This may of course be a justification for a medical qualification and overlooks the fact that most elite athletes are well aware of their bodies' limitations. The increased ease with which elite performers can seek advice, because of the fact that sporting officials are beginning to realise the important cost of injury (Howe 2001), along with the associated popular press, which focuses on a wide array of sports-related topics, has meant that athletes have become better consumers of sports medicine, rather than just simply patients.

For simplicity's sake I have been referring to the traditional patient as a 'patient-athlete', but these individuals could be more correctly defined as athlete-consumer-patients (ACPs). When an injury occurs, there is a certain degree of urgency; however, if the sporting performer is not an elite participant and they do not have private health insurance, they may be required to wait weeks or even months for physiotherapy. Most professional sporting clubs and associations have their own treatment staff, which enables them to see to injuries as soon as they occur.

Another option for pain and injury treatment is osteopathy, which is an alternative form of medicine that is more holistic than that provided by the physiotherapists. The treatment of injury provided by an osteopath is essentially performed by the manipulation of the skeletal system. This is often accompanied by heavy massage to loosen muscles around the various joints in the body before realignment of the spine can safely take place. Pain and injury related to heavy physical contact or overuse of the body can be managed in this way to speed the return to full fitness. This type of treatment is most often undertaken as an alternative to visiting a medical doctor, as traditional Western medical practice has been slow to embrace more holistic medical practices. As the world of sport begins to become increasingly commercialised, more alternative medical practices have been sought, as the 'expense' of having ill or injured performers increases. Sports clubs and governing bodies are continually looking for the best manner in which to manage the treatment of injury when it hits their prize assets, and alternative medical practices are increasingly being considered in this regard.

In fact, commercial sports medicine clinics are now increasingly employing osteopaths in the belief that the demand for their services is soon to increase.

The impact of politics and commercialism on injury treatment

Since the Second World War, elite sporting performers have been increasingly interested in getting help from any field of research that could possibly increase performance. Medicine was and continues to be the most obvious place to get help in the elimination of injury. Because not all the answers are readily available in Western medicine, sports medicine, perhaps more than any other branch, has adopted a more sympathetic approach to non-traditional treatment practices. It is this attitude that has led to an increased tolerance by the medical fraternity towards such methods of treatment as massage therapy and osteopathy. Lately this tolerance can perhaps be seen as an attempt by medical professionals to maintain hegemonic control over elite sporting performers as they seek to get the best possible treatment, which until recently was outside the remit of Western medical treatment.

The enhancement of physical performance has become paramount as the politicisation of sport has grown particularly at the international level, since sporting success became synonymous with nation-building. Another factor besides currents of nationalism was the ready availability of greatly increased rewards, particularly but not exclusively material rewards, brought on by sporting success. Both these processes have had the consequence of increasing the competitiveness of sport, and one aspect of this increasing competitiveness has been the down-grading of the traditional values associated with taking part, accompanied by a great increase in the value attached to winning.

Whorton (1992b) has suggested this shift could be put down to the American 'frontier' philosophy of the self-made man who had a desire to use sport as a vehicle to obtain success. In the late nineteenth century, as a result of this new spirit the Americans easily defeated the British at their 'own games' of rowing and athletics. These defeats did not sit well with the British public or their sportsmen; therefore, those involved in sport began to examine ways in which the British could regain their pre-eminence. Good international performances began to be achieved by adopting the more scientific training methods used by the Americans at this time. However, this was a short-term solution as the participants in international competition were amateur and found it difficult to reach ever-increasing levels of proficiency within the time constraints dictated by work. A shift to professionalism occurred (as discussed in Chapter 2), which allowed athletic performance to take precedence over work for at least the period of time during which the sportsman was able to compete with the best. The consumption of sports medicine, therefore, can be seen to be an important link between politics and sport, and was established as the British developed the desire to reaffirm their position as the world's greatest sporting nation.

This was not the first time in history that sport and politics became inseparable, as the ancient Greeks used sport as a method of symbolically maintaining political superiority. However, since the collegiate competitions between the United States and Britain, the association between sport and politics in the international sporting arena has been inseparable. One of the most infamous occurrences of the sport–politics relationship occurred when Hitler used the 1936 Olympics as a spectacle to confirm racial superiority.[2] Since the Second World War the relationship between politics and sport has been heightened by two occurrences.

First, during the Cold War the communists did battle with the capitalists on the sports field rather than with their more destructive nuclear arsenals. Within this context, sporting competition took on a value far greater than that of the sport itself. Sport became a symbol of superiority in East–West relations. The need to establish how many medals each nation won at the Olympic Games can be seen as a reflection of this philosophy. As many governments came to see international sporting success as an important tool of propaganda in this capitalist–communist struggle, so those athletes who emerged as winners came increasingly to be treated as national heroes, with rewards to match. This even occurred within Britain, where the media often refer to winners as English or British. More often than not, if successful athletes come from outside England but from inside the British Isles, their local national identity is ignored and they are referred to as British.

Second, to a great extent this process has more recently been associated with the development of independent nation-states in Africa, which has seen the emergence of outstanding athletes whose international success has been a major source of pride in new nations. Governments have often sought to use these sporting successes to help establish a national identity in a context that is more appropriate in the eyes of a modern world. In the early 1980s, when apartheid was at its height in South Africa, a young black man named Sydney Maree left South Africa for university in the United States. There he became one of the best milers in the world. When he was due to return home, so that he could be a symbol of the apartheid regime (and run world records within South Africa's borders), he sought political asylum and eventually he became a US citizen.

Since the politicisation of sport has been increased, there has also been acceleration in the commercialisation of sport in the West. Although winning an Olympic medal has been an honour since the establishment of the modern Olympics in 1896, the increase in monetary reward has been enormous over the past two decades. As a result of this trend, many sports that were once amateur have had to become professional in both approach and name in order to limit hypocrisy. Athletics, for example, has reached a point where the top competitors in Britain can legally earn several million pounds in one season alone. It is also apparent that many other nationally ranked athletes are able to make a marginal living as full-time competitors in hopes of obtaining the level of performance that is required for the big pay-day. This scenario exists today in rugby union (Howe 1999; Smith 2000), but what is of importance here is how the notion of political superiority as seen in sporting success affects the further development of sports medicine.

As mentioned earlier, sports physicians saw sporting performance as providing the study of physiology with experimental data (Hoberman 1992), with the emphasis being placed on the discovery of physiological laws rather than the application of these discoveries to athletic achievement. Increasingly, the emphasis that has come to be placed on winning and on breaking records for club and country has dramatically changed the relationship between athletic performance and sports medicine. At the turn of the twentieth century the promotion of sporting success initiated the commercialisation of sport. The massive proliferation of professional foot races and cycling competitions in the Rhondda Valley region of South Wales can attest to this (Gwyer 1990). Most of the participants and organisers were of working-class stock and therefore had different social values from those of the largely middle-class medical fraternity. It was considered appropriate for sportsmen of the working class to benefit from medical intervention, but the 'pure' middle-class amateur would never dream of taking such an advantage (Allison 2001). Ever since 1945, when transportation links around the globe began to improve dramatically, the need for nations to appear distinctive has given rise to many a reinvented tradition. Like other pursuits, sport became an arena where this distinction could be made – the symbolic battlefield where one nation pits its mettle against another. Therefore, these middle-class medical researchers, who often lacked the physical qualities required for sporting success, lent their brains to the national cause by increasing the athletic performance of the nation's athletes. They did so by making their scientific findings accessible to sportspeople and coaches through the medium of the club doctor and physiotherapist.

In this manner, the symbiotic relationship between sport and medicine can be seen as egalitarian since both medical scientists and elite sporting participants derive what they consider to be benefits out of the relationship (Waddington 1996: 184). Medical experts gain an ever-expanding knowledge of human physiology, and elite sporting performers benefit in terms of improved athletic performances. Between nations, however, there has, over the past fifty years, been secrecy as to how athletes are able to enhance their performances for the good of the nation.[3]

If there is a symbiotic relationship between sports science/medicine and the elite sporting performer, the balance appears to be in the favour of the scientists. In Chapter 1 it was suggested that two types of sport medicine – theoretical and practical – exist. Theoretical sports medicine takes time to be fully developed into practical procedures for medical intervention.

Therefore, the physiologist obtains data from elite sporting performers well before there will be any practical outcome for the performer. This dynamic of course places the power very clearly with the sports science/medicine experts, but is in an odd way comforting, since the status quo is maintained whereby participants are exploited by those indirectly involved in the performing of elite sporting practice.

Summary

This chapter has explored the importance of injury in a sporting world that has increasingly become regulated by the goals of commercialism. Sports medicine teams and the elite sporting participants that they treat using a plethora of treatment methods are at once working for the same ends. The ultimate goal is to have the performer injury free so that they can earn their 'keep'. Medical teams are under pressure from both sports management and, at times, the performers themselves to 'fix' injuries immediately. This ultimately disempowers the elite sporting performer to the point where they are willing to adopt non-traditional medical practices in order to speed recovery. Assuming these are legal, the benefits both for the education of Western medical practitioners and for the sporting participant can be twofold. Injuries may be cured more quickly using alternative medicine such as osteopathy and the sports medicine clinic will ultimately benefit from the links that it has made with the alternative practitioner, and will be enabled to become the gatekeeper to this important knowledge.

Both injury and the issues surrounding pain, discussed in Chapter 4, lend themselves, in part, to the development of lay knowledge, owing to their ambiguous nature. This lay knowledge is important because it can be used by elite sporting participants to keep the medical fraternity on its toes. Lay knowledge is put to the test when an elite sporting performer attempts to negotiate the culture of risk that exists in all sport cultures to one degree or another.

Chapter 6

Risk culture as a 'product'

The role of injury and pain in the professional sporting context has been examined in the two previous chapters in order to establish the important use to which sports medicine has been put in trying to minimise their occurrence and severity. When pain and injury occur, the elite sporting participant has several options: to give up the sport; to let the body heal naturally with minimal medical intervention; or to actively rehabilitate the injured area with the advice of a sports medicine expert. Unfortunately, decisions with regard to what to do with an injured body are not always the concern simply of the sporting participant alone but may affect a large number of individuals within the participant's social network (Nixon 1992, 1993b). The social environment surrounding every patient-performer may heavily influence decisions made in times of pain, and with each choice comes a degree of risk. Risk in the context of the sporting community refers to the danger of any structural or emotional damage as a result of participation in sporting activity by an elite sporting participant. In other words, risk is a product of sporting participation. The choice to continue in sport through the use of sports medicine – which is employed in the professional sporting environment – may appear to be limiting risk, but the use of sports medicine can often mean that the sport is already embedded in a particular risk culture.

This chapter will begin with a brief exploration of risk and its relation to culture. A discussion of risk and the use of performance-enhancing drugs will follow this. Lay knowledge and its role in the socialisation of elite sporting participants are of importance, as well as the social networks in which these individuals interpret messages regarding risk. The chapter will finish by examining the body and risk before closing with the suggestion that risk in the elite sporting context manifests itself in a cyclical manner.

Risk and culture

There has been some interesting research done on the nature of risk culture within the social environment surrounding sport. It is Frey (1991) who first referred to the culture of risk in sport, but perhaps more important to this current chapter is the work of Nixon, who explored the relationship of pain, injury and risk in sport (1992, 1993a, b, 1996). Nixon's work has illuminated many of the key concerns that social scientists are increasingly often beginning to explore in the ever-greater critique of professionalism and sport. In the field of anthropology it is the work of Mary Douglas (1966, 1985, 1992) that is of great importance. Douglas (1992) sees risk as a social construction that is interpreted through human actors as a response to the danger that exists. Responses to risk are culturally specific, and because of this, an understanding of the habitus of sporting environments as highlighted in Chapter 3 is of great importance when one is exploring risk in its cultural associations. The distinctive habitus of the professional sporting performer entails, in part, the necessity to maintain a livelihood, and as a result, the taking of risk may be considered a normal component of performance enhancement:

> Risk taking . . . in the work context may be considered part of an overall strategy for career advancement. The notion is that once a person has reached a certain level in their career they may need to take a risk – in order to achieve long-term goals.
>
> (Lupton 1999: 156)

Elite sporting participants may habitually respond to risk, which suggests that in the field of play, when their body is 'absent', choices about risks and whether to take them may be unconscious.

A fundamental component of the habitus of most elite sporting clubs is that players wish to perform to the best of their ability on every occasion and, as a result, train in order to achieve ever-greater levels of fitness, thus enhancing performance. Improved fitness can be a risk since there are cases where fitness can be more of an illness than a state of physical well-being. As already mentioned, some athletes have been shown to be so physically fit that their immune system is suppressed (Shephard and Shek 1994). This suppression, however, is most common in elite athletes who compete in endurance sports, such as long-distance running, and have a very low percentage of body fat – which is uncommon among power-based sportsmen like the players involved in professional soccer and rugby union. As each new level of fitness is achieved, more risks are taken with the body, since the harder a sporting participant trains, the more physical (and perhaps emotional) stress there will be that has to be endured. When the individual is confronted by the possibility of ever-increasing rates of injury, they must choose how much risk they are willing to take. Such important decisions are the markers of risk culture.

Risk culture is present in every level of sport, since injury does not just affect the elite. However, it takes on greater importance in the world of the elite/professional, as a result of the greater investment in time and/or money being made in training for enhanced performance. For anyone adopting the lifestyle of an elite athlete, in which leisure time is filled with preparation for enhanced performance, or taken up by training that the sports participant is paid to undertake, an element of risk continually exists since physical performance is fundamental to this distinctive habitus. These individuals are 'confronted by risk' through the possibility of injury. In essence, then, risk consists in consciously knowing that I might become injured, but going ahead in spite of that knowledge. In this way, risk culture may be seen as a choice of lifestyle. While some of the risks of enhanced performance may be unconscious to sporting participants who are habitually trained to perform, they become objectified by the presence of pain and injury.

Risk culture, therefore, is elusive, and this chapter will undertake an examination of risk culture in order to establish a better understanding of the desire of sporting participants to improve their performances on the field of play, at any cost. In view of the significant implications of the physical risks and costs of sport participation, it seems important to understand how and why athletes accept the risks and costs of participation in sport.

The risk of using illicit drugs

One of the most-discussed issues related to risk culture, and one that has been an area of considerable research, is the use of illicit performance-enhancing substances (Laura and White 1991). The consensus of social attitudes is against the use of illicit drugs (such as anabolic steroids) not only because of the health risk that is associated with their use, but also because the use of such drugs is contrary to Western notions of normality. It has also been noted that using anabolic steroids will make women more manly (Mansfield and McGinn 1993). On the other hand, arguments for men not using such drugs are often based on the risk of physical and psychological illness. It is well documented that sporting cultures such as body-building and the people involved in them are well aware of the risks that drug use entails (Klein 1995; Monaghan 2001), but the quest for the ideal body is all-consuming. Risks that body-builders will take are summed up in the phrase 'Life's too short to die small!' (Klein 1995: 112). Most sports that require strength, speed or stamina may be susceptible to illegal performance-enhancement. As was discussed in Chapter 1, rugby is full of players who are taking the legal substance creatine, which replicates the enhanced performance qualities of training that are obtained with anabolic steroids.

Athletics is perhaps the best example of a sport that has had its reputation tarnished by scandals that involve illicit drugs. Most people will be familiar with the events surrounding the Canadian sprinter Ben Johnson at the 1988 Olympic Games. Evidence from the inquiry in Canada after that event (Dubin 1990) indicates that athletics is not the only sport that is turning a blind eye to the problem. Jennings and Simson (1992) suggest that the root of the problem lies with the International Olympic Committee (IOC) and its former president, Juan Antonio Samaranch. In their text they suggest that the power of the investors (who pay for valuable advertising rights associated with the Olympics) is such that, in order to keep its 'money tree' growing, the IOC has needed to hush up controversies that might have damaged the 'noble' Olympic ethos.

One of the problems lies within the philosophy of *win at all costs*, which has become an integral component of the sporting world as a result of the political values[1] attached to sporting success and the role the mass media play in personifying them. This philosophy is only the root of the problem. To stretch the analogy, the athletes can be likened to a tree's leaves in that the faces may change from season to season but the underlying structure remains the same. As athletes' careers come and go, the fact still remains that sport is riddled with drug use. In spite of relatively drug-free competitions such as the Barcelona and Atlanta Olympics and the more recent International Association of Athletics Federations (IAAF) world championships, there have still been cases of drug suspensions outside major championships. The accusations by athletes directed at the successful Chinese middle-distance runners related to drugs use after the 1993 world championships (Frecknall 1993), and the more recent problems of nandrolone (Ferstle 1999), are clear examples of rules being breached. In the case of nandrolone, the use of legal food supplements is supposed to have produced a positive test, which has led to athletes having to take even greater control over their bodies.

The risks that are involved in the use of illicit drugs in sports are all too apparent to the medical fraternity:

> The question facing the medical practitioner, society at large and the sport in general, concerns the relative dangers that are presented by the use of powerful drugs in a non-therapeutic situation, when there exists because of them the possibility of damage to the individual through serious side-effects of the drugs, damage to the sport through the introduction of unfair competition, and damage to society at large through the erosion of its moral fabric.
>
> (Anstiss 1992: 101)

This quotation highlights two important elements of the debate surrounding the use of illicit drugs. Most medical writings on drug use in sport refer to the harm of their use (Grayson 1999), whereas the discussion surrounding the moral argument have largely taken place within the philosophy of sport (Gardner 1989; Hoberman 2001). Philosophers (Brown 2001; Simon 2001) have also articulated concerns regarding the use of drugs in order to enhance performance. Within this debate, harm may be seen as the actual consequence of using performance-enhancing drugs, while the risk of using such substances is their potential harmfulness. By encapsulating discussion of the illicit use of drugs in a risk-laden discourse, rather than one that illuminates harm as medical literature does, sporting administrators and those individuals increasingly in control of the lives of elite sporting performers (e.g. agents, coaches) are able to actively encourage a culture of risk. If harm is eliminated from these discussions, the risks, while costly, may seem worth taking, as Holowchak (2002: 75) demonstrates: '[S]ince so much of competitive sport today is about winning, our investment in performance enhancement is immense. When, if ever, is the cost too great?'

Risk culture, then, may be seen as a dome that entraps health and positive physical performance in the body of elite sporting participants. Only when confronted by injury and pain are elite sporting participants forced to decide whether to risk continued performance by evaluating training to enhance fitness or to halt activity till the injury heals. The desire to conform to an idealised body image has put pressure on the general public to develop a healthy lifestyle, and as a result, an ever-increasing segment of the population is dealing with varying degrees of risk. What is apparent, from the perspective of an elite sporting participant, is that little risk is taken while a participant is satisfied with their on-pitch performance. At times when performance enhancement is required, risk culture takes a paramount role within the participant's individual sporting habitus. This to some performers, means risking health through a new method of training that includes the use of illicit drugs that they may feel are necessary to allow their body to perform at the level that the mind desires. The final decision varies as much with the individual as it does with the individual sporting network.

Lay knowledge, socialisation and risk

Elite sporting performers are continually immersed in an environment where the acceptance of risks is normal. As time passes, individuals begin to gain an understanding of their bodies but also of the importance of staying injury free. Levels of acceptability of risk vary depending on the degree to which it is embodied in the habitus of a given sporting community. Each individual sporting participant is surrounded by layers of distinctive habitus and therefore is confronted by contradictory interpretations of different cultural ideas and symbols. Sporting participants see their bodies as machines that can be trained through the use of physical habitus. This is not to say that all elite sporting participants have a detailed understanding of exercise physiology, but rather that they have an inherent perception of how the body functions because their performances in training and competition continually test the body's physical limits. As a result, an elite sporting performer's lay education in exercise physiology could be seen as a history of the injuries that they have endured. This catalogue of injuries is what brings the body to the attention of the sporting participant and gives them a better understanding of how the body works. Because of the 'invisibility' of the body while sporting participants are injury free, and in spite of the fact that the habitus of sport conveys a relatively coherent set of messages about risk, pain and injury, it is difficult for the participant to understand objectively what these messages mean. Risk culture establishes a normalised response to pain and injury where the discomfort of the body and the choices that are made to heal it are seldom seen as risky.

Discussions of pain and injury are so regular in sporting communities that new research has proliferated since the beginning of the 1980s, when the focus of social theory increasingly revolved around the concept of embodiment. Work by Kotarba (1983) explored the culture of sport and the idea of playing in pain, and how that impacts upon the individuals involved. A growing number of scholars have highlighted the impact that pain and injury have in sporting contexts (Nixon 1989, 1993a; Roderick et al. 2000; Walk 1997; Young 1993). This research suggests that attitudes towards risk affect most individuals regardless of the type of sport in which they endeavour to participate. For example, dealing with risk can be seen to be part of the culture surrounding body-building (Monaghan 2001). In his ethnographic study of body-building, Monaghan highlights the fact that what appears to be risky business for the unenculturated may be part of normal cultural practice to the body-builder. It is clear that 'risk-taking in bodybuilding, similar to risk-taking among others adopting active lifestyles, offers the possibility of gains as well as losses.' (Monaghan 2001: 183). This point is key. Adopting a lifestyle choice which involves the training that is required for high-performance sports does often become risky simply because training at a high level of intensity can mean that injury is only around the corner. In sporting environments, what is of fundamental importance is how participants become socialised into taking risks.

Nixon has established that the popular sports media are an environment where messages about the social role of the sporting participant are illuminated

> [A]thletes are exposed to a set of mediated beliefs about the structural role constraints, structural inducements, general cultural values, and processes of institutional rationalisation and athletic socialisation that collectively convey the message that athletes ought to accept the risks, pain and injuries in sport.
>
> (1993a: 188)

This study suggests that the risk that accompanies pain and injury in the context of elite sport is somehow statistically normal. In a study of US college wrestling, Curry (1991) suggests that a 'culture of risk' has such an impact on participants that it actually normalises responses to injury that to the non-participant would seem extreme and often unacceptable. The grip of risk culture is so strong that if you express concern regarding injury, you may become marginalised from the rest of the sporting community (Nixon 1993a, b).

The culture of risk that has been highlighted in the work of Curry (1991) and Nixon (1993a, b) can be seen to be further developed by Young (1993) and Young et al. (1994) in the context of exploring how masculinity and violence are useful concepts that relate to the nature of risk culture. Certainly, in the cultural environment surrounding sports such as rugby union and (ice) hockey, issues of masculinity and violence are of fundamental importance since the physical contact inevitable in both these games may portray norms of masculinity as well as being a breeding ground for violence. In fact, a sport that is more contact oriented may be more open about risk than one that is non-contact. It takes little or no time for an uneducated observer to establish that if you play rugby or (ice) hockey, you are going to risk both pain and injury with every match. The nature of these games makes this quite explicit. The difficulty is that once the participant is part of the particular sporting culture, they become immune to many of these 'obvious' messages about pain and injury and then can be drawn into a culture of risk. The nature of socialisation means that it will seldom be 'complete', which is to say that there will be other influences in the participant's life that may encourage them to examine the risks, but whether these influences are stronger than the lure of the culture of the chosen sport can be seen only in hindsight. The difficulty is managing this acceptance of risk to which participants become accustomed.

In Britain there is concern for the health of individuals and issues related to access to medical treatment (Joyce 2001; Macauley 1997b). Elite sporting participants must often rely in the first instance upon their GP to pass them on to a sports medicine specialised physician unless they have access to private treatment through a club or sports association. In the professional sporting world, where results are paramount, the culture of risk can be seen to be working in harmony with a lacklustre provision for treatment of sporting injuries. If the culture of risk, as suggested by Nixon (1993a; see also White et al. 1995), has the impact of eliminating the talk of pain and injury in various sporting environments, by marginalising those who engage in such discourse, this will benefit those providing medical services. There will be less interest in appropriate treatment, as a result of this treatment being counter to cultural norms. As well as discouraging those individuals who will not sacrifice their body for the cause of enhanced performance, it enables medical professionals to see to participants who make sacrifices for the betterment of the team, nation or sport.

The danger of this approach is that a culture of risk will become so entrenched that participants, coaches and medical teams might all become embroiled in a 'fog' that leads to the long-term acceptance of pain and injury that is at the heart of risk culture. Professionalism dominates the contemporary world of high-performance sport. In this environment there appears to be pressure for sports that have remained amateur to establish practice that is not dissimilar to the practice of those engaged in by professional sports, including embodying a culture of risk. Monaghan (2001) has suggested that risks that appear unacceptable to those outside a sporting culture may not even be seen as risks to those on the inside. This is of importance, since lay knowledge of the body, whatever the sport, may help to eliminate the thought of risks that appear to be ever-present (see Chapter 8). Work by Messner (1990, 1992) suggests that a personal conceptualisation of masculinity acts as a filter which, when incorporated with external influences, such as a culture of risk, may influence a sporting performer to accept pain and injury and continue to compete. Some sports with heavy physical contact and with almost certain 'injurious outcomes reinforce and naturalise notions of masculinity that value physical dominance' (White et al. 1995: 158).

Socialising as a team within the elite sports community in North America is often perceived as counter-productive to the achievement of the individual goals of each participant. There is an inherent dualism in club organisations in North America. Clubs are structured either as recreational or elite/professional and it is seldom that these two groups interact. All professional sports clubs in North America are run as corporations, and therefore members of the community can impact upon the club only if they are financial shareholders. The self-contained environment of the high-performance clubs is where risk culture in the sporting community lays its most solid foundation. Here the majority of socialising that occurs is between intensely competitive individuals whose discussions often focus on their aches and pains, and how they performed in spite of them. These reactions, manufactured within the communities concerned, have often been supplemented by the reactions of hegemonic authorities. Respected individuals of the sporting community frequently glorify the character of athletes who endure a high pain threshold, thus sacrificing themselves for the team and ignoring the personal consequences. Athletes who choose to talk openly about their pain and injuries risk stigma, especially if the pain and injuries have invisible sources. Because of the nature of the lifestyle of an elite sporting participant, they may be willing to take great risks because in the short term they will be financially well rewarded. However, in this environment risk is apparent only when an athlete is injured. The relative importance of this risk may be muted by the quality of treatment provided by the sports medicine team. Nixon (1993a) has suggested that in the social environment of professional sports the issue of risk is often obscured, since elite sporting performers are aware that there are high-quality treatment facilities at their disposal. Of course, after the performer is no longer of value, the provision for treatment of injury will be removed.

An example of this disbelief in a player's potential to overcome injury is the case of Bo Jackson, who was a superstar in two big-time professional sports: baseball and American football. This case shows that where enormous amounts of money are involved, even megastars have to confront risk culture head-on. While engaged in a football game, Jackson sustained a career-ending hip injury. The injury was so bad that the hip required replacement, and after surgery even walking was problematic for him. Several attempts on the part of Jackson to come back to baseball were horrific. This man, once one of the best-rounded athletes, could not even jog around the bases when he hit a home run. Eventually, after more surgery, he was able to play at a level that resembled his old self, at least on the playing field. However, what will be the long-term implications of such forced participation? Sporting franchises generally show little compassion in cases such as this, since when it looked as though Jackson would never play again, his team sold him, once one of the most valuable commodities in sport, for a dollar.

In British rugby and athletics clubs, situations exist that are distinctly different from those found in the North American system, which has a profound effect on the grip that risk culture can have on the sporting community. After their creation in the Victorian era, the rugby and athletics clubs can be seen today, at least internally, as egalitarian institutions in that it does not matter whether you represent the club's first team or its eighth. What is important is how well you socialise at the bar after the day's matches are over. Even if you are a first-team star, you stand a better chance of being ostracised if you do not go for drinks than if you are the 'slippery fingers'[2] on the seventh side but are always willing to spend time in the local with clubmates till after last orders. In this communal structure, risk culture is less likely to become embedded into the social fabric since the reasons for participating in the club's matches are often as many as the number of players, and therefore the socialising will be more light-hearted and designed to reduce post-match stress.

Professional sport has, to a certain extent, changed the club ethos of Britain. The days of amateurs playing their sport at the highest level have all but disappeared (Allison 2001), and sporting clubs that embraced professionalism yet have tried to maintain an egalitarian environment (see Chapter 7) struggle with the balance that needs to be maintained. In the ever-increasingly competitive world of professional sports there appears to be little room for half-measures such as semi-professionalism at the elite level. The social network, where the pull of habitual action towards taking risks exists, is also of importance.

Elite-participant social networks

The social network that surrounds elite sporting performers can have both positive and negative impacts on whether an individual becomes entrapped within a culture of risk (Nixon 1992, 1993b, 1996). Support from family and friends is crucial if a participant is to make an informed choice about treatments available for pain and injury. The ability to make an informed choice may be heavily influenced by the participant's position within the sporting community concerned. Nixon (1992) suggests that social networks inside sport, for which he coins the term 'sportsnets', are the main influence in messages that are received by the participant in relation to a culture of risk. It is within sportsnets that the distinctive habitus (see Chapter 3) of various sporting practices is learned. It is here that pain and injury are 'normalised'. A conflict exists between the individual's own social support network and those that are more explicitly tied to the sporting environment in which they are engaged, particularly as the sportsnet is where the hands-on day-to-day training takes place, which is key to performance enhancement and the maintaining of status as an elite sporting participant.

The tension concerning which of these networks of support to listen to is complex in the environment of professional sport. Those involved in professional sport want the most out of their athletes, which is understandable. Contracted elite sporting participants need to distance themselves effectively from the culture of risk so that this can be mediated by their other social support network, which is their friends and family. Difficulties can surface, however, when the two networks are one and the same. When parents are coaches, for example, their success can from time to time outweigh the notion of well-being for their child, and there clearly is tension in this type of relationship (Dyck 2000). It is of course important to remember that most often it is extreme cases that are being discussed in this approach. However, increasingly there appears to be an emphasis on elite sporting performance, and in these cases it is often difficult for people to avoid negative social support that may lead to long-term injury or disability.

The normalisation of pain, which often causes disabling injury, is perplexing. If a career in sport is ended prematurely as a result of an injury that is seen as normal, the person in retirement as a disabled ex-participant may become marginalised since, depending on the severity of the impairment, they are 'abnormal' in the view of the larger society. In spite of this, elite sporting participants appear to act in a logical manner when confronted with issues about whether to accept the risk that may be inherent in the sport in which they compete. There are, of course, only a limited number of alternatives when one is confronted with pain. An injured participant may seek medical attention to alleviate the pain and cure the underlying injury, or perhaps decide to rest the body for a time or even consider retirement. Each of these approaches has value, and the response for a participant will depend on numerous factors. First, decisions may depend upon the social support the participant receives from family and friends as well as on the sport-specific social support that an injured participant receives. Second, an important factor is how serious the injury is and what amount of rehabilitation will be required for the performer to return to complete fitness. This is a key factor, because it is well documented in some professional sports such as American football (Huizenga 1994) that there is heavy pressure, or a risk culture, which often forces players back into the game before they are fully recovered, often with the help and support of the medical staff. Finally, the age of a performer may impact upon their desire or ability to recover from a long-term injury; they may decide to retire, whereas a number of years before, retirement would not have been considered an option.

For Douglas, risk may be seen as a contemporary concept to substitute for traditional notions of misfortune. In the context of injury related to the participant in sport, this understanding can be seen to have some currency: 'Whose fault? is the first question. Then what action? Which means, what damages? what compensation? what restitution? And the preventative action is to improve the coding of risk in the domain which has turned out to be inadequately covered' (1992: 16). Clearly, in the cultural environment of sports injuries we can see all these questions being asked. It is the notion of prevention of risk that the notion of risk culture, discussed above, fails to address. Nowhere other than through retirement are the risks associated with sporting participation going to be eliminated. Changes in the laws of games such as rugby union (see Chapter 7) may in part be a response to the increase of prevention, but only not playing the game guarantees the elimination of the risk in participation. In a cultural environment where the ability to sometimes handle great amounts of pain is valued (Nixon 1996; White et al. 1995; Young et al. 1994), participation will always entail a degree of risk.

Clearly, risk perception must be seen as specific to individual sporting participants. To those who are inside a sports-specific culture of risk, where the status of participants is often marginal to other concerns (Frey 1991), there may be no power with which to facilitate the change in sporting culture. Therefore, pain and injury become rationalised to such an extent that they normalise the presence of physical hardship within sport. This is, of course, on one level, what elite sport is all about: the pushing of physical limitations. However, when unnecessary risks are taken as a result of social pressure there may be a need to re-evaluate the structure of elite sporting practice. The sporting body may be a good place to begin this examination.

Risk and the ideal body

Over the past couple of decades there has been a development of concern about the problems associated with pain and athletic performance. While the obtaining of an 'ideal' body is often a preoccupation in some cultural environments, realistically most people realise that such a quest should only be an attempt for self-improvement. Concerns about bodily appearance, which are often enhanced by the mass media, carry great powers of persuasion. In order to achieve a 'perfect body', risks are often taken (Monaghan 2001), depending on the social environments surrounding the sport and sports club in question. In other words, the influence of mediated images and peer pressure may be minimised when an individual has both self-esteem and an accepting social environment. The environment in elite sporting contexts teaches participants to manage their fear of risk and the accompanying pain and injury by deflecting serious discussion away from these concerns. Transforming the body into a high-performance machine takes years of dedication as well as the ability to avoid the pitfalls of pain and injury that the risks of high performance often entail.

With the advent of the mass media, body image began to transcend geographical regions, which in the past could maintain a unique identity; a more globally normalised concept of body image is today increasingly apparent. In concert with the media, consumer culture has influenced the discourses of sport, leisure and health by appropriating the desire to manipulate the body and using it to garnish more productive advertising. Western society is currently dominated by the desire to look young, healthy and beautiful, and to be exciting. The sporting body, for the general public as well as for the elite or high-performance athlete, is firmly articulated in the ideology that has established the body as the major focus for consumerism. As a result, participation has become fundamentally controlled, to the extent that a 'system of expansive discipline and surveillance produces normal persons by making each individual as visible as possible to each other, and by meticulous work on persons' bodies at the instigation of subjects themselves' (Hargreaves 1987: 151). While this interest in sporting bodies may be seen as a recent historical development, body image has a long history of importance in the social sciences. In anthropology there have been attempts to address questions concerning the body and how differing cultural understandings relate to European colonialism (Lock 1993; Turner 1996).

There has been a fascination at least since the time of the ancient Greeks with the phenomenology of the body. From this period a naked male body portrayed images of strength, whereas naked female bodies, after the establishment of Christianity, involved notions of shame or sex. 'Old' bodies were never more than 'shame-full'. Certainly, early works of art may be seen as fine examples of the perfect human form. Through the use of remnants of previously dominant cultures, a chronology of normative bodily values could be determined that would establish what physical characteristics were in vogue at given historical periods. The key element that such a sequence would demonstrate is that dominant images of the human form are diachronically variable. Today, institutions such as the Olympics have produced many 'Greek gods' in the human form of athletes (Daley Thompson, 1980 and 1984 Olympic gold medallist in the decathlon, is a prime example). What makes an understanding of culturally constructed norms of body image so important is that as a result of mass-media exposure given to high-profile athletes, the fitness craze continues to gather momentum, acting in many ways as a catalyst for parallel developments in sports medicine and sports-related industries such as dietary supplements and health food, as well as sport shoes and the manufacture of equipment. This continues to have the effect of increasing the number of individuals who have become more aware of the importance of a healthy lifestyle as a means to objectifying a 'perfect' body image. The push for some form of toned or trim body inevitably leads to sporting participants increasing the risk which they would normally be exposed to, as some individuals have to train harder than others to achieve the same ends.

No longer does the 'Greek god' aesthetic stand alone as the bodily ideal, since the individuals behind the forces of commercialism have realised the limits of marketing only one ideal bodily form (Gruneau 1993: 98). While the sporting body is more broadly idealised, a variation of the ideal body now exists. For example, athletes who perform at basketball, (ice) hockey and marathon running at the elite level will have different physiques because of different functional requirements of their chosen sport. However, these sporting bodies are all idealised in the media and thus encourage the public to achieve one of the ideal body types by using the products endorsed by the individuals whose form is desired. The reason why such a connection between consumer and sporting cultures is possible, according to Hargreaves, 'is their common concern with, and capacity to accommodate the body meaningfully in the constitution of the normal individual' (1987: 151).

There is of course a wealth of knowledge that indicates conclusively that a healthy diet and moderate exercise can improve the quality and length of life (Lüschen et al. 1996). Nowhere are the conceptualisations of the ideal body and the healthy body more clearly shown as synonymous than in the various media of advertising. Although there is evidence that physical states such as obesity put undue stress on the heart, thus making an individual a candidate for a heart attack (and we know that watching our caloric intake while eating a healthy diet along with cardiovascular exercise on a regular basis may reduce this risk), the ideal body type as portrayed in the mass media may be just as harmful. Certainly, contemporary female models (Naomi Campbell et al.) cannot be a healthy ideal to which young girls should aspire. These women may be naturally super-thin, but physical and psychological problems that result from trying to be so thin, such as anorexia nervosa and bulimia, can be life-threatening (Nixon 1989). Yet it is these images that continue to fuel the fitness boom,[3] all in the quest for the perfect body. As a result of more participation in activities designed to better the 'self' physically, whether through aerobics classes, lunchtime runs in city parks or semi-competitive intramural sports at university, this influx of participants has placed great stress on the medical system, which has been forced to adapt as a result.

It has been seen throughout this book that the disciplined body, emblematic of its specific sporting habitus, is the lowest common denominator in sport and that, as a result of the mass media, the global village shares a similar image of 'perfection' in terms of the norms of physical appearance for both genders. There are risks involved in the pursuit of perfection, and while everyone has a propensity to take risks (Adams 1995), the desire to do so varies with each situation and the potential reward. Achieving the body of an elite sporting participant is not enough for those competitors themselves. The risks taken by professional or elite amateur sporting participants in the daily grind of training increase as their desire for yet better performance becomes their new goal.

Not every individual can attain the perfect body. While this is a self-evident statement, the world of the disabled is not immune to the pressures of conformity of the body.

'Imperfect' bodies

While the public and the elite athlete alike strive to obtain the perfect body, at the same time there has begun a movement towards the integration of individuals with imperfect bodies into sporting communities. With the push of legislation in countries such as the United Kingdom and Canada, the disabled are being included or mainstreamed in all walks of life. In the international sporting world, wheelchair races have been part of the Olympic programme of athletics since 1984 as a demonstration event. In one respect this can be seen as an apparent step to merge perfect with imperfect, but the preoccupation of society with the ideal body image has placed unnecessary stress on the self-esteem and general well-being of individuals, both able and disabled, who will, for one reason or another, never obtain society's idealised norm.

While financial reward is still minimal at best for the disabled sportsperson because of a lack of media attention, there is a feeling in the disabled sports world that, rightly or wrongly, sporting excellence is a valid stepping stone for acceptance into society at large as well as a powerful tool in building self-esteem. This is derived from the understanding that increased personal worth can make strides towards destroying societal stereotypes as a result of the individual's positive example. Because of the nature of many athletes' disabilities, sports medicine's curative aspects play an important role in keeping these athletes 'on track' in order that they may attempt to attain their goals. Many impairments, such as cerebral palsy, can denote muscular imbalance through specific areas in the body. When an athlete who is impaired in this manner begins heavy training for such activities as distance running, a fine line must be drawn between working the muscles that are inherently weak, so that they become stronger, and the maintenance of flexibility, which is reduced as the muscle is strengthened. This problem of course is faced by everyone who exercises. However, the nature of the impairment and its tendency to increase spasticity in affected areas complicate the athlete's problems in the area. Constant care by massage and physiotherapy is the best way to reduce the chance of chronic injury.

Risk of increasing the degree of disability is a definite possibility with some impairments. However, because some disabled athletes have been indoctrinated into risk culture, it is hard for them to adopt what non-sportspeople would see as a sensible approach to training for sports participation. A disabled athlete, such as the author, has a different relationship with risk as compared with an able-bodied elite sportsman. While elite rugby players are healthy and working towards enhanced performance, they are free of their body (as previously mentioned), whereas elite athletes with cerebral palsy are never 'free' of their body because the impairment entails that while they are in motion, the body is 'visible' to the participant. This is to say that most sporting participants are known to perform physical skills without conscious thought. A sporting participant with cerebral palsy has much less control over the most ordinary activities such as walking and running, which means that risk is more apparent to such an athlete, since increased physical awkwardness is bound to lead to more pain and injury. Regardless of whether an elite sporting performer is seen as perfect or imperfect, the push to enhance their performance means that they will be confronted with a cycle of risk.

The risk cycle

The impact of the media on notions of acceptable body forms places a great strain on individuals who wish to conform to socially acceptable norms. Lay knowledge of both anatomy and physiology that is generated from years of preparation for enhanced sporting performance is a useful tool when the body breaks down, and may be seen to limit risk taking within sporting environments. Risks associated with occupations such as manual work and high-performance athletics (Kotarba 1983) illuminate the importance of how individuals may negotiate pain and injury. Lupton has suggested that lay knowledge of risk is reflected upon by social actors who balance what they hear from 'experts' against their understanding of the world around them: 'The existence of varying perspectives on "risk", among both experts and lay people, suggests that the phenomenon of risk is a production of competing knowledges about the world' (1999: 106). If this is indeed the case, then elite sporting participants, while not immune to risk culture, are not likely to be as easily persuaded as the work of Nixon (1993a, b) suggests.

While the habitus of elite sporting participants has continually evolved, the underlying ethos of sporting excellence achieved through individual commitment and pain is still valid today. Here I am referring to what in Chapter 4 was discussed as positive pain (or, for the purpose of clarity, 'fatigue'). It is felt that all elite sporting participants recreate positive pain in their training regimes so as to delay the onset of fatigue in competitive situations. This is achieved by exposing themselves to ever-increasing levels of fatigue in training. In order to achieve this end, a performer may need to increase the risk involved in their training as they push their body ever harder. At some point in the pursuit of excellence the athlete may increase training to such an extent that the pain becomes negative and hence a signi-fier for injury. In this case, then, the risk taken has not paid dividends. Roderick argues that 'Athletes are not "empty vessels" on arrival at top-level sport. Rules, beliefs, attitudes and patterns of behaviour (i.e., cultures) are formally and informally learned by children' (1998: 73). The cultural devel-opment of individuals is not removed from influences outside their sport but occurs within the subcultural influences imposed upon them through continued participation such that an embodied acceptance of risk is acquired over years of exposure.

Importantly, though, the notion of risk suggests there is some choice. Work by Szerszinski *et al.* suggests that

> The idiom of risk presupposes ideas of choice, calculation and respon-sibility, so that whether the risk attitude prevails or even makes sense in a given area of life depends on the degree to which that area is regarded as fixed and inevitable, or as subject to human agency.
>
> (1996: 12)

Another interpretation of risk is that it can be seen as a balancing act. Adams (1995) likens the human perception of risk to a thermostat, whereby the perceived danger and the rewards related to it are balanced by our propensity to take risks. Because the notion of risk as it relates to elite sporting performance implies the idea of choice, it could be argued that what has been called risk culture is misleading. Perhaps a term to describe what is known as a culture of risk or risk culture would be 'cost culture', because, as we have seen, at some level decisions are made as to the cost, social as well as financial, of maintaining an involvement in sport in the face of the risks of pain and injury.

Cost culture exists in so far as elite sporting participants are concerned, since they are constantly discussing the risks and sacrifices that they are making in order to be part of the team. However, it is only the players who are on the fringe of such teams that are vulnerable to the overt influ-ence of risk. Cost culture does exist, but it exists as a rite of passage for the players who are trying to make the squad. Only when star participants' performances are in decline do they have to work within cost culture, much as they had to when they were up-and-coming performers. Comments by a couple of players who once played for Valley RFC highlight this view of risk.

> In order to make the squad as a youngster you have to take risks . . . train and play through injury . . . until they [the coaches] see your value and leave a place open for you in your absence as a result of injury. The sacrifice of the body in the beginning of a career can be great.
>
> (Notebook 2: 17)

The use of the term 'sacrifice' is very important here since the clubhouse was full of supporters who were willing to take the risks of pushing for a spot on the squad.

> This gammy knee is a result of trying to make Valley's first XV. I played a couple of years for the Athletic [seconds] and played well. Then I was called up when I was carrying a knee strain . . . after playing through it for two games I couldn't walk. . . . I was replaced by [a player who went on to play over 300 games for the firsts] and the rest is history. My knee gives me lots of gyp now but at least I got to play for the firsts!
>
> (Notebook 2: 40)

Risks are taken by athletes in order that they may achieve the best levels of performance possible, but (as mentioned earlier) a risk that must be rationalised exists only in conjunction with pain and injury. My observations indicate that once a player reaches a secure position at the elite level, a reliance on risk culture is minimised. Therefore, first-hand observations of cost culture at Valley RFC were not as evident as they perhaps would have been had the study focused on an average club side. This cost culture can be seen as existing in the social network that surrounds an athlete throughout their career. Whether or not it affects the approach of an individual to their given sport is clearly dependent on the level of ability that the performer has achieved and when and with what regularity they sustain serious injury. On the way to fulfilling their ability, risks may be taken, and likewise when performances begin to slip. Once again risk will be influential, but, importantly, there are costs that must be weighed against the benefits of continuing to compete and train in order to perform well within the chosen sport.

Figure 6.1 illustrates how the cycle of cost culture may be established for an elite sporting participant. By attempting to enhance performance, the elite sporting participant may be confronted by illness (injury), at which point they will turn to the sports medicine practitioner for help. Once health is restored, sporting success may be achieved; however, in time the participant may wish to enhance their performance to a greater degree, and thus

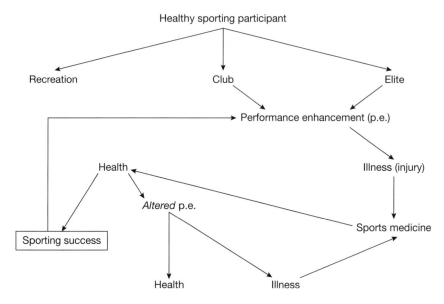

Figure 6.1 Sports-based cost culture.

the cycle repeats itself. Risk may be seen as being outside a transparent casing or force-field that surrounds a sportsperson who is healthy and seeks enhanced performance, since risk becomes self-evident only when injury and pain confront them.

Lyng (1990: 859) uses the concept of 'edgework' to articulate the experience of participants in dangerous activities. Edgework is about the ability to maintain control in risky environments where mental toughness is seen as key to not giving in to fear.

Observations that were made in the context of rugby union suggest that risk is taken by a player who has to struggle to be first class (Howe 2001). There appears to be a point in every participant's career where the risks involved in pursuing participation at the elite level become too great and they become resigned to playing at the level they are currently at. Shift in the focus of a participant's goals can be due to a number of factors such as other interests, the discovery of talent in another sport, or life situation (e.g. marriage and/or children). It is clear that until such life-altering events are passed, sportspeople will take risks in order to achieve improved performance. Lupton suggests that 'Risk-taking becomes the mark of someone who is ambitious and not content with remaining at a plateau in their career. The importance of personal flexibility is again implicated in this notion of risk-taking' (1999: 156). It is this flexibility that could be seen as the link between the notion of risk and the concept of cost as it relates to sporting culture. Seldom is an individual *forced* to take risks. At one level or another, an elite sporting participant weighs up the cost of continuing in sport.

The problem that exists for athletes is that risks can often be hard to see. There may be talk of risk taking place in sport, but until the onset of pain resulting from injury, risk is not a primary concern to the sporting participant, since the evaluation of the risks of participants has already occurred within cost culture. What makes the situation dangerous is that it is difficult, particularly for members of that culture, to isolate risk. The 'invisibility' of risk in sporting environments makes conscious understanding of it problematic.

Summary

In this chapter I have argued that risk is a product of sporting participation, and is most apparent with the onset of pain and injury. What is most important, however, is that this risk, as highlighted by scholars such as Nixon (1992, 1993a, b), Young (1993) and White *et al.* (1995), is a product distinctive of that particular sporting culture where cultural capital is accrued by those who are willing to risk their health and well-being for a better performance. The reward for performing in a state of pain is often high, but it is wrong to assume that participants are sheltered from the concept of risk. Enculturation into a cost culture takes years to develop fully, and most participants' social worlds are not limited to the environs surrounding sport. As elite performers are confronted by pain, and therefore injury, they are faced with a decision as to whether to risk continued training and competition by evaluating the costs that are involved in their continuing to do so. These issues are not simply the focus of concern for elite performers: more and more, members of the general public who wish to conform to idealised body types are dealing with varying degrees of risk culture. It is apparent that minimal risk is taken while an individual is satisfied with the level they are performing at in the world of elite sport. However, as soon as that level of performance begins to suffer, cost culture takes a paramount role within the participant's individual sporting habitus.

Part III

Theory into practice

Chapter 7

Distinctive community
The Welsh rugby club

In the cultural context of South Wales, rugby is more than a game. It is fundamentally linked with Welsh identity (Andrews and Howell 1993; Smith and Williams 1980; Williams 1991). For a number of historically significant reasons surrounding England's treatment of colonised regions, there has often been a quasi-revolutionary reaction in the form of nationalism when games have started to be played in these places (see Williams 1991). Although the English introduced rugby, it became a symbol of Welshness as it became apparent that the Welsh were just as good at it as their English oppressors. In the case of Valley, a town of importance in Welsh industrial history, sport has long had a special importance both as an amateur practice and as a professional concern (Gwyer 1990). Performance at the elite level of Welsh rugby is an important part of community identity for the people of Valley, and it is for this reason that changes in the game as a result of professionalism (Howe 1999, 2001) have had an impact on the habitus of Valley RFC.

This case study will explore the importance of injury in the context of rugby at Valley RFC, but before it does so, this chapter will examine other data collected in relation to the game of rugby in the early 1990s. Such a comparison will increase the understanding of pain and injury in the context of the rugby world more broadly, before we look at the distinctive nature of Valley RFC. After exploring the statistical similarities between data collected in Valley and data collected elsewhere, the chapter will illuminate issues related to the rates of injury in the game of rugby. In the era of professionalism, when more often than not, players are wearing more padding and therefore tend to be more physical in the act of tackling, rates of injury are increasing. To what extent the altering of the rules of the game has impacted upon this is unclear. The comparison of rates of injury prior to professionalism, while useful, needs to be done with caution. Clearly, the game of rugby union is changing rapidly. One of the elements of the game that has not been transformed is the talk of pain and injury. The latter part of the chapter will focus upon 'talk' of pain and injury at Valley RFC as a vehicle for exploring the distinctive habitus that is part of this club.

Injury statistics: a comparison of evidence

The statistical importance of injury as a result of sports participation has not been properly addressed in the United Kingdom. However, there has been a call to establish a case register especially designed to look at the problems of injury in rugby union (Garraway *et al.* 1991). Media attention has concentrated on the few tragic events in which injuries received while participating in rugby have resulted in death or permanent disability. However, a much broader spectrum of injuries occurs and goes unnoticed by the public, and it would be a rather difficult task to detail all injuries in a sport such as rugby union. Work has been done, for example, using the referee's match reports (Sharp *et al.* 2001), which have been designed by the Scottish Rugby Football Union as a way of determining the number of injuries that occur. This is based upon data concerning the number of replacements and substitutions during a game. However, these data could be inaccurate because of the injuries that do not get reported, or those that are not 'real' but are theatrics played out for tactical reasons.

Part of the problem with comparing injury rates in rugby is that older statistics may be a result of old rules. For example, in 1969 a law was introduced disallowing direct kicking to touch[1] outside the 22-metre line. This increased the playing time during which players were exposed to the chance of injury. By introducing the bonus point system (for more tries) during the 1995/6 season the Welsh Rugby Union (WRU) has encouraged more play with the ball in the players' hands and therefore increased their risk of getting injured.[2] It would have been interesting to compare the rates of injury recorded in this current study to those of the 1995/6 season, since this study's data do not cover the period of the new points ruling. Because there is greater pressure on clubs to score tries, players will be more fatigued by the end of the match, thus creating a more likely environment for injury to occur. Minor rule changes have brought about a reduction in the incidence of serious neck and spinal injuries (Davies 1992). Stopping the full three rows each side of the scrum crashing head to head is believed to have helped save necks, as has penalising the deliberate collapsing of the scrum once formed. This reduction may also be a result of reduced emphasis on set pieces and a greater focus on open play. Figure 7.1 shows that the periods just before half-time and full time are usually the times when most injuries occur. The figure illustrates data collected at a qualifying tournament for the 1995 World Cup.

It is important to realise that the term 'injury' in the data illustrated in Figure 7.1 refers to any time when the physiotherapist may be required to attend to a player on the pitch. Therefore, the statistics represent an accumulation of the knocks and bruises as well as more serious injuries that may require the replacement of a player. This statistical analysis supports my own observations at Valley RFC, as well as those of Davies and Gibson (1978),

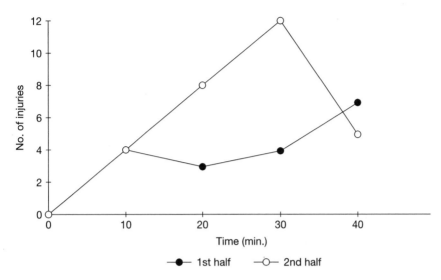

Figure 7.1 Injury through match time. (From Wekesa *et al.* 1996.)

who have suggested that over half the injuries that occur on the rugby pitch take place in the last quarter of the game.

Although there appear to be no quantitative data to support such a claim, my observations suggest that the later stages of a training session also provide the most cases of injury on any given training night. The increased rate of injury towards the end of a match and the end of a training session is believed to be a direct result of fitness levels. As fitness levels improve, as they must at the elite level in the commercial age of the sport, there will be a related decrease in the amount of serious injury, as physical fatigue will become less of a factor until there is a correlative increase in the demands placed on players. This increase in demand for better levels of fitness as well as higher expectations of performances will mean that cost culture (see Chapter 6) becomes an important influence in the lives of elite players.

Rates of injury

How does the incidence of injury at Valley compare to that of other rugby-playing communities? In the Sheffield Study by the British Sports Council (Gwyther 1995), a random sample of 28,000 16- to 45-year-olds were asked about their sporting activities during a set four-week period. What emerged was that although 30 per cent of all incidents were due to soccer, the real villain was rugby. Soccer was played by 10 per cent of the sample while rugby was played by only 1 per cent. Rugby's injury rate per 1,000 occasions of participation was 100, compared with 64 injuries per 1,000 in soccer. Similar research being undertaken in New Zealand has a much larger scope. The Injury Prevention Research Unit (IPRU) was established in 1990. Data on sport and recreation suggest that there are on average seven fatalities, 4,500 hospitalisations and 92,500 emergency attendances each year (Chalmers 1994) in a country with a population of approximately 3½ million (similar to that of Wales). A current analytical study undertaken, also in New Zealand, by a research unit known as the Rugby Injury and Performance Project (RIPP) uses a prospective cohort design involving 356 players (of both sexes) to identify the risk factors and protective mechanisms for injury prevention in rugby. As well as being New Zealand's 'national' sport, rugby union has the highest injury rate of any sport in the country.

One of the reasons that the sports injury figures are so closely scrutinised in New Zealand is the presence of a national no-fault injury compensation scheme. Statistics shows that sports injury is a major problem. Sixteen per cent of all claims during 1992 were a result of participation in sports. Therefore, it is in the national interest to reduce the risk of injury. It could be argued, therefore, that if other nations had similar insurance schemes, they might be more inclined to record injury statistics. While the National Health Service, in the United Kingdom, provides 'health care for all', the poor quality of treatment of sports injuries has forced many sports partic-ipants to seek private help (Joyce 2001). It is not so much that treatment at the time of injury is poor, but rather that the after-injury care needs to be improved. For most doctors, rehabilitation appears to be synonymous with rest; however, for the dedicated sportsperson, rehabilitation should ideally be proactive. Entry into physiotherapy clinics that are funded by the NHS can take a long time and therefore athletes are often forced to look for alternatives.

John Davies, medical officer to the Welsh Rugby Union, acknowledges that there is a great deal of injury in rugby but claims that the game is now on the way to being made safer. Rule changes and the tightening of rules that have long existed have made a huge contribution, according to Davies, in the reduction of the risk of injury in the game:

> During the 1970s 30% of injuries were due to foul play but that has been reduced to 8%. Touch judges can now draw the referee's attention to foul play, and penalties seem far more common than they were twenty years ago.
>
> (quoted in Gwyther 1995)

However, as things stand, 50 per cent of all injuries still occur as a result of legitimate tackling. This is despite intensive training on the right and wrong way to do it. Players are now allowed to wear soft padding on their shoul-ders, which may in time reduce the number of players injured in the tackling phases of play. The structure of the knee has affected the rate of injury in tackles, since a tackle may force the knee in a direction in which cartilage and ligaments are not designed to move. With professionalism in rugby, results matter, and as a result the tackling in a match has become more severe. In recent years, in fact, tackling to inflict pain and therefore reduce morale in the opposition has become more commonplace. This transformation may have occurred for a number of reasons. First of all, the impact of American football could be seen to have led to a shift in the manner of tackling. In that code of football, confrontation is part of the game with every play, not just during set pieces such as rugby's scrums and line-outs. Also, when the ball carrier is brought down in a tackle, there is no continuation of play. Because play stops, the tackle can be more physical, since the player on defence does not have to hurry to his feet after the initial tackle, to chase the play/ball. Furthermore, the belief that equipment such as that worn for American football would reduce the number of injuries is a fallacy, since the equipment hinders the body's natural flexibility mechanisms in areas such as knees. The other reason heavy tackling is becoming more common is that nations such as Canada that are becoming a force in world rugby have players who initially trained in conflict-style football[3] and therefore are much more aggressive on contact than their counterparts in the British Isles. In this regard, many people have argued that to make the game safe, you would have to remove tackling altogether, which would change the game greatly. The game would certainly be altered by removing the tackle; however, touch rugby[4] is a very popular co-ed game which is played by both skilled rugby players and supporters alike during the summer months and has benefits since it can contribute better ball-handling skills.

Injuries that occur during scrummaging develop more regularly in school games, as the young players have not developed the skills and strength that are necessary for safer scrummaging. In a South African study, Scher (1991) shows that although only 30 per cent of those in his sample were less than 18 years of age, this group made up 80 per cent of those who injured their spinal cords while scrummaging. The media coverage of recent cases also highlights the problems surrounding the quality of refereeing at youth level. The young are more at risk because they are learning the game, and therefore a firmer hand is needed in administering penalties and instruction. By adapting the rules of the game in order to teach skills safely, serious injury related to scrummaging in young players may be minimised. A former medical officer to Rugby School has stated that in thirty-four years he never had to deal with serious neck injury. Tackling seems to be the most common phase of the game for injury: 'Outstandingly the most important area of injury is the tackle; the corollary of this is that the boys must be relentlessly taught how to tackle and how to ride a tackle safely' (Sparks 1985: 75).

Injury in Valley Rugby Football Club

While the total number of rugby players for whom I have a detailed injury history is rather small in comparison to that in some published studies, the results will be contrasted to see whether any similarity has arisen. The playing positions have been collapsed, to enable a more fluent reading of the tables. Therefore, wing, centre, prop, lock forward and wing forward are all combined results of the two positions that exist during a match since there is a transference of role within these groups. For example, it is hard to distinguish between an inside and an outside centre when one is trying to determine when and how they are injured. Table 7.1 shows how the frequency of injury by position has changed. In this study, which was conducted over a three-year period, O'Brien (1992) recorded a total of 120 injuries among fifty players. The investigations I conducted in Valley were over a period of two years, but injury statistics were gathered for a year and a half with approximately the same number of informants; seventy-eight injuries of a serious nature were recorded. By serious I mean an injury that would keep a player out of a match.

One of the biggest problems in recording the incidence of injury is that collection of such data, while appearing objective, can be very subjective. While I was in Valley, the injuries that I found it possible to record most accurately could be termed non-playable. By this I mean either an injury that caused a player to leave a match and not return or one sustained in training that kept him out of the next match. Playable injuries such as cuts, bruises and certain strains are more difficult to monitor, and therefore, while I acknowledge the importance of their existence, in terms of the overall health of players they are not included in my injury statistics. This is because the reporting of such 'minor' injuries by players could be erratic and therefore would make my statistics less reliable. Information collected on 'minor'

Table 7.1 Frequency of injury by position

Position	Roy (1974)		Van Heerden (1976)		O'Brien	
	%	(rank)	%	(rank)	%	(rank)
Full-back	9.5	(6)	10.5	(3)	15.3	(1)
Wing	10.5	(5)	12.0	(2)	12.3	(4)
Centre	9	(7)	10.5	(3)	14.0	(2)
Outside half	8.5	(9)	7.5	(10)	7.5	(7)
Scrum-half	7	(10)	14.2	(1)	3.2	(10)
Prop	9	(7)	8.4	(8)	12.9	(3)
Hooker	11	(2)	9.1	(6)	11.2	(5)
Lock forward	11	(2)	8.4	(8)	6.4	(8)
Wing forward	11	(2)	10.0	(5)	10.7	(6)
Number 8	14	(1)	8.6	(7)	6.4	(8)

Source: O'Brien (1992)

injuries, however, has been used in many of the ethnographic 'snapshots' throughout this book. Overuse injuries were also a significant factor in the study, as they directed the research towards the idea of the seasonality of injury: they appear to occur most frequently during the pre-season training routine when players are getting back to match fitness.

Several of the injuries that were recorded throughout the investigation in Valley could be distinguished as chronic in that they took longer to heal than is reasonable. In these cases, either the injury was misdiagnosed by the treatment staff or the player may have developed a problem that could have an impact on whether or not his career continued and on whether (and if so, when) surgery might be required to correct the problem. This type of injury was recorded only once for statistical purposes, because, while the injury would no doubt been of great significance to the player concerned, it may affect the reliability of the data set.

Table 7.2 shows how the frequency of injury by position at Valley RFC compares with that disclosed in O'Brien's (1992) study. The difference in the distribution of injuries across the playing positions could be caused by several factors. First of all, the players highlighted in the four studies may have different resilience to injury. Second, the players who were recorded in the two studies may have been playing a different style of game. For example, Valley RFC plays a game which is very physical among the forwards early in the match; however, as the game progresses, a faster service (of the ball) to the backs is initiated. None of the studies consulted elaborates on which type of game the participants in the study are playing.

Table 7.3 shows how the positions that were most prone to injury compare in terms of the area of the body that was injured. Players in the two positions illustrated sustained enough injuries to allow a reasonable comparison of the regions of injury between forwards and backs. Table 7.4 shows the two most injury-ridden positions as well as that of wing forward to allow comparison with the data from Valley.

Table 7.2 Frequency of injury by position, Valley Rugby Football Club, February 1994–June 1995

Position	%	Rank
Full-back	6.4	5
Wing	7.7	4
Centre	18.0	2
Outside half	9.0	3
Scrum-half	2.6	7
Prop	9.0	3
Hooker	6.4	5
Lock forward	5.1	6
Wing forward	28.2	1
Number 8	7.7	4

Table 7.3 Comparison of injury at two
positions, Valley RFC (actual
numbers), February 1994–June 1995

Part of body injured	Position	
	Centre	Wing
Knee	1	3
Back	1	1
Shoulder	5	1
Leg (below knee)	2	3
Leg (above knee)	0	5
Arm/hand	3	3
Head	0	2
Other	2	4

Table 7.4 Comparison of injury at three positions

Part of body injured	Position		
	Centre	Wing forward	Full-back
Knee	3	2	3
Back	3	3	4
Shoulder	2	2	2
Leg (below knee)	2	1	3
Leg (above knee)	1	2	1
Arm/hand	1	0	1
Head	3	2	3
Other	2	1	0

Source: Adapted from O'Brien (1992)

While these statistics of injury are somewhat inconclusive, it appears in the case of Valley RFC that players in the positions that are in movement when heavy physical contact is made are the most likely to get injured. At the elite level of the game, injury is less likely to occur in open play, such as a tackle on the wing or in the closed play of the scrum. The statistics from Valley suggest that action at the side of the scrum and in the centre of the pitch will be areas where there is a greater risk of injury.

In future, as the game continues to evolve, one of the methods of determining injury rates at various positions will be to examine the player position make-up of a club. Valley RFC had a number of quality players at the position of wing forward (flanker). While at first glance it may appear strange that a squad of limited size would have a number of good-quality replacements not able to get a game, in the light of the injury statistics this appears to represent a form of injury management. A similar situation was not managed as well at the position of centre, where the club was often short of support when injury occurred. As a club becomes more successful, its ability to draw quality players will be improved. This will eliminate the 'overwork' of some players in specific positions.

However, should a club's fortunes falter, the situation may become even worse. The make-up of the squad may be seen as an attempt at injury management, and, in the case of Valley RFC, a task that the coaches in the 1990s handled with foresight. The increased number of flankers means that there is plenty of injury cover for the most injury-prone position. In addition, the physique of the flanker allows for such a player to be an acceptable emergency replacement for the positions of lock or number eight. In future, with long-term detailed injury histories being compiled by the team physiotherapist, a more accurate evaluation of the likelihood of injury will be able to be established. This, however, is no guarantee of success in managing injury, since to regulate injury entirely is impossible.

Physical stature and positional variation of injury

The game of rugby places specific demands on players occupying the various positional roles. The fact that people with a range of physiques and physical attributes are able to play in the same team makes rugby unusual when compared with many other team sports, where homogeneity of physique and of physical performance attributes are common. Although the forwards are often considered 'ball winners' and the backs 'ball users', players within these broad groups have different tasks during specific phases of the game. Previous descriptions of the anthropometric and physical performance profiles of rugby players have shown that forwards and backs differ in terms of these characteristics (Lee et al. 1997; Quarrie et al. 1996).

In the current study, the prop forwards were the heaviest, slowest and least aerobically fit players. They possessed highly endo-mesomorphic body types and typically rated very low in terms of ectomorphy. Previous work has indicated that individuals possessing endo-mesomorphic body types typically have better performance on strength and power tests than those of less robust body types. Thus the physiques of the props probably reflect the demands placed on them for strength and power when competing for the ball in scrums, rucks and mauls. The hookers are similar to the prop in terms of mesomorphy but are generally lighter and less endomorphic, and more aerobically fit. Casual observation of the game at its highest levels by some members of the supporters' club at Valley has suggested that

> hookers have tended towards a more 'prop-like' physique over the past two decades, as the demands on strength during set pieces [scrums etc.] have increased. We are not blessed with that sort of size at [Valley] . . . but size does not always lead to greater conviction in the loose.
>
> (Notebook 1: 23)

As the locks play a major role in contesting possession in the line-out, height and jumping proficiency are considered assets. Consistent with the findings of Quarrie *et al.* (1996), the main difference between the locks and the back-row forwards is in terms of height. The jumping ability of the locks is not any greater than that of other forwards, but it appears that long-term leniency[5] in the rules of lifting in the line-out has led to increased height among those playing in the position. When the rules were tightened in the past and lifting was not allowed (often during international matches), the increased height of the lock forward was not a great benefit, as a lack of co-ordination of the tall men in the second row was often a drawback during loose ball play.

The loose forwards (wing forwards and number eight) are assigned the task of gaining and retaining possession of the ball in loose play, and are therefore expected to be aggressive tacklers and to be quick over short distances. Loose forwards at Valley are generally taller than the front-row forwards but shorter than the locks. The loose forward could be considered the all-round athlete of the game. At Valley RFC an indication of this is evident in the player who, as well as being capped over thirty times for Wales in rugby, has also played a number of seasons on the Welsh basketball squad. On the other hand, the blind-side flanker is slightly more endomorphic than his counterpart in the open side. These players also have less speed and general aerobic fitness but often more strength and power, as the physicality of tackling is greater on the blind side. (The *blind side* is the side of the scrum that is closest to the touchline during a scrummage. It therefore varies with the position of the scrum on the field. The other side is known as the *open side*; as its name suggests, it has more open space in which play can take place. See an example of a scrum in Figure 7.2.) Fifteen of the twenty-two serious injuries to wing forwards recorded during my study were to the blind-side players. It could be argued that there is a major difference in the play on either side of the scrum. One of the blind-side players was very prone to injury, and a member of the medical treatment team commented to me the first time I saw one of the blind-side flankers in the treatment room: 'This player is your thesis! He has chronic problems with his hips and knees which makes him my most frequent visitor. It is tough for me as I can only seem to relieve his problems – not eliminate them' (Notebook 1: 6). Part of this player's injury problems is visible, as he is heavily knock-kneed and has commented to me that, if it had not been for the problem with his knees, he would have played rugby at a higher level.

The players occupying different positional categories within the backs also differ in their roles in the game. Because of the speed which the scrum-half possesses in comparison to the forwards he is seldom heavily tackled, and this is perhaps the reason why in my study of Valley RFC, players in this position have suffered the least from injury. In the study by Van Heerden highlighted by Conor O'Brien (1992) (see Table 7.1), the high rate of injury

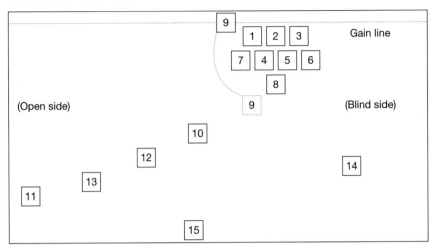

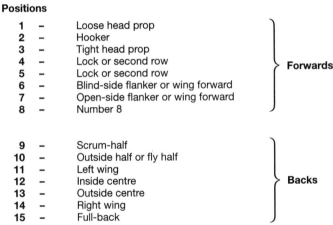

Positions

1	–	Loose head prop
2	–	Hooker
3	–	Tight head prop
4	–	Lock or second row
5	–	Lock or second row
6	–	Blind-side flanker or wing forward
7	–	Open-side flanker or wing forward
8	–	Number 8

Forwards

9	–	Scrum-half
10	–	Outside half or fly half
11	–	Left wing
12	–	Inside centre
13	–	Outside centre
14	–	Right wing
15	–	Full-back

Backs

Figure 7.2 Players' positions at the scrum. The scrum is a method of putting the ball back into play, after play has been stopped by the referee. The scrum-half on the offence places the ball into the scrum at the gain line and then ideally receives it again at the base of the scrum for distribution to the backs. The defensive side would be the mirror image of the team formation on the opposing side of the gain line. For full details of how the game is played see *Laws of the Game of Rugby Football* by the Welsh Rugby Union.

among scrum-halves may in fact be due to their playing behind a weak pack of forwards and/or chronic injuries. The pairing of half-backs (scrum and outside halves) must attempt to control the possession of the ball obtained by the forwards, and decide whether to launch attacking or defensive plays. At the outside half position, injury rates most certainly depend on how often individual players get rid of the ball by kicking. The first choice outside half was such a star that data recorded for this position may have taken on greater importance as a result of his impact on club performance; my observations were probably more detailed when he was injured, as he is constantly under the spotlight. The half-backs are often the shortest and lightest of the positional categories; however, while this is the case with scrum-half, the outside half had a more physical presence than average in this position. Besides his kicking, it has been suggested that another reason why he won over eighty Welsh caps was because he is a great tackler, a skill where his physical size was no doubt an advantage. The traditional small stature of the inside backs is an advantage in many respects, however, since it allows them to be more mobile and therefore avoid the hard-hitting forwards.

Centre backs are the most robust of the backfield, and because of the way these backs charge into the plays, it is not surprising that this is the second most injury-prone position in the current study. The data sample from Valley RFC contained two centres who were in their early thirties. Both these players suffered from chronic injuries: one had a knee problem that required surgery during the summer of 1995 and the other had a chronic problem with his abdominal muscles. These two individuals no doubt swelled the injury statistics at the centre position. Outside backs (or wings) are the true sprinters in the game, and as such they are often tackled one on one and hence avoid serious injury as a result of their pace. Because of the specific requirements of each position in the game, positional training is very specific. For example, those in the front row of the scrum (see Figure 7.2) must work on the strength of their necks and shoulders to avoid injury, much as the wings or scrum half must work on running speed in order to avoid tackles. Valley's fitness co-ordinator at the time of this research suggested:

> Rugby is a game that a person with almost any physique can play because all positions require varied skill, which must be developed. I give each player a position-tailored fitness programme. Today training has to be specific because the game is so competitive. If you don't train you get injured and then someone else gets your match fee.
>
> (Notebook 3: 45)

Seasonality of injury

During the first couple of months of my study (January to March 1994), one hamstring injury was recorded. In the last month of the 1993/4 season, four hamstring injuries were recorded. It seems likely that the quality of the playing field must be a factor in the increased incidence of such injuries. As the pitches around South Wales begin to dry out, the game becomes quicker and more explosive. This shift in the manner of playing as a result of better conditions puts more strain on different parts of the body. The data from Valley RFC indicate that hamstring strains were also problematic during the beginning of the season when the pitches were still hard and dry from the summer. At both these times, the backs began to wear thermal tights or Lycra shorts under their kit in order to keep this region of the body warm to minimise strains.

Overuse injuries were most common at the start of the season, as players were eager to get playing but did not have adequate fitness levels. Many of the injuries were a result of unsupervised fitness training and were of a minor nature (and are not included in the data sample). Problems such as shin splints were common, as many of the larger players did not have the proper footwear to use for jogging. Also, there were a lot more sore, stiff muscles at this time of year, no doubt in part owing to poor preparation for training.[6] Not surprisingly, the physiotherapists spent considerably more time giving massages at this time of the year than during the season, as the players' bodies adapt to doing heavy training during the early part of the season.

Talk of pain and injury at Valley RFC

As has been discussed earlier, the human body is the centre of performance in all sporting contests and therefore is of fundamental importance when discussing pain and injury. Throughout my study I was struck by the manner in which players reported their injuries to me. Generally there was a desire to talk of the injury only if it was related to training and the goal of becoming a better athlete. If the pain and injury were a result of what could be seen as physical inadequacy on the part of the athlete, then the consequences for the player's life outside the sport became the focus of conversation. Most of the injuries that I recorded were of an acute nature and therefore so was the pain. If a sports injury becomes chronic, this often means the end of a career, and fortunately there were no such injuries while I was with the club. I became concerned with how and why pain and injury varied from player to player and how this variety depended on the treatment that was administered by the medical support team.

In Valley the disclosure of pain, and therefore injury, took an unusual pattern. Players tended to be the most public about minor pains and injuries.[7] However, what is clear is that the loudest complaints were made about injuries when the player concerned played on. If a player broke his forearm, the pain was obvious, whereas if the injury was playable, then the player concerned would let it be known that he was not pain free. This served two purposes. First of all, it gave the player the option of blaming any blemish in his performance on the injury. Second, it would give the player elevated kudos within the club because of his ability to handle the pain and champion the club's cause at the same time. The determination to succeed on behalf of the club is one of the components of the habitus of the club. A second-row player at Valley RFC regularly reported problems with his back in the practice just before an important match, which was a convenient way to defend himself against any shortcomings in the quality of his perform-ance. When the pain is indicative of a serious injury, only then does the question of risking long-term health come into question.

Earlier I suggested that pain is in fact the marker of injury. The treatment of injury after the onset of pain can be a problematic process. From time to time it is possible for the medical practitioner to misdiagnose an injury because they are not taking into account all the relevant information. Examining data samples shows, rather alarmingly, how minor injuries have turned into more serious ones because the medical staff were treating the wrong ailment. However, as there are no rigid rules about the elimination and/or severity of duration of pain (in part because of the subjective nature of the concept), it may not be the most accurate indicator of injury.

The role that pain played in affecting the treatment of injury to a player can best be highlighted in the most significant injury case during my study, which involved a leading Welsh international who missed several games during the 1994/5 season with what was considered to be a hamstring injury. The injury had come about during an important cup match and he had continued in the match despite pain in the area of his hamstring. As a result, he was kept out of the club's Cup semi-final, which Valley lost.[8] During the following season the medical team was unable to detect a broken collarbone that the club's international star had sustained. Because of this late diag-nosis he was unable to take his place at outside-half for Wales for the first three matches of the 1996 Five Nations Championships, all of which were lost. In this specific case, X-rays were taken but they did not appear to indi-cate a fracture. If the player had been more vocal about the pain he was in, then the injury could have been properly treated. The player commented:

> You may think I'm thick but the pressure for me to play is unbelievable. When no fracture showed [on the X-ray] I thought, 'hell, it [the pain] must be in my mind'. . . . Now with the injury like it is I may lose my spot on the Welsh squad.
>
> (Notebook 3: 20)

In some cases the pain of an injury may be a better indicator of an injury than the diagnostic equipment used by the sports medicine team. This in itself raises a rather interesting question as to how the level of pain toler-ated by an individual on a daily basis affects the quality of service that they receive when they become injured. Because of the subjective nature of pain, an understanding of how each player reacts to it may become important in determining the functioning of sports medicine clinics. Research done on both male and female American collegiate sporting participants suggests that '[they] typically play while hurt to the extent possible and get help when their pain level reflects an injury that prevents them from performing' (Nixon 1996: 83).

At Valley RFC the habitus at the club allows for open communication between the sports medicine team and the players. It appears that players will often seek medical treatment before an injury becomes serious. Squad size has a lot to do with personal communication and availability of medical treatment. At a large US university, high-quality sports medicine provision is considered paramount (see Nixon 1993b, 1996), but there may be too many elite sporting participants for each individual to be given the proper care and attention required. Valley RFC, on the other hand, only has a squad of thirty-six players and a treatment staff of four (including the doctor). A player commented:

> One of the physios is always about . . . if I feel any real pain I go to him right away. . . . I have missed several opportunities to play for Wales in the past because I was concealing an injury, so I don't want to miss my next crack.
>
> (Notebook 1: 29)

In spite of this availability, it is impossible to detail the level of pain accurately, no matter how well the treatment staff knows the player. In regard to the collarbone fracture sustained by the club's international star, the amount of pain that he was willing to persevere with at the start of an international campaign would arguably be greater than that which he would consider acceptable for a regular club league fixture. Each competitive situation has a relative value to the player preparing to perform in it, and the more important it is for the player to play in a match, the more pain they will be willing to overcome.

Accessibility to a sports medicine clinic is paramount to the way an elite sporting participant deals with pain. If a player can drop in to see a physiotherapist when they have a minor complaint, it will reduce the chances of serious injury. The advent of professionalism in rugby union and the desire of both the club and the players to protect their investment in the sporting body has made inaccessibility of treatment a thing of the past at Valley RFC.

Data recorded at the club suggest that within the community of players there are three levels of pain. The private level, the locker-room level and the public level could all be shown to exist at any one time (Howe 2001). As suggested earlier, the level depends on the seriousness of the injury that the pain is marking. However, what is unusual about sporting subcultures is that often pain is associated with a specific action that is unique to that activity. If a player damages his upper body, pain may be present only when he is performing that movement, and therefore the pain may be contextualised within an environment associated with the specific movement.

Discussions among the players often focused on pain as much as injury because injury was seen as an indication of inferior biomechanics. The idea of injury detracts from an athlete's notion of perfection on the pitch, in spite of the fact that every player at Valley was injured over the two years when I was in residence. There was a definite correlation between the type of injury, the pain that was involved and the way it was discussed. Players would often talk about their injuries as if the mechanical failure of the body was a character flaw. Referring to a chronic problem with his forearm, a player stated:

> It is not so much the pain of breaking this thing [arm]. To have it happen so often really gets me down. Maybe [the coach] is right. It is about time I try to change my tackling 'cause every time I start playing good I get injured again.
>
> (Notebook 3: 23)

It is clear, then, that injury may make you reassess yourself as a player and, perhaps even more importantly, as a person so as to not undermine your self-confidence. Therefore, with an injury of a serious nature there is little kudos to be gained by talking of the pain. With injuries that are related to overuse of particular parts of the body, most often aggravated by too much training, the talk of pain increases.[9] A long-serving centre, for example, from my arrival at the club was continually struggling with sore abdominals, which he suggested arose from

> the type of work that I do as well as all the training to make me a better player. Remember, when you play in the centre it is important to have strong abs, and at times I push myself too hard . . . the pain gets – well, bad. You gotta remember that you gotta push that barrier if you want to keep your place at my age.
>
> (Notebook 1: 31)

In his eyes, then, in order to keep his place on the squad it was important for him to be able to tolerate pain.

Attitudes to pain vary among individuals even within the same subculture, and at Valley RFC, players would appear to be under more pressure to tolerate pain while their position within the squad is under threat. In other words, a player may be more or less vocal about the pain depending on what advantage he thinks it may bring. For example, he might feel that if he mentions the pain he was in after a match in which his performance was below par, he may be able to save face as it will be considered that his game was poor as a result of carrying an injury. Likewise, if a player receives a minor injury in training and he could easily be replaced by another individual, then there is a tendency to conceal the pain and injury, especially if there is a rotational system in practice at his position whereby he may be able to play only every third game (as was the case at open-side flanker throughout the 1994/5 season at Valley). If a player concerned is a certain starter for every match and much better than his understudies, the chances are that he will do less to cover up the pain and injury that he may be feeling, since having to cope with a pain may hinder his performance and in the long term may affect his chances of being the club's number one.

Whether this is a result of the recent adoption of professionalism or the result of the habitus of the club, it is too early to tell. It is true that Valley has created a club 'to die for' (Howe 1999), and I would argue this ethos is controlled by the presence of risk culture, since performance enhancement and risk are related (see Figure 6.1, p. 124). The coaching staff and key players may express how going through pain and injury give the players opportunities to prove and display their character, but when confronted with anything more than scratches and bruises, the coaches and officials expressed concern for the well-being of the players. The team manager commented:

> It is important especially for newcomers to the club that they realise the level of commitment we expect in their play. To shy away from a painful tackle is not tolerated; mind, if there is a serious injury our first concern is for the health of the player.
>
> (Notebook 3: 27)

A case that brings this to light in Valley was that of a player who in the 1994/5 season arrived from Cardiff RFC. After playing several friendly matches he hurt his back. Because he had yet to establish his value to the squad, team officials were reluctant to pay for the operation that would cure his problem. Eventually he was able to get fit, and at the end of the 1995/6 season he won the squad's 'most improved player' award. This is a successful case where the risk was 'worth' the result, and certainly if he were to be injured now, the club would not take a risk with his fitness; he has shown his worth. Therefore, risk culture's importance has been minimised (for the time being) as far as the player is concerned.

> Last season [1994/5] I was on the verge of making the squad and I had to push my body in order to get the break . . . the pain was frightening and I was frustrated that the club would not pay for the operation . . . fortunately it all worked out in the end.
>
> (Notebook 5: 13)

Some injury treatments may work only in the short term, and my data suggest that the selection of treatment method was not always successful and the same player might be out with the same injury after being 'healthy' for just a short time (Howe 2001). This is an indication of a number of possible problems. First, the player may be unable to handle the physicality of the game. Second, it may be an unlucky coincidence. Finally, it may be a flaw in the method of treatment administered for the injury. An injury that was recorded can illustrate this point clearly. A player with a history of Achilles tendon problems had once again sustained an injury to that region while negotiating a tight bend on loose ground while competing in an international match. Because of the case history of such ailments, the assumption was made that he had re-aggravated this old injury. While the pain was considerable, he was unable to go through the familiar routine to get back to fitness. However, on a chance visit to his podiatrist to have his orthotics re-glued, it came to light that he had broken down the devices that were designed to stabilise his running gait, and therefore the recent Achilles injury was merely a symptom of the problem that he was having with his feet. It is therefore important to realise that pain may also be a marker for an injury to which it is not directly related.

If pain and therefore injury start to become chronic, then a number of choices have to be made: do you retire from your sport or do you have an operation that may save and even prolong your playing career? For example, a scrum-half for the local sports college partially dislocated his shoulder shortly after my arrival in Wales. With treatment the injury began to get better. However, once the player began to do more training in the weight room in order to further enhance his performance, the added tension of tight muscles in his shoulders has led to the diagnosis that the shoulder has been dislocated since the original injury. As his shoulder gets tighter, the pain increases and there is a lack of general mobility. Now the athlete must decide whether to have an operation or to retire from rugby. Another choice that must be made in this and many other cases is whether or not to have a private operation (which would cost several thousand pounds) or to wait possibly for several years for the same treatment on the NHS (Joyce 2001; Macauley 1997b).

Summary

It has been shown that rugby's different positions can lead to differing rates of injury, and in a sport where some players are physically larger than others, the injury rate can be expected to be high. The fact that sportsmen's bodies can vary greatly in terms of factors such as flexibility can also have an impact on whether or not they are prone to injury. Rule changes made by the game's administration, the WRU, over the past twenty years have been designed to make the game safer as well as more spectacular. At Valley RFC the sports medicine team have recently begun accumulating detailed medical histories of injured players in the hope of enabling the team to determine objectively how to keep players injury free and ready to perform. Determining the probability of injury will remain problematic; however, through close examination of the medical history in correlation with data on injury at each playing position, it is possible to construct a squad in a way that limits the likelihood of decline in performance as a result of injury.

What clouds this logical development of a squad is the talk of pain and injury, which is often used as a barrier to mask the true feelings of players in times of distress. Injury is a financial burden to professional rugby clubs such as Valley RFC, which have limited resources, and therefore developing new plans for managing the phenomenon is of fundamental importance.

Chapter 8

Elite distance runners

In comparison to other sports, running is a simple physical activity. All children use it as a component of play, and as a result, the sport of running when engaged in as a serious pastime is often conflated with the ideas related to children's play because for those who do not run, it is reminiscent of childhood.

Running as a mass cultural phenomenon developed in the 1970s, particularly in North America with the win of the American Frank Shorter in the 1972 Olympic marathon (Cooper 1998). The 'running boom' accelerated in North America during the 1970s (Curtis and McTeer 1981; Jorgenson and Jorgenson 1981; Lance and Antshel 1981), and people began to associate positive images with the sport of running or jogging. The development of this phenomenon was not unique to North America but was also occurring in the United Kingdom at about the same time (Smith 1998). Mass participation in running was not seen as necessarily important to those involved in the sport of athletics (of which distance running is a component), though potentially it did initially have an impact on recruitment to athletics clubs. The boom in jogging did give rise to the idea that running for whatever reason, whether for fitness or sport, was not an unusual activity for people to engage in during the last third of the twentieth century. The focus of this chapter is elite runners, but it is important to situate these individuals in an environment where running is not a 'strange' pastime; rather, what distinguishes them from joggers and ordinary runners is the level of commitment that they direct towards the sport.

This chapter will explore the cultural context of an elite athletics group that comprised some of the top middle- and long-distance runners in the United Kingdom from the mid-1990s to the present. The account that follows is ethnographic, with observations undertaken as I took an active part in the training and culture of the group. What will be highlighted here is the way this group dealt with pain and injury in a sport where sports medicine support is provided on an individual basis. The training group was predominantly male. Female participants were not excluded, but their involvement was limited and infrequent, and as a result, the impact of female runners on the culture of the group and its understanding of pain and injury has been limited. From the outset, this distinctive sporting cultural environment will be explored before attention is drawn to the role of pain and injury play in shaping the culture of the group.

Cultural context

The distance running group that is the focus of this chapter was based in South Wales and was part of one of the region's most successful athletics clubs. Athletics by its very nature is an individual sport, and as a result, clubs are often broken up into smaller training groups that generally cluster around coaches with particular expertise. Whether their speciality is sprints, hurdles, vertical jumps, throws or distance running, the athletes generally spend most of their time with a particular discipline coach, especially in larger clubs. The club as a whole would come together for league matches, but even then it would be divided by sex, since the men's and the women's leagues were held on the same weekend at different venues. It is important, therefore, that the training group be seen as part of a bigger whole.

In the context of South Wales, athletics is seen as a sport of limited consequence. Rugby dominates the Welsh as an important cultural symbol (Andrews 1991, 1996; Williams 1991) of their physical prowess, and in spite of a lack of international success over the past twenty years, rugby is still the nation's sport. Athletics, on the other hand, which has produced Welsh legends such as Steve Jones (the former world record holder for the marathon) and Colin Jackson (the world record holder in the 110 m hurdles at the time of writing), seems to gain appreciable attention only every four years, when the Commonwealth Games briefly becomes the centre of attention. The Commonwealth Games is the only sporting occasion outside rugby and soccer internationals where Wales as a nation is represented on the world stage, and athletics takes centre stage. During the intervening years, while Welsh athletes might shine at major international events, they are representing Great Britain and Northern Ireland, which clearly takes the focus away from their Welshness. It is perhaps for this reason that so many of the training group dismissed rugby as unimportant to them since it often robbed fine athletics performances of an opportunity in the spotlight – there may have been an 'important' rugby fixture that needed column inches to promote it in the national newspaper. The dislike for, or rather ambivalence towards, the game of rugby might have been a result of Wales lacking success on the international stage, and yet the media still have an unquenchable thirst for the game. What is interesting is that as soon as elite runners 'retire',[1] as did several athletes within the training group, they begin to pay more attention to sports such as rugby:

> When I was wrapped up in my world of training and racing I didn't care about anything other than getting the miles in. It was about getting ready for the next race. I could not have cared less about anything other than running. Now that I am out of the sport I take pleasure in watching Cardiff [RFC] because I now have no need to be so focused in [my] free time.
>
> (Notebook 5: 12)

The commitment to training, in the social circle that this training group inhabited, may to an extent have blinded the members of the group to the world around them, and this is something that often happened when the performances began to decline.

> My training has been **** poor lately and it really makes me want to go out and enjoy life. There has to be more to life than running and at times I feel trapped in the circle of heavy training and racing that I just wish to break free. But then my running starts to pick up again and then I am hooked.
>
> (Notebook 5: 15)

Several informants expressed similar sentiments with regard to the love–hate relationship they have with the sport. Much of the training was done individually, with structured training evenings on Monday and Thursday, and the group would get together for their long run of up to two hours on Sunday. In between times, the twice-a-day training was often done solo unless the training route used crossed that of another member of the group. This isolation could make the times when things were not going well on the running front very dark indeed.

Since most of the discussion on training nights was, unsurprisingly, about running, if things were not going well for a particular athlete while they were for the majority of the group, the pressure within the group placed upon that individual would begin to build. Because of the focus upon 'talk of training and racing', the group was often an unforgiving environment if an athlete was not performing well. Light-hearted 'banter'[2] for one athlete confident in their current progress could be seen from the outside as being hurtful, and only the most resilient of athletes felt comfortable being in the group long-term. There was in fact a hard core of six athletes from a mixture of backgrounds who were regularly part of this bantering circle, while another handful of athletes could be seen as part-time members of the group.

Structuring the season

The controlled progressive overloading of the body is fundamental for successful training (Martin and Coe 1991; O'Toole 1998). Distance running groups will structure their season to follow this basic training premise. It is not the purpose of this chapter to explore the rights and wrongs of middle- and long-distance training, for there are many excellent training manuals currently available from which keen and enthusiastic coaches can develop a training schedule that will suit their charges (Martin and Coe 1991; Noakes 1991; Watts *et al.* 1982). The group that is the focus of this study paid close attention to the structuring of a season, and the athletes in conjunction with the coach established the perimeters of the seasonal structure. The season for the group was largely broken up into four components, though these are uneven in length. From October to March the focus was on strength and endurance, and for most of this period the athletes would concentrate on building strength endurance. Racing during this period may take the form of cross-country or indoor track events, but unless the athlete is targeting the major winter championships (like the World Cross-Country Championships – which several of the group have competed in), the focus at this time of year is to improve strength so that when the summer season begins, the athlete is stronger than the previous season. May to August is the track or road racing season, when more attention is paid to developing speed and speed endurance. The spare months at the end of the two 'seasons' are designed for recovery, whereby the athletes in September and April will take the first two weeks off with no running and then run once a day for the next couple of weeks before beginning more serious training.

What has been outlined above is an illustration of how the season might be structured. None of the athletes in the study sample followed this exact plan because the coach met athletes individually to tailor their programmes to their needs and desires. For example, sometimes a major outdoor championships is held in the early autumn, and therefore the start of the track season for an athlete targeting the major athletics championship of a given year (for example, the 2000 Olympics in Australia was held during the Northern Hemisphere's autumn) will be later in the year to allow for the peak performance to come at the right time. It is also important to realise that the schedules are not set in stone because work commitments and/or injury can make the preparation that is required to compete at the elite level impossible. In these circumstances the coach and athlete have to sit down and discuss a new direction and/or another way forward. Because even the most detailed preparations do go wrong, it is important to be able to handle positively situations such as injury and loss of form, and the sign of a well-prepared athlete is an ability to overcome such obstacles.

> It is impossible to overemphasise the importance of injury prevention and treatment to the career of a successful athlete. It has been noted that the champion athlete is very often one who has attained a high level of lay expertise and downright craftiness with regards to injuries, whereas novices seem to keep getting hurt.
>
> (Marty Liquori, in Noakes 1991: 465)

The lay knowledge that is highlighted here is very important, particularly in the manner in which it may be in constant conflict with the culture of risk that is a product of much of the banter that is part and parcel of the interactions within the group. In other words, lay knowledge, or a basic understanding of the biomechanics and physiology of the body might be a part of an athlete's understanding of an injury situation, but rational judgements based on this knowledge may be hindered by the culture surrounding the athlete's training group.

Because of pain's subjective nature, it is often difficult for an athlete to distinguish whether the pain they are experiencing is going to be a help or a hindrance in relation to their desire to enhance performance.

Zatopekian pain

Positive pain and the importance it has in the training cycle were highlighted in Chapter 4. It is clear from observations conducted with elite distance runners that it is the management of this type of pain and the attempting to eliminate the more negative pains that impede the progression of an athlete in serious training that are fundamental to producing better performances. Key to a productive season, and ultimately the career of the athlete, is the ability to deal with positive pain and keep negative pain at arm's length. This is more difficult to achieve than might be anticipated.

> Fatigue and muscle soreness are quite different from overtraining or staleness, although they may exist during such states. They are normal physiological elements of what may be termed the training process, which is defined as a set of interactions between a stimulus and a response intended to initiate adaptive (beneficial) physiological changes.
>
> (Martin and Coe 1991: 254)

Zatopekian pain can therefore be seen as positive fatigue and muscle soreness, but the difficulty in distinguishing these from the negative is problematic, as recent research into overtraining in endurance athletes illuminates (O'Toole 1998). The management of training, therefore, is crucial for an athlete to maintain a positive outcome from their efforts. Because much of the training undertaken by elite distance runners is done in isolation, it requires a degree of lay knowledge to allow them to achieve the correct balance.

A periodical of the sport in the United Kingdom, Athletics Weekly, which has been published for over fifty years, is testament to the fact that maintenance of a long period of injury-free training can almost seem unusual. On a weekly basis, athletes return from near-career-ending injury to race successfully, only to be sidelined six months later with another injury. Major injuries are one of the key issues highlighted by this publication, as well as promotion of various athletes, clubs and regional associations. However, more dangerous perhaps are the pain and injury that are not 'highlight' material and therefore may appear invisible. These are the small 'niggles'[3] that confront athletes from time to time and will be familiar to anyone who has run for any length of time. One of the group suggested:

> The trouble I have is that I am never really injured. I just have various problems with 'niggles' that keep me from being ready to perform at my best. I can handle the pain of training week in week out but I am continually breaking down in a minor fashion . . . to the point where I am questioning myself as to whether it is in the mind.
>
> (Notebook 5: 17)

The ability to deal with Zatopekian pain and to see its importance as a training tool, then, can come into conflict with the desire to be a pain-free athlete. Pushing the body in training is necessary if it is the athlete's desire to perform better from one season to the next. Elimination of minor injuries might be solved by implementing a preventive approach such as a more comprehensive regime of stretching that will allow the athlete more flexibility over time (Noakes 1991), thus reducing many simple niggles:

> Since I have begun a stretching regime I have been able to eliminate the needless odd day off that seems to be always required after a tough session. My body now responds more positively to training with intense levels of pain, and the proper warm-down helps me recover more fully.
>
> (Notebook 5: 12)

The simple act of prevention, which is part of a stretching regime, seems a rather logical step to maintaining fitness for the strenuous routine that elite runners follow. When running twice a day is factored into at least part-time work, it is often the little things, like the fifteen minutes of stretching before and after a run, that are eliminated so that as much running time as possible can be squeezed into the day. Of the runners in the group, only one had had six months as a full-time athlete. The majority were in full-time employment, and therefore often paid little attention to comprehensive stretching regimes until it became apparent that they were beginning to pick up more and more niggles. In this sense, then, the catalyst for taking up stretching may be seen as the appearance (Leder 1990) of the athlete's body as a result of various pains and ailments.

Athletes gain an increased understanding of their bodies, as is the case with elite sporting performers more generally, when they have to deal with pain and injury. An elementary understanding of the biomechanics of the human body is one of the by-products of a long career in the sport of distance running as a result of seeking to treat and understand those niggles and pains that mark injuries that athletes receive, and athletes' digesting of advice as to how to return to running. The sediments of all the cumulative treatments provide the athlete with a reasonable understanding of how the body works, and the art of maintenance, while at one level ingrained in the habitus of elite runners, is often suppressed unconsciously when pain and injury are not present.

This understanding of the body is allied to the notion of seasonality of the sport, since inherent in this approach to training is the desire to build rest and recovery into the yearly schedule. The coach of the group suggested:

> Rest at the end of the winter or summer season is as important as the training itself. In fact, it should be seen as part of your training programme. Many of the top African runners are known to take a complete month's rest after the summer season, which enables them to fully recover and get ready psychologically as well as physically for the season ahead.
>
> (Notebook 4: 57)

The Kenyan athletes are known for their ability to produce phenomenal performances, and, while debates rage as to the benefit of being born and training at altitude, what is certain is that they train incredibly hard (Bale and Sang 1996: 157). Intensive training is undertaken by the elite distance running group that I studied, but there was an underlying feeling that if they were to rest, it would have a detrimental impact on overall fitness. In fact, as the case of *Athletics Weekly*'s merry-go-round of injury and then return to fitness suggests, athletes from all disciplines in the sport would be well served by having the confidence to implement rest as a fundamental part of the training regime. One of the athletes commented:

> I know I am really flying not just when my racing and training times are good but when I am not afraid to take a few days off. For me it is a sign of being ready for something big when I have the confidence to miss a session if I feel fatigued. After all, there is no point in just going through the motions.
>
> (Notebook 5: 14)

It is important for these athletes to be in tune with their bodies. The ability to distinguish negative from positive pain can be increased by listening to the body and having discussions with the coach. Determining when the body is overtired and therefore should not be induced into positive pain can determine whether or nor an athlete has a successful season. Positive pain that is associated with heavy training can turn into negative pain if the body is in a state of fatigue before the positive pain training is introduced. In many respects, then, being an elite distance runner is like living life on a knife-edge. On the one hand, the athlete wants to push the envelope of fitness by dealing with increased levels of positive pain; and on the other, there is a desire to stop the body from breaking down from overwork. 'The same personality – independent, introverted, single-minded, self-reliant, self-confident, distrusting – that enabled me to excel as an athlete in full health hindered me when I became an athlete in pain' (Frank Shorter in Noakes 1991: 465).

The character that makes an elite distance runner successful, then, can be part of the problem. The nexus between the isolation of the training of a long-distance runner and the idea that negative pain is bad is filled by the social discourse around pain and injury within the training group. If an athlete takes it easy in a group training session, the banter is sprinkled with colourful synonyms for cowardice regardless of whether the athlete is in negative pain or injured. Experience and a complete understanding of the group habitus leads to a self-assured athlete feeling as though he belongs, while a novice in the environment might feel unwelcome. Of course, if the athlete is indeed taking it easy in training, such discourse will act a spur to a better performance in the session.

With the coach present, concerns of pain and injury and their detrimental impact on the enhancing of performance are openly the focus of discussion. Among the athletes, however, advice to one another is loosely sprinkled with heavy sarcasm that appears to be one of the few ways in which the athletes communicate as a group. This can be seen in many respects as a product of what Nixon (1992, 1993a) has referred to as a culture of risk. In a sense, the sarcastic banter is a way of shielding oneself from the fear of failure due to the frailty of the body. The discourse that the group engages in, while helpful as a vehicle for easing the tension of the session to come or the one just completed, might act in a sinister manner as an environment that could breed a lack of self-confidence. As an experienced international runner when I joined the group, I was warned, 'The boys are very intense; don't let it upset you . . . the way to deal with them when they "have a go" is to give it right back!' (Notebook 4: 2). From that day forward, not many serious words about training were had as a group; rather, the banter flew around, and serious fears about pains and injuries were left for one-on-one chats between athletes and, more often than not, the coach. The culture of this particular group illuminates the importance of Zatopekian pain in setting the stage for the manipulation of the body through the use of specific training that uses pain positively.

Pain threshold

Zatopekian or positive pain is a useful way to increase the body's immunity to pain. By using training that incorporates a gradual increase in the amount of positive pain they are exposed to in the environment before a race, athletes will be better able to handle the rigours of competition. Publications that are designed to assist coaches and athletes articulate the difficulty of balancing positive and negative pain, but not necessarily in these terms. Martin and Coe (1991), for example, refer to the difficulties of stress management where training is really an act of balance to allow progressive exertion of the body, but incorporating appropriate rest into the training cycle means that the athlete's body does not become over-stressed. Another training manual includes a chapter entitled 'When Things Go Wrong' (Horwill 1982). This is fitting, since the tensions involved in the training process means that the act of improving an athlete's threshold for pain is full of difficulties.

Elite distance running athletes who produce performances of high standard in competition often find it easier as their training gets tougher. A member of the group suggested:

> I had been out for three months with a hip injury and as a result I struggled for the next three months being absolutely knackered, but as my body got used to the pain of heavy training everything seemed to fall into place. I am now faster and stronger than I was before. Perhaps the break did me some good after all!
>
> (Notebook 6: 23)

There appears to be a trend for the athletes in the group to see the positive side of time away from running after they have returned to full fitness, but at the time the body breaks down, seldom is the positive side of the enforced 'rest' articulated. Often the athlete is consumed with the fear of losing race fitness, particularly if the injury comes at a crucial time of the season:

> I know being injured is not the end of the world but I am afraid [about] what I will lose. All winter long I have been putting high-quality and [high-]quantity sessions into the bank and now I can barely walk. If I am out for several weeks I am afraid I will have missed my chance to run well this season.
>
> (Notebook 6: 12)

The reality is that a couple of weeks' rest may have a positive impact on this informant, as it did on the previous one, but this athlete lacks the foresight to see that a break might be a good thing. Importantly, the good coach–athlete relationship that exists might enable this athlete to realise the positive side of injury. If much of the season's preparatory training has been done, then an enforced rest is not always a bad thing.

Because of the individual nature of the sport, progress can easily be determined by measuring performances against those of the previous season and the athlete's personal best, but for the elite distance runner the sport is seldom about a simple run against the clock. Elite status is determined, to some degree at least, by how well you perform against others. Ideally, when heavy training is ongoing, the athlete does not need the distraction of the performances of others to 'upset' their preparations, but performances of the group and others both nationally and internationally was a central focus for the group's banter. The ability to deal with the banter that made up these discussions and to stay focused on the task at hand was a hallmark of the core members of the group. Those who were not able to manage this task either faded away from the group or gave up the sport at the elite level.

Intense long-term training is the foundation for improving the capacity to withstand positive pain. As a result, athletes need to avoid injury to enhance their pain threshold. Paradoxically, an elite participant's everyday threshold for pain increases as a defence mechanism, allowing them to train in the absence of an affordable sports medicine clinic. For individual, largely amateur, elite sporting participants, the cost of private sports medicine treatment can be prohibitive. One of the athletes in the group was looked after medically by the British Athletics Federation (now known as UK Athletics) and another was part of a similar Welsh scheme (Elite Cymru), but for the most part, the group was left to its own devices when it came to medical treatment. The use of the National Health Service (NHS) for this purpose was almost a waste of time, not because of the quality of treatment but because of the length of waiting lists to see a specialist or even a physiotherapist. Therefore, owing to the cost of rapid private treatment (which often varied in quality), the majority of the group sought treatment only for the most serious pains and injuries. This attitude has been endorsed by medical doctors who have developed programmes to encourage participation in running. In his successful book *Lore of Running*, Noakes, a qualified sports medicine physician, suggests the following 'Ten Laws of Running Injuries' (1991: 452):

1 Running injuries are not an act of God.
2 Each running injury progresses through four grades.
3 Each running injury indicates that the athlete has reached the breakdown point.
4 Virtually all running injuries are curable.
5 X-rays and other sophisticated investigations are seldom necessary to diagnose running injuries.
6 Treat the cause, not the effect.
7 Rest is seldom the most appropriate treatment.
8 Never accept as a final opinion the advice of a non-runner.
9 Avoid the knife.
10 There is no definitive scientific evidence that running causes osteoarthritis in runners whose knees were normal when they started running.

While these 'Laws' were never articulated in this exact manner by any members of the group, action in times of injury suggests that years of involvement in a sport in which there is a distinct lack of accessible sports medicine have produced a situation in which many of these principles were embodied in the habitus of the group. While most of the 'Laws' are self-evident, number 2 contextualises the relationship between niggles and more serious injury. While a niggle might be contextualised as discomfort that is present but does not alter training, injury limits training or prohibits it altogether. Treatment of injury when it arrives must, in the light of the principles behind these laws, be carefully considered, particularly because the serious manner in which the athletes treat their sport means that it is fundamental to their identity: 'I am really not myself when I am not running. The spare time I have when I cannot train twice a day leaves me at a loose end. My running in a sense defines me' (Notebook 6: 24).

The maintenance of an identity was one of the reasons given for a member of the group becoming a qualified massage therapist upon retirement from running. This was a helpful sideline to his other employment and was seen by him as a way to stay involved in the sport:

> I got interested in massage because I kept breaking down. Little niggles often became serious problems, so I felt if I trained in massage I would be able to understand my own injury problems but also make a little money on the side 'cause there are not many of us [therapists] who really know the sport.
>
> (Notebook 5: 94)

Services such as relatively cheap massage are invaluable to a runner who is always trying to get more out of their body. Massage after a heavy training session or race speeds the body's recovery by the removal of lactic acid from the muscles (Martin and Coe 1991), and so the athlete can contemplate training more intensely more often if a massage therapist is close at hand. Indeed, many of the world's top athletes have massage therapists on retainers so that they will be available whenever they are needed. Of course, the simple act of getting a massage does not mean that an athlete can train to improve their pain threshold every day; rather it means that the time in between specific training sessions is more likely to be niggle free. The body is then more likely to respond when the athlete asks it to do specific intense training, which is required to improve as a runner.

As the sport of athletics becomes more commercialised, and as a result, more and more athletes adopt a professional approach to their bodies, the need for more specialist sports medicine treatment has become apparent. As mentioned above, several of the athletes were on government programmes that enabled them to seek out the best treatment for injuries, but many committed runners have yet to reach elite status and may fall foul of injury before their potential is realised. Some sports medicine experts suggest that the runner should be able to determine the cause of their injury:

> Because running injuries have identifiable causes, it follows that the runner, the person closest to these causes, should be in the best position to analyze and correct them. Furthermore, the development of virtually all running injuries . . . is a gradual process . . . the runner will have a fairly long warning period.
>
> (Noakes 1991: 487–488)

This process of determining the nature of injury and correcting it can also be managed within an effective coach–athlete relationship.

Management of injuries

The management of injuries can be time-restricted and expensive. Developing a training schedule that favours Zatopekian pain over negative pain is difficult to establish and maintain. As a result, from time to time an athlete's body will break down. Adoption of preventive measures such as massage and stretching regimes is fundamental to the maintenance of a pain-free and therefore injury-free athlete. There are, however, a number of tools that the athletes in the group under investigation adopted to minimise the inconvenience of pain and injury within their lives as elite runners.

Adoption of a training diary is a useful tool when it comes to managing pain and injury. Because much of a distance runner's training is done in isolation, it is important that the training that is done away from the watchful eye of the coach be recorded as accurately as possible. This does not just mean an accurate detail of the training session just completed, such as whether it was a road or an off-road run and to what intensity it was completed. In the current technological age, with inventions such as heart rate monitors an athlete is able to record his or her heart rate throughout the run and, with the use of a computer interface, download this material onto their personal computer. What such technology will not do is tell you how you are feeling. It is true that an athlete's heart rate may give an indication of how the body is performing physiologically, but this is only a guide. It is the perceived effort on any given training session that is key. If a runner feels that they are working at a given effort and the heart rate monitor says otherwise, it is sensible for the runner to 'listen' to their body.

By recording how they feel in terms of effort for each session, as well as distance covered, time and conditions, an athlete will be able to monitor their health as a lay practitioner might. Also of importance is the recording of various niggles that crop up from time to time. These may be fleeting, one-off entries in the training diary, but may just as easily appear over a period of a week. In this case the athlete may wish to consult a massage therapist or physiotherapist so that the niggle does not become compounded. When numerous niggles begin to appear with increased regularity, this can be seen as the 'early warning signs' that serious injury could be just around the corner. In the context of the elite runner, any injury that keeps them away from running for more than a couple of days is perceived as serious. However, in spite of the fact that most of the group kept diaries that they updated daily, the ability to see these trends developing was often masked by the athlete's commitment to improved performance.

One of the runners who was poor at keeping an up-to-date training diary commented:

> I didn't really think there was much need to keep a training diary. The coach knows what training we do every day so I never felt there was much point, but if you think of it as a way of avoiding injury, it then really has a purpose.
>
> (Notebook 4: 34)

In spite of this revelation, during one of our many discussions this athlete continued to be poor at managing his training diary. This became apparent when the coach used to read through the diaries to match his interpretation of the training we were doing outside his gaze with the form that was shown in his presence during training sessions. As a tool, the training diary is a useful way for both coach and athlete to attempt to manage the onset of serious injury.

Discussions with the coach also facilitated the creation of an environment that was suitable for attempting to manage injury. The coach saw the core of the group at least once a week, and for those times when he did not, every five to six weeks he would collect and scrutinise the training diaries, looking for trends in the group's training. Each athlete was treated as an individual when it came to the establishment of training sessions and the monitoring of training diaries, but if the needs of the small group of athletes were served at certain periods in the season by doing similar training sessions, then it gave the coach an opportunity to see how the group as a whole was progressing. By comparing the training diaries of each athlete, the coach was able to determine the health of the athletes to a certain degree. If he saw that one athlete was getting injured regularly and others were not, he could compare what each athlete had been doing. Of course, some runners are more susceptible to injuries than others, and over time the coach will be able to manage training programmes in the light of this.

> You are all individuals. *Scrutinise* the diaries to see how I can improve your training, particularly when someone is new to the group. It helps

me get to know what works for an athlete and what doesn't. The onus is on the athlete to be honest in his diary, otherwise the system breaks down.

(Notebook 5: 56)

It is clear that for this system of injury management to work, there needs to be mutual respect between the coach and the athlete. The time and dedication required on the part of the coach, which are given with no remuneration, are great. It means that, unlike in sports such as rugby and football, where coaches are highly paid at the elite level, the work of most coaches in British athletics circles is a hobby. In order for the coach to get the most out of the athletes, the way the athletes are managed in the absence of a coach is important.

Equipment

One way of limiting the limited basic injuries and niggles is to make sure your running equipment is in good repair. The equipment used in the sport of distance running is limited. Basically, all you need is a good pair of training shoes and appropriate clothing. In the age of consumerism there is a proliferation of these products on the market. One of the ways to avoid injury is to select the appropriate shoes (suitable for the mileage covered weekly, the surface trained on and the biomechanical nature of the runner's foot), which can be purchased through a specialist running shop. Over the years a runner becomes familiar with the type (as distinct from the brand) of shoe that biomechanically suits them. This is important, since it is the foot that absorbs the initial impact with the ground, and therefore good footwear is essential.

Problems can develop, however, for the elite athlete who does not change their shoes regularly. The members of the training group, who were consistently doing at least seventy-five miles per week, needed to replace their training shoes every six weeks. This can be a considerable financial burden over the season. While several members of the group were given free shoes and clothing by manufacturers of specialist running companies, some other athletes would often risk serious injury by literally running their shoes into the ground.

My shins and lower legs have been sore while running for a week or two now. I know I have to get another pair of daps [shoes] but I can't afford them until the end of the month. Hopefully I can keep away from injury until then.

(Notebook 6: 27)

For those lucky or good enough to secure sponsorship for running equipment, there was never a need to force this type of injury problem upon themselves. However, for the others in the group, the financial penalty involved in performing at the elite level simply resulting from the cost of running shoes could lead them to risk injury.

Achilles heel

When injury confronts an elite distance runner, the body, perhaps not surprisingly, most often breaks down in the lower extremities (Horwill 1982; Satterthwaite et al. 1999). While runner's knee is a common injury, the two most serious injuries that confronted the group were focused around the area of the Achilles tendon. One of these cases developed as follows:

> An athlete who had represented Britain on the track, cross-country and roads began to complain about pain in the area of his heels. Over a period of four to five weeks this became very severe, and while the athlete had in the past suffered from mild Achilles tendinitis, his feeling was that this problem was not quite the same. He had developed a similar sensation as a youngster and had been unable to run for some time. After several months of attempting to determine the cause of the problem and with the development of a lump on his heel about the size of half an egg, the athlete decided it was time to see a specialist. By adapting his running shoes and buying brands other than the ones he was contracted to wear, he was able to continue training heavily with the help of various orthotic devices.[4] Eventually the athlete had these large lumps surgically removed from his heels. Five weeks after returning to running, he was in good enough shape to win the AAA Championship over the half-marathon distance on his first serious attempt at the distance. Unfortunately, in the six months that followed, the lumps on his heels returned, and with them the pain and discomfort of running, and this talented athlete decided to retire.

While several of the runners in the group suffered problems with their Achilles tendon, this case was one that ultimately forced the retirement of an athlete in his prime. Perhaps if the athlete had paid more attention to the pain when it first started to occur, he would not have developed such an acute case. However, because the injury had first appeared in his youth, it may have had something to do with the primary biomechanics of his running technique, which is often hard to transform.

Time away from running could have also been managed by the use of 'running' in a swimming pool, allowing the athlete to make a gradual return to running instead of the rapid return that he did make. Elite runners, when they are injured, often 'run' in swimming pools with flotation devices, and this takes the strain off the legs and can allow for healing as well as enabling them to maintain at least some degree of fitness. The activity has become a popular treatment for overuse injuries such as Achilles tendinitis and is even marketed with a line of products, such as flotation belts, as 'aqua-jogging'. It was perhaps adopted from the technique that has been used with race-horses for some time. However, while activities such as this are useful when it comes to maintaining a level of fitness for the runner, the boredom that can be a product of this activity often forces runners back to the chosen sport before they are ready. It might be the obsession with running that forces the elite runner back from injury too quickly. 'The basic cause of [running] injuries is a desire to improve mixed with a little foolishness' (Hughson 1980: 23).

Summary

The habitus that pervades this particular training group is tied to the balance between positive and negative pain. The group were professional in their approach to the sport and to the management of injury and pain. Seasonal structures as well as monitoring of training diaries allow both the athletes and their coach to attempt to keep injuries at bay. The monitoring of niggles that creep into a runner's diary is key to achieving the management of the onset of serious injuries, as well as the more commonly documented stretching regimes (Brook 1986). The banter or discourse that takes place between the athletes, while generally good-natured, harbours a culture of risk that can impact upon whether or not the athletes will listen to their bodies by balancing Zatopekian pain and rest. This constructive act will, if adopted, minimise the onset of negative pain and its accompanying injury.

Chapter 9

Bodily dysfunction

The Paralympics as an arena for risk

The cultural environment surrounding Paralympic sport has been rapidly transformed over the past twenty years. This transformation is a result of the Paralympic Games shifting from an athlete-centred event to one in which the desire for corporate financial backing has increasingly been the target. A shift in the philosophy of the organisation responsible for the quadrennial sporting festival, the International Paralympic Committee (IPC), has meant that concerns for the athletes are often articulated only through innovations in sport science and medical provisions. Whether these are the general sport science ideologies designed to facilitate appropriate structuring of the sport or, more specifically, the clinical environment where pain and injury are treated, they both play important roles in discussions regarding elite sporting participants who are impaired. This chapter will focus upon athletes with impairments who have been involved in the Paralympic Games. For the purpose of this chapter, impairment will be defined as a physical abnormality such as the loss of a limb or lack of use of the legs that might distinguish one class of competitors from another. Disability, on the other hand, is the social impact impairment has upon the individual.

Since 1988 there has been an increased importance placed upon debates surrounding issues of classification. Impaired athletes are classified in order to provide an equitable system for competition that relates to the type and degree of impairment. The classification system is continually being re-evaluated in an attempt to improve equity, and this, along with a desire to provide high-quality medical facilities for the athletes in order to facilitate an enhancement of their performances, is a key issue within the Paralympic movement. The data presented in this chapter have been collected using the method of participant observation. As a member of four Canadian Paralympic teams (1988–2000), I have actively attempted to chronicle the changes that have been occurring within the disabled sporting movement. The importance of developments in the professionalisation of sports medicine, as seen throughout this book, will be the primary focus of the observations discussed below.

Cultural context

The Paralympic Games are an international sporting event that is second in size only to the Olympic Games. One hundred and twenty-five nations were involved in the games of 2000 in Sydney, Australia. Since 1988 there has been an increasingly close relationship between the Olympic movement and the Paralympic Games, with the Paralympic Games being held in the same city and using the same venues as the Olympics. Closer links with the Olympics developed in 2001 into an official agreement that was signed between the International Olympic Committee (IOC) and the IPC, which limits the Paralympic Games in size and scope (IPC 2001b). Ultimately this will have an impact on the opportunities available for athletes with impairments because of the complex structure of elite international sport for this population. This in turn will have a direct impact on the risks that participants are willing to take to achieve their Paralympic dreams.

The Paralympic Games have traditionally been an international sporting forum for athletes with varying degrees of impairment to demonstrate their abilities, and the complexity of the classification system is one of the ways in which these games are distinct from the Olympic Games. Paralympic athletes compete in a number of disability categories: blind, amputee, cerebral palsy, wheelchair users and mentally challenged. Within each of these disability groups there are more specific classifications, so that, for example, there are eight distinct classes for participants with cerebral palsy.[1] With multiple classes within most disability groups, running international sporting events for this population of impaired athletes can become a logistical problem for the IPC. In the 2000 Paralympic Games there were fifteen 100-metre final races for men and eleven for women in the sport of athletics. If this is compared to the two events that ran at the Olympic Games, it takes little imagination to appreciate some of the difficulties that might be involved in staging the Paralympic Games. Within this population of elite sporting performers it is their impaired bodies that make this sporting culture distinctive, and it is to the issues related to them that we now turn.

Marginal bodies

Work in the field of disability studies has suggested that individuals with impairment are pushed to the margins of society (Oliver 1996; Thomas 1999). This is not distinctive to individuals with impairment, as people going through rites of passage are often seen to be in the same state, which Turner (1967) refers to as liminality. Within the context of commercialised sport, which has been one of the central themes of this book, impaired sporting participants can be seen to exist in a liminal state. Until relatively recently, the only exposure that Paralympic sport received was found not in the sports pages of newspapers or the sports review on the evening television news but in the 'Life' section of various forms of popular local press (Howe and Reeves 1999). As a result, sporting excellence was not the focus of this type of coverage, but was a by-product of wider discussions related to how individuals overcome their impairments. News reports of this nature are disabling since in effect they are increasing the social barriers between elite sporting participants with impairments and those without.

Since the late 1980s there has been a considered effort on the part of the IPC to force the issue of sport for impaired people into mainstream consciousness (Steadward 1996). For this effort to be successful, society's view of what is an acceptable sporting body needs to be altered. In an environment where the body is essential such as sport, imperfection becomes evident. DePauw examines how sport marginalises the impaired and argues that we need to re-examine the relationship between sport and the body as it relates to disability:

> Ability is at the centre of sport and physical activity. Ability, as currently socially constructed, means 'able' and implies a finely tuned 'able' body. ... To be able to 'see' individuals with disabilities as athletes (regardless of the impairment) requires us to redefine athleticism and our view of the body, especially the sporting body.
>
> (1997: 423)

Hahn (1984) suggests that because sport for impaired people is based on physical tasks, those in this community who are not as physically able as others become further marginalised. The problem is that sporting performance, including the Paralympics, glorifies physical ability. As a result, more severely impaired competitors are being marginalised within the Paralympic programme because their bodies do not fit the image that is associated with the ideal able body. These elite participants are being given sporting opportunities in events like boccia,[2] which is removed from the environs of the athletics stadium and swimming pool that are the focus of most media attention during the games. This makes the more severely impaired participant liminal to the games. The involvement in competitive sport, of impaired performers, is in effect accepting the social definitions of the importance of physical prowess – in essence disabling them (Hahn 1984). This is an important point, though somewhat problematic in nature, since most of my informants see their sport as a vehicle that if used properly can lead to their empowerment.

> Sport is about ability and my ability is limited by my disability. Performing at the Paralympics does make me feel that I can conquer all the world has to throw at me. It makes me feel better when I know I have given my best in competition.
>
> (Notebook 7: 45)

Paralympians are grouped by their ability to perform in the sporting arena within impairment groups. Classification- and performance-specific technologies that are used by these groups distinguish Paralympic sport from the mainstream. A team of classifiers normally consists of a medical doctor and a sports technical officer[3] who together follow guidelines so as to best determine an individual's class. The process of classification is normally carried out only when the individual first becomes involved in Paralympic sport and when they go to their first major international competition.

While classification is seldom mentioned in coverage by the media, it is another form of marginalisation for the more impaired individuals. In essence, the classification develops a degree of normality, where the less impaired athlete and their sporting performance are considered more significant than those attributed to more impaired individuals. It has been suggested that the reason classification is not an issue discussed in most of the media coverage of the Paralympic Games is that the public will find it confusing: 'Able-bodied classification is readily accessible and easy to understand, whereas classification of athletes with a disability involves a medical exam, requires an anatomical determination, is complicated, and is difficult to explain to the public' (Steadward 1996: 32). It is important to realise the agenda behind such a statement. The IPC wants to reduce the number of classes to create a more media-friendly environment (Cole 1999). By reducing the number of classes of competitors, much of the confusion regarding how Paralympic events are staged will be eliminated. It is paramount that the public who read about disabled sport are aware of the existence of such a system. Without such an education there will be a lack of understanding of the variety of performances across impairment groups, which will confuse the public and diminish any sporting spectacle for impaired people.

Representation of athletes with disabilities in mainstream media may be conceived as leading eventually to the marginalisation of their 'otherness'. The removal of the liminal status of the least impaired Paralympians could be facilitated by the media coverage surrounding the Paralympics, bonding the distinctive sporting habitus and the sporting news. In 1984 intense media exposure of international sporting festivals transformed the Olympics from a sporting event into a mediated commercial sporting spectacle. For the Paralympic movement, this shift began at the 1988 Paralympic Games in Seoul, South Korea. Coverage in Canada and the United Kingdom of the Paralympics had previously been contained in 'human interest' sections of local and regional newspapers, far removed from the sports pages (Howe and Reeves 1999). Subsequent Paralympic Games were a catalyst for the improved quantity and quality of media coverage; however, this increased exposure lacked authenticity. Ethnographic research conducted since 1986 suggests that if mediated representation of the disabled sporting community is to benefit the athletes, it must be informed by the habitus of the

Paralympian. A major component of the habitus of a Paralympian is artic-ulated through a broader discussion of classification.

Classification

Classification is present in many sports. It usually takes the form of age grading, weight grading or separation of the sexes. Systems of classification have been put into place in disabled sport in an attempt to achieve equity in sporting performance between groups of impaired individuals. Initially the classification systems were established within distinct impairment groups. Classification was designed for the elite level of sporting competition and developed to provide an equitable playing field on which athletes with impairments could compete against one another. Throughout the history of sport for impaired people (see DePauw and Gavron 1995), the development of sports organisations of athletes with varied impairments may be seen as a product of the organisations' attempts to make the classification system as equitable as possible. However, some specific sports organisations have argued that classification within impairment may be seen as oppressive if the system is understood in a hierarchical manner. DePauw (1997: 421) has suggested that 'The classification system implies that the athlete at the lower end of the scale (i.e. class 1) is of less worth because of the socially con-structed roles of "physicality, masculinity and sexuality".' If not properly managed, these systems of classification may lead to a transformation of disabled sport that could lead, in turn, to the marginalisation of more severely impaired participants within sport, as was mentioned previously.

Owing to logistical and corporate pressure placed upon the IPC, there have been moves over recent years to transform the classification system. Currently there is a shift to an integrated model of classification, one designed to promote integration between impairment groups (Vanlandewijck and Chappel 1996). This type of system allows for sporting competition between athletes with differing impairments. Research in the field of sports science suggests that certain impairment groupings can compete together because their functional skill for the sport is at a similar level of competence (Richter 1993). The result of this type of discussion, backed by scientific research, is known as the functional classification system, and the system has been adopted in the sport of swimming at the Paralympic Games but has not been welcomed by all sporting federations for impaired people (Richter et al. 1992).

A major problem with the use of a functional model of classification is that it makes it difficult to determine the role of training – the 'training effect' – on a competitor's ability. In other words, the physical act of classi-fication may be seen as problematic. Classification is complex, and it is rather difficult to determine how much the functional equity of classification is related to the amount of training that an athlete devotes to enhance their performance. It is possible that such a classification system could encourage a culture of underachievement among some groups (or rather individuals) so that they can stay in a less functional class. Failing the functional assessment, while unethical, could increase a performer's personal reward. Issues related to cheating in the process of classification have become very important now that money is involved in the sport (BBC 1994). If a Paralympian is in a more competitive class, their chances of winning medals become reduced, thus acting as a demotivator as far as training is concerned, at least until the participant's classification has been established. Not surprisingly, protests against classification have been observed to be increasing since this research began.[4] In essence, the functional classification system is a response to a desire to reduce the number of classes to provide a more competitive sporting environment in which these athletes can compete. While some have argued that this will improve competition and hence the marketability of the movement (Steadward 1996), others have argued that such systems are inequitable (Richter 1993; Richter et al. 1992). The system has clearly not been perfected.

It had been proposed by the IPC that a combined system for athletics competitors in wheelchairs should be in place before the 2002 World Championships, but because of lack of agreement between the individual sporting federations, this has not gone ahead. There are many problems in combining all wheelchair athletes. For example, the nature of the impairment in spinal injury means that wheelchair users differ in the degree of power they can generate while racing, as this varies with the location of the lesion on the spine. In the case of wheelchair-based athletes with cerebral palsy, it is an issue of motor control while racing a chair (Richter 1999). Therefore, combining all the users of wheelchairs in athletics becomes rather problematic. How an equitable classification system is determined is key to the streamlining of events. Sports scientists and medical professionals have been working at solving these problems for years (DePauw 2000). Issues of classification are continually contested within the IPC, and there is some way to go before all concerned parties are in agreement. Since taking on a role within the IPC Athletics Committee, following the 1996 Atlanta Paralympic Games, I have not been to one IPC meeting where classification has not been a hotly contested issue. This is because each sports federation for disabled people wants to do what it feels is best for its competitors. With five federations, each with its own classification system believed to be in the best interest of its competitors, organising multi-federation events could be problematic. The IPC, which is responsible for looking after individual sport world championships for all groups as well as the Paralympic Games themselves, has had difficulty managing these events and the complex classification systems to the satisfaction of all federations.

Managing classified bodies

The bodies of impaired athletes have continually been judged in relation to an able-bodied 'norm', and the standards of play and performance are compared with those in mainstream competitions. This can have an adverse effect on participation rates within sport for the impaired, because

> It is through the study of the body in the context of, and in relation to, sport that we can understand sport as one of the sites for the reproduction of social inequality in its promotion of the traditional view of athletic performance, masculinity, and physicality, including gendered images of the ideal physique and body beautiful.
>
> (DePauw 1997: 420)

Sport is an embodied practice, and hence many people who possess less than normal bodies may shy away from the masculine physicality associated with sport. At times, because of the complex classification system that exists, there are simply not enough athletes to stage events at the Paralympic Games. In the sport of athletics there need to be six athletes from four nations entered in any event for it to be included in the programme. By the 2004 Games in Athens, the IPC also requires there to be ten athletes on the ranking list before an event will become viable. If there are not enough athletes to hold individual class events, then events will be combined.

In field events, such as the shot-put and discus, the IPC has implemented the use of scoring tables (similar to those used in the decathlon and heptathlon) to allow for the equitable combining of classes. The tables establish for each class what performance is worth 1,000 points, and results are compared to determine which athlete has achieved the most points and is therefore the winner. For track events, tables could be established, but the implication for the spectacle make it highly unlikely that they will be adopted. Imagine the athlete coming across the finish line in fifth place being awarded the gold medal! Therefore, if two classes are combined in a track race, the chances of the athlete from the more severely impaired class winning the event are minimal. As a result of this lack of a level playing field, national Paralympic committees are not likely to support an athlete who has little chance of winning a medal, and the event may not have enough athletes to fulfil IPC requirements for it to be part of the programme. Moreover, the unpredictability of injury may limit the opportunities for athletes to compete at the highest level:

> One of my events at the games was cancelled because one of my competitors was not selected by his NPC [National Paralympic Committee] and two others were out with some form of injury. I am thankful to be

here and represent my country, but what real chance do I have against these guys?

(Notebook 7: 42)

The classification system as set out by the medical professionals and administered by experts from the individual sporting federations has led to an ongoing political battle between, on the one hand, those who volunteer on behalf of the federations and, on the other, the IPC. The federations such as the Cerebral Palsy International Sport and Recreation Association (CP-ISRA) believe that their classification system is equitable and that any changes made by other bodies are inappropriate.

We [CP-ISRA] have a tried and tested method of classification. A classification team is made up of a medical doctor, a physiotherapist and a sports technical person. The burden of classification – of getting it right – is therefore shared amongst the experts.

(Notebook 5: 84)

In fairness to the IPC, many of the changes that it wishes to impose upon the federations with regard to classification are related to making events more competitive in terms of the number of participants competing for each Paralympic medal. The idea is that more spectators will be drawn to the games if fewer medals are awarded and the competitive pool for each medal is larger. However, such a move is counter to the roots of disabled sport, in which rehabilitation and participation were the founding principles (DePauw and Gavron 1995). It is not surprising, therefore, that there is a conflict between the disability-specific federations of the IPC, with the elite sporting participants, who risk pain and injury, often being caught in the middle of these disputes when their events are cancelled:

I train hard. In fact my body hurts all the time, but there will be no Paralympics for me 'cause there are only a handful of athletes around the world who compete in my event that are in my class – you can understand what the IPC is doing but it hurts when it comes so close to home.

(Notebook 7: 34)

Unfortunately, the cancellation of events has largely occurred in the more severely impaired classes and in women's events, whereas one of the goals of CP-ISRA is to champion the cause of just these groups, which, even within the federations, seem to lack competitive opportunities. Living in one's impaired body is a gendered experience. Men who have physical, sensory and intellectual impairments face a threat to their masculinity (Gerschick and Miller 1995), but once they have come to terms with their impairment, society is traditionally more accepting of men being involved in sport, impaired or otherwise (Hargreaves 2000). This is highlighted by the fact that women involved in the Paralympic Games are a minority and, at both the 1992 and 1996 Paralympic Games, less than a quarter of the competitors were women (Hargreaves 2000: 206). The complete and strong, aggressive, muscular body is the most tangible sign of maleness. As physicality has traditionally been considered an admired male trait, sporting bodies represent a pivotal form of 'physical capital' for disabled men, more so than for disabled women.

This notion of 'physical capital' is a construct of Bourdieu (1984), and is a result of his awareness of the body's importance in structures of dominance and the bearer of symbolic value. Muscularity is felt to have high physical capital. In other words, having a good physique has a currency or value within wider society. Someone with an impairment who uses a wheelchair, for example, may not have the ability to develop a physique that is highly sought after in society at large. Not every 'able' individual can do this either, but they do possess a body that is 'normal'. For this reason, the athlete with an impaired body becomes aware of their difference, if for no other reason than by comparing their physical performance to that of their 'able' peers.[5] Because of the fear of the impaired falling behind 'normal' individuals, parents, teachers and coaches have unknowingly hindered the development, socially and physically, of young impaired individuals by creating what can be called achievement syndrome – the idea that the impaired are successful in spite of their disability (Camilleri 1999). Achievement syndrome may in fact be one of the reasons that paternalism is apparent in Paralympic sport, at least at the grass-roots level. As Paralympic sport transforms itself into a commercial spectacle, there is less room for individuals who find comfort in paternalistic environments.

Achievement syndrome is a trap that the disabled sports federations and the IPC are working hard to avoid. Specificity in the sporting experience and the mainstreaming of the training of many Paralympians, at least in the Western world, has helped considerably. The advent of sport-specific technology has also helped. This has been a benefit not only in the realm of performance enhancement but also in the ability to eliminate minor injuries that can be caused by sporting equipment that was made for another purpose (e.g. the hospital wheelchairs used for racing at the early Paralympic Games).

Technology

Able-bodied high-performance athletes rely on technology in their day-to-day training (Hoberman 1992; Shogan 1999), yet when athletes perform in sports such as athletics, the technology they use within the sporting arena may be completely absent from view. An able-bodied athlete does not take technology with him to the start of an Olympic 1,500-metres final (though it could be argued that his clothing and footwear are products of advanced technology). In the case of the wheelchair 1,500-metres demonstration held at the Olympics, the technology for movement (the wheelchair) is explicit:

> When persons with disabilities use technologies to adjust the participation in 'normal' physical activity, the use of these technologies constructs this person as unnatural in contrast to a natural, nondisabled participant, even though both nondisabled participants and those with disabilities utilize technologies to participate.
>
> (Shogan 1998: 272)

Technology such as racing wheelchairs and flex-feet (artificial legs biomechanically designed for running) has enhanced the performances of athletes whose impairments benefit from their use. While this is good for the groups concerned, it marginalises further those athletes who do not use technologies directly in their competitive performance. Technology has much to do with high-quality wheelchair performance, as does the ability to stick to a rigorous training schedule. Because the high-end wheelchair athlete is able to perform at the same level as, or better than, an able athlete, the abilities of these athletes are obvious to the public. On the other hand, it might be more difficult to see the ability of the performance in the case of an athlete who has cerebral palsy that affects both legs, and runs 100 metres much more slowly than their 'able' counterpart.

The possibility of new bodies for the disabled is provided by sport-specific technology. In elite disabled sport there are increasing numbers of athletes with mechanical, artificial designed bodies that are creating new sporting potential. Technology has the capacity to 'normalise' the disabled body, to produce 'sporting cyborgs'. Those who have the most sophisticated aids are those from the West, and they are the athletes who have the greatest chance of winning medals and breaking records. As a result, the Paralympics risk becoming a show of radical technology, rather than a show of athleticism, leaving behind those from the developing world who do not have at their disposal performance-enhancing technology. One athlete who benefits from flex-foot technology has suggested:

> Since I started using this leg I have been able to train harder. I now have only minor problems with the swelling of my stump. This technology allows me to train and perform better. The comfort once you are used to the leg means that I am sure more amps [amputees] will get into track . . . and that can only be a good thing.
>
> (Notebook 7: 50)

The key, then, to some technological advances is not only an increase in the quality of performances but a reduction in the number of injuries sustained as a result of biomechanical inefficiency. Much like the adoption of a running prosthetic limb, the new technology involved in wheelchairs helps eliminate many injuries, particularly to the shoulders. An athlete who competed in the Sydney 2000 Paralympics commented:

> Since I have started using a [wheel]chair built for me I don't have to reach for the push rim. I can push harder for longer without suffering too many injuries. When I compare this to my chair ten years ago the technology is unbelievable – much better for my shoulders.
>
> (Notebook 7: 23)

Research carried out on injuries suggests that as many as 40 per cent of injuries to competitors using wheelchairs occur to the shoulders (Davis and Ferrara 1995), perhaps owing to the fact that it is the shoulder that is fundamental to the process of pushing a wheelchair. Of course, as the technology improves, and racing wheelchairs become lighter and more ergonomically designed, the risks involved in the act of 'pushing'[6] will be reduced. Over time, though, injuries that are still commonplace within this sporting community are due less to the technology than to participants' desire to further enhance their performance. For instance, as wheelchairs get easier to push, they are going to be pushed harder more often:

> This is my first custom-made [wheel]chair and it has really helped me improve. I used to have shoulder trouble all the time 'cause I couldn't sit completely comfortably in it. Now when I am injured it is because I am over-training.
>
> (Notebook 7: 4)

As the technology improves, particularly for amputee and wheelchair athletes, the aim is to allow the impaired body to perform at a level that is equal to, if not better than, that of able individuals. The provision for sport science support in the form of both technological innovation and medical provision has a part to play in the recent improvements in performances among Paralympians.

Medicine and the impaired body

As was highlighted in Chapter 3, the body is the primary tool with which sporting participants have to work. The difference for the impaired individual is that their body is physically, cognitively or sensorially impaired, and, as a result, an elite sporting participant may need their sporting environment to be adapted in order to facilitate an accessible environment for their performance. There has also been a shift in the need for adaptation to sporting environments and/or sporting participants, as demonstrated by the use of prosthetic limbs and wheelchairs, and the push to continually refine this technology.

Much of the technology used by Paralympians is becoming desirable for members of the impaired community who are not elite sporting participants; the consumer market is growing around these technologies. The real benefits are that more people are being attracted to Paralympic sport, and some of the top performers are able to benefit financially from corporate sponsorship. This new market has meant that the push for enhanced performance, which is a marriage between good sports medicine and sport science, has meant that elite sporting performers with impairment who do not benefit from advances in technology such as flex-feet or wheelchairs are often seen as less than serious. An ambulant athlete with cerebral palsy suggested:

> Performances right across cerebral palsy sport are improving. The athletes are much more serious and professional about their training and the results are coming, but the world-class performances are not improving at the same rate as the amps [amputees] or wheelies [wheelchair athletes] because our performances are only based upon technology that is visible, which seems to be the new face of the Paralympic movement – minor disability enhanced by high-tech science.
>
> (Notebook 7: 14)

Consumer culture sells aesthetic images of the normal (Featherstone 1991), and issues related to health promotion such as dieting are often marketed in the context of what is aesthetically pleasing. The push of the body beautiful has been referred to by Glassner (1992) as the 'tyranny of perfection', and can impact on the impaired who do not benefit from the use of technology as much as the amputees and wheelchair users. In the case of elite sporting participants with impairment, the lack of perfection in their physical form means that their sporting achievements are not perceived as being as important as the fact that they have overcome impairment:

> It is frustrating ... There once was an article about a serious injury I had sustained and all the reporter had to say is [that] these things are [to be] expected when your running gait is not normal. This is of course a valid point but able-bodied elite athletes get injuries as well. In a sense the article was highlighting my lack of normality, not my commitment to my sport.
>
> (Notebook 7: 17)

The frustration that this sporting participant feels towards the public perception of sport for the impaired may also be seen to manifest itself in the way in which medical developments around issues of impairment have developed:

Prosthetic medicine is dedicated to physical normalisation and is devoted to the artificial alteration of both function and appearance, but it enters the realm of biopolitics because it uses the normal body as its tribunal and blueprint for action, and treats the impaired body as a spoilt entity that must be hidden and corrected.

(Hughes 2000: 561)

Elite sporting participants are more concerned about the function of aids to be used in conjunction with their body, and if developments in technology enhance sporting performance (in the way that many of the prosthetic racing legs worn by the top Paralympic amputee sprinters enhance performance), then aesthetics is secondary. In disabled sport, because function and not aesthetics is the goal, there is no shame in impairment. Medical professionals who have come across physical difference are helpful in the fight against pain and injury:

Once I have been to a physio a few times they understand my situation. Their training tells them how 'able' bodies work but most listen intently to what I say about how I manage injury, and then they are well on the way to helping me heal.

(Notebook 7: 14)

This comment articulates my understanding of medical treatment. Once a medical practitioner fully realises the nature of an athlete's impairment and the importance that the individual places upon high-performance sporting pastimes, they will do their best to help and heal injury. In the environment surrounding the Paralympic Games, the medical staff (doctors and therapists) selected for the Canadian medical team were chosen because of the high-quality experience they had in treating impaired sporting participants.

The management of pain and injury is key to the success of the elite participants, but also the national Paralympic committees as well as the IPC. Therefore, at the level of the individual, the nation and the IPC, provision must be put in place to minimise the onset of pain and injury. On an individual level, an elite sporting participant must limit the onset of injury by engaging in preventive medicine. The development of stretching regimes and mobility exercises is very important on a daily basis. To me, as an athlete with cerebral palsy, the need to maintain flexibility during my career was fundamental to my staying away from injury. Self-management of programmes of stretching is vital to all elite performers, but the specific nature of cerebral palsy, where a high degree of spasticity will result if a rigorous stretching regime is not followed, makes it paramount. Much as for the informants in Chapter 8, the need to monitor 'niggles' that crop up is important to keep injury at bay. Because of the unusual stresses and strains that are forced upon the impaired body that is eager for enhanced sporting performance, injuries need to be monitored by the national Paralympic committees as well.

There is a fear on the part of some working in the field of disability studies that the medical treatment of impairment disempowers those who in wider society are seen as lacking normality:

> Increasingly, medical solutions to impairment can be interpreted as aesthetic solutions and genetics represents the promise of the final solution – the definitive elimination of prenatal congenital impairment and in consequence – as the causal logic of the medical model suggests – disability itself.
>
> (Hughes 2000: 563)

While this may be the case in society more widely, those working with impaired elite sporting participants in the sports medicine field often seem to remove the impairment from the equation. A doctor of sports medicine commented to me, 'If you keep running you are going to cause yourself a permanent disability to your Achilles' (Notebook 4: 45). The irony in this statement, of course, is that I have been impaired by cerebral palsy since birth, and regardless of whether I continue to run or not, I will often be seen as disabled. This is a clear example of how a medical practitioner can see past the impairment when they are treating a Paralympian. What is evident here is the cost that the high-performance participant may have to pay if they risk their health by continually trying improve their performance.

Impairment, pain and injury

The drive of individual participants, nations and the IPC to improve the quality of performances at the Paralympic Games has led to a desire by all parties to be financially rewarded for their commitment to sport. However, it is often difficult for the general public to see the ability in some of the performances of individuals with impairments. This can result in stigmatisation of a young person who is interested in sport, and may, perhaps more importantly, also have an effect on how sport for people with impairments is structured. Elite sport is concerned with enhanced bodily performance, yet how is this shown with a collective of impaired bodies? Marketing sport for the impaired is problematic when the general public may not know about sport opportunities for the impaired.

One approach has been to market the Paralympics in the image of a worthy charity (Cole 1999). What happens on a more regular basis is that participants' records are increasingly being noticed by the outside world. The move towards ever-improving performances places greater strain on the participants to push their bodies to the physical limit. This is, of course, no different from what occurs in mainstream sport, but it places a great risk of sustaining pain and injury as, in a similar fashion to the other case studies in this volume, more sacrifices are made in an attempt to improve performance.

The difficulty with Paralympic sport, with its complex classification system, is that a participant can train for years, only to be told months before the games that their event has been cancelled owing to lack of entries. To the competitor who has been making sacrifices in the aim of achieving great physical performance, this does not seem fair:

> I have been the world record holder in my class for a few years now. My goal is to continually improve my performances. As a result, my shoulder keeps getting injured. I keep pushing my body and then the IPC turns around and cancels my event at the Paralympic Games – it is not fair.
>
> (Notebook 5: 78)

The cancellation of events is not a hardship that Olympians have to deal with, and therefore in a sense it is a distinctive feature of the Paralympics in the world of elite sporting events. Being injured at one time or another as a result of training for sporting excellence is not distinctive to the impaired community.

Ferrara and Peterson (2000) review many of the key studies related to injury and sporting participants with impairments, and their data indicate that rates of injury are not dissimilar to those in 'able' sport. The only difference appears to be a reduction in participation due to impairment-specific conditions: 'Numerous authors have cited illnesses/injuries such as pressure sores, decubitus ulcers, urinary tract infection, autonomic dyreflexia and other conditions that have caused a reduction in participation time' (Ferrara and Peterson 2000: 139). Non-impaired sporting participants would not experience these types of conditions, but their existence accounts for only a small percentage of injuries recorded. The notes taken by medical practitioners are a rich source of data on injury and impairment, however clearly all injuries are recorded.

When data are collected at events such as the Paralympic Games, there may be reasons for participants not to seek treatment for their injuries. Athletes might think that disclosure of an injury might lead to their removal from the team.

> It really is a pain in the butt. Several weeks ago I sustained a serious injury that will no doubt impede my performance at these games but it is so important for me to compete . . . my family have spent a great deal of money to come and watch me perform.
>
> (Notebook 7: 17)

The Paralympics come only every four years, so the elite sporting participant will often take risks with injury either by not disclosing it to the medical team or by competing in spite of advice to the contrary. Medical treatment is readily available to all participants during the Paralympic Games. The Paralympic village in Sydney, during the 2000 Games, included a comprehensive medical clinic, and most Western nations took their own treatment staff. Canada, for example, took sixteen medical staff, including three sports medicine doctors and thirteen therapists of various descriptions. This medical team was designed to look after all the needs of the 162 Paralympians on the Canadian team. In this way, all the Canadian competitors could receive treatment as and when it was required.

In contemporary Western cultures there has been an increased investment in Paralympic sport, and the result of this has been the marriage of the desire of impaired sporting participants to achieve that potential with the support and facilities, such as sports medicine back-up, to allow them to do so. For a long time, mainstream sport did not consider Paralympians as elite (DePauw 1997), but today those with the physical skill, and given an acceptable number of like-minded individuals with the same impairment, can show the world that impairment is not an obstacle. Pain and injury, however, can be an obstacle. The stress that some impairments place upon the body means that access to sports medicine treatment is paramount.

The fact that pain and injury are issues that are becoming increasingly important in the sports medicine literature surrounding disability means that Paralympic sport is reaching maturity in the sense that commercialism has forced those involved in the sport to put the fitness of the participants on the agenda. No one would be interested in watching the Paralympic Games if the athletes, as a result of injury, were unable to perform to the best of their abilities. In many respects, the new importance of proper treatment for pain and injury that is emphasised by countries such as Canada means that Paralympians are important national assets. The attempts to manage injury across the Paralympic movement are as positive a sign of the maturing of the IPC dream as the launch of the 'Doping Disables' (IPC 2001a) is a negative sign. Both are evidence that Paralympic sport has grown up.

Summary

Transformations that have taken place in Paralympic sport have occurred in both sport science and medicine. Paralympians are now treated in a similar fashion to Olympians when it comes to alleviating both pain and injury, but treatment is organised so that Paralympians can concentrate on achieving even greater performances at a social cost. In spite of increased acceptance for the Paralympics in society generally, the push to reduce the number of classification categories has meant that the more severely impaired athletes who lack the aesthetically pleasing bodies that the International Paralympic Committee wishes to use to market the movement are being forced out of those sports that are considered the shop window.

Pain and injury manifest themselves in Paralympic sport in ways similar to those in mainstream sporting contexts. The difference here is that owing to the complex classification system and the need for technological innovation in terms of mobility apparatus such as racing wheelchairs, impaired bodies that are shaped into acceptable forms (through the elimination of severely impaired athletes from the public eye) have ultimately hindered the development of IPC sport. Distinctions in classification mean that if injury randomly hits a number of competitors in the same class, an event at the Paralympic Games may be cancelled. With such a small number of competitors in some classes, the IPC might take event cancellation as a sign of a lack of interest on the part of the athletes, but this is seldom the case. A closer link must be established between the registration of injury and the IPC in order that events that have low numbers of competitors (and these are often the events with the severely impaired or female athletes) are given every opportunity to take place in the Paralympic Games.

Conclusion

This book has examined the transformation of Welsh rugby union, British distance running and Paralympic sport on two levels: that of the sports organisation and that of the individual elite sporting participant. Each of the case studies lends weight to the thesis that the embodied practice of sport in a professional environment places significant stress on elite sporting participants. Professional sporting participants have better medical provisions than were available to the competitors of yesteryear, but these have come at a price. The relationships between commercialism, medicine and sporting bodies were investigated in order to establish the importance of pain, injury and risk in the contemporary sporting world. This conclusion synthesises the different strands of argument presented throughout the book that professionalising forces in elite sporting performers perceptions' of their bodies have led to changes within the methods of treatment of injury. This has in turn had an impact on the structure of the sports in which they are involved.

Part I of the book set the foundation for the argument by exploring the development of sports medicine and the shift in dominance of amateur ideology in sport to a new dominant paradigm of professionalism. It concluded with an exploration of the body and notions of embodiment as articulated by Bourdieu, Foucault and Merleau-Ponty among others. Part II more specifically set out the parameters for the social examination of pain, injury and risk. Building on work by Howard Nixon (1993a), White *et al.* (1995) and Monaghan (2001), among others, it examined the importance of this triplex of concepts within a commercial sporting environment where the sporting body is managed. Part III utilised Bourdieu's concept of habitus and Foucault's ideas regarding the disciplined body in three distinct case studies – Welsh rugby, elite distance runners and Paralympians – and explored pain and injury using the ethnographic tool of participant obser-vation. By using the work of Bourdieu (1977, 1992), Foucault (1979) and, to some extent, Leder (1990) and his discussion of bodily absence, these case studies neatly illuminate issues that formed Parts I and II of this book.

Each of the case studies articulated a distinctive habitus that gave a more nuanced understanding to the treatment of pain and injury. The distinctive cultural environments produce a collection of attitudes towards pain and injury that enables those involved in each case to understand the appropriate response required to mediate a continuing involvement in their chosen sport. If this fails, and the costs that an elite performer has to take in order to participate become too great, they may be lost to the sport. The push for enhanced performance by elite sporting participants, coaches and administrators transforms the training of physical habitus, which ultimately has an impact upon the environment surrounding a sport. The exploration of professionalisation of sports medicine in these cases has gone some way towards developing an anthropological understanding of the way in which sporting cultures ultimately protect themselves from fragile bodies. In adopting cultural responses to pain and injury that eliminate the fear of risk in these sporting environments, coaches and other sporting officials are empowered at the expense of elite sporting performers.

Throughout the first part of this book, I have shown that leisure activities have undergone a transformation from being a sport with an ethos of amateurism designed to promote egalitarian competition and pleasure for the participants, to a spectacle more driven by a concern for consumption by spectators. As a result, sports such as rugby union and athletics have become primarily concerned with the profit that can be gained from 'fielding' a successful team. The specific case of the habitus at Valley RFC articulated in Chapter 7 exhibits qualities that bridge the divide between the amateur and professional worlds of sport – worlds that may, at first glance, appear dissimilar. The principal agents of the transition to professionalism are the players. Before they began to receive explicit payment for professional performances, the players' commitment to the levels of training required to perform as elite participants was not unlike that of their professional colleagues in other sports.

For a long time the sports administrators at the International Association of Athletics Federations (IAAF) as well as the Welsh Rugby Union (WRU) began to gain financially from the efforts of the participants through the investment of sponsors. Eventually, elite sporting participants also began to demand payment. This transformation in attitude by participants was almost complete by the mid-1980s and coincided with the development of the International Paralympic Committee (IPC). The elite sportsmen and -women felt it was their right since it was their sacrifice, in the name of the spectacle of sport, that made the sporting activity a marketable commodity. In the case of Valley RFC, in order to meet the contracts and expenses of players, the players and administrators had to transform their habitus by taking the initiative and selling their product (elite rugby union), in conjunction with other top clubs throughout First Division Rugby Limited, to the largest possible audience, without losing sight of the values on which the success of the club had been based (Howe 2001). Commercialism in the case of Valley RFC is about meeting the expenses of a successful squad and enabling the development of a unique bodily habitus in its players through which the club will be able to, with limited resources, embrace the attitudes of professionalism.

For distance runners, the need to secure the use of an agent to gain access to top-flight racing opportunities meant that runners on the edge of elite status were often excluded from events in which significant prize money was available. These same individuals would also have limited access to high-quality sport medicine, and therefore were often left to rely on the lay knowledge that they had acquired from their time in the sport. Balancing training, racing and work against the risk of injury has often meant a premature end to a 'career' in athletics. The same can also be said for the Paralympian. It is only every four years that the spotlight is on Paralympic sport; thus the opportunity for these elite performers to secure sponsorship is limited. In countries such as Canada and the United Kingdom, financial support is available to the best of the elite performers, and medical provision is part of these packages. The majority of Paralympians do not receive government funding and are likely to become disenchanted in time of injury and eventually leave the sport without fulfilling their potential.

In the second part of this book, I explored in detail how elite sporting performers put the most fundamental of human tools, their bodies, through the risk of pain and injury in order to achieve a performance intended to satisfy the expectations of their sporting community. Drawing on this material, the case studies in this book illustrate the relationship between the body and a particular sporting culture. Following Turner (1996), the community that surrounds each of the three cases highlighted in this book may be seen as a particular somatic society in which political and moral dilemmas are related through the medium of the human body.

Risk culture

Risk culture, in the context of elite sporting performances, may be seen as a dome that entraps health and positive physical performance in the body. Only when confronted by injury and pain are sport participants forced to decide whether to risk continued performance, by evaluating training to enhance fitness, or to halt activity until the injury heals. What is apparent, from the perspective of an elite sporting participant, is that little risk is taken while a player is satisfied with their competitive performance. At times when performance enhancement is required, the existence of risk is paramount within the participant's individual sporting habitus. Whether or not this means risking health through a new method of training that includes the use of illicit drugs which the performer may feel are necessary to allow their body to perform at the level that they desire, the final decision varies as much between individuals as it does between the sporting environments.

Risk cultures exist in professional sport in so far as elite sporting participants continually discuss the sacrifices that they make in order to perform at the highest levels that they are able to achieve. Only the participants on the fringe of selection (whether as a member of a team or as an individual), however, were vulnerable to overt influence from risk culture. In the light of this, risk culture may be seen as a rite of passage for the participants who are trying to move on to higher levels of competition.

Risks are taken by sporting performers in order that they may achieve the best possible levels of performance, but, as mentioned earlier, a risk that must be rationalised exists only in conjunction with pain and injury. My observations indicate that only when an elite sporting performer reaches a secure position at the highest level can a reliance on risk culture be minimised. In first-hand observations, risk culture among British distance runners was not as evident as it might have been if the study had focused on an average club with sub-elite aspiring athletes. However, if this research had been conducted with the average club runner, the results might have been different. This culture of the risk dome surrounds an elite sporting performer throughout their career. Whether or not it affects the approach of an individual to their given sport is clearly dependent on the level of ability the athlete has achieved and when and with what regularity they sustain serious injury. When they are on the way to fulfilling their ability, risks may be taken. Similarly, risk culture will be influential once again when their performances begin to slip.

Cost

It has been shown that risk culture is a dynamic force within the distinctive habitus of a sporting club. Its influence on the habitus of the individual sporting participant within the sports club, however, may be seen to be balanced (if not offset) by the presence of a culture of cost. Within cost culture, the ultimate decisions take place as to whether the elite sporting performer will accept the risks of physical damage that continuance in their sport may entail. If the sporting performer's social spheres do not extend beyond that of the habitus of the sports club, then their capital in cost culture and their experience in its use will be limited. While risk culture may surround the individual, at any given level of performance it will never directly affect them (provided they are in a healthy state). It is only when pain and injury confront them or when there is a significant change in their capital (economic, symbolic or otherwise) that they are confronted with risk. It is at the interface with risk culture, therefore, that cost culture exists, where the individual has to assess the value of continuing to compete in the sport. In consequence, cost culture, in the context of the case studies illustrated in this volume, may be seen as a regulator of lifestyle signalled by pain.

A fundamental component of the habitus of a successful sporting club is that participants wish to perform to the best of their ability in every competition, and as a result, train in order to achieve ever greater levels of fitness. As each new level of fitness is achieved, more risks are taken with the body, since the harder an elite sporting performer trains, the more physical and perhaps emotional stress develops and has to be endured. This can sometimes take the form of positive pain, which is a term used to describe the fatigue that an elite sporting performer goes through in the course of trying to enhance performance. The negative side of this use of positive pain is the not knowing when the ability to cope with pain will lead to injury. When the performer is confronted by the possibility of ever-increasing rates of injury, choices must therefore be made as to how much risk they are willing to accept. Such decisions are the markers of cost culture.

For anyone adopting the lifestyle of an elite sporting participant, whose leisure time is filled with preparation for enhanced performance or, for the professional athlete, paid training, an element of risk continually exists since physical performance is fundamental to this distinctive habitus. However, the only time such competitors are confronted by risk during competition is when they become injured, since until that time their body is 'absent' (Leder 1990). At this time there is nothing to relate to the risk that is so pervasive in sporting culture. In this way, cost culture may be seen as a choice of lifestyle in that the risks of enhanced performance are not apparent on a daily basis to the subjective sporting participant but are objectified by the presence of pain and injury.

When an elite sporting performer is confronted by injury, they become physically aware of their body both as the embodied self and, more importantly, as a layperson educated in the practical elements of exercise physiology and biomechanics. This education is a diachronic link to the injuries suffered by the performer, since the understanding of the body is enhanced by the treatment of pain that indicates the presence of injury. It has been suggested that powerfully mediated images of sporting participants coping with pain force athletes to accept its presence in their professional careers. Those who complain about its presence are seen in a negative light. This in turn harbours and reinforces a risk culture (Nixon 1993a). The long-term observations undertaken for the three case studies in this volume suggest that the immediate social environment surrounding an injured sporting participant acts as a buffer that turns risk culture into cost culture. Elite sporting performers intimate that social networks provide a safe environment to discuss whether the costs of participation are worth the risk. In other words, undertaking a simple cost–benefit analysis helps the injured athlete, with the help of close family and friends, to acknowledge risk, and supports an informed decision about whether to continue to train and compete, rest the injury or retire. In this way, cost culture is used to monitor individual decisions that are made about how to deal with injury.

Discussions of pain and injury will always take place in the environment surrounding elite sporting performers. Much of the discourse surrounding pain and injury is often a product of the masculine environment surrounding sport (White et al. 1995). The machismo associated with these discussions should not always be taken literally, since when an elite sporting performer is confronted with more than a minor injury, the discourse about their ailment is abandoned. The elite performer becomes concerned with two things: whether the injury is playable, and, if not, for how long they will be sidelined and whether they can accept the cost if the risk taken by playing while injured impairs their health over the long term. In this environment, high-quality medical provision often helps elite sporting participants to make a decision.

Professionalised medical provision

In professional sport, more importance is given to the management of injury, since the loss of key performers may damage results obtained by the club as well as the financial viability of the organisation. The conduct of sports medicine practitioners is regulated by a code of ethics produced by the World Medical Association (WMA) designed to govern the behaviour of those doctors involved in the treatment of sports injury (Grayson 1999). This code of practice was established in 1980, and clearly it was felt to be important to distinguish how serious the level of the participants' involvement is, since these regulations ask medical staff to ascertain at what level each of their patients is engaged in their sport. How sport fits into the lifestyle of a patient is key. For an elite amateur or professional participant, the lay knowledge that an individual gathers about their body and its functioning is likely to be greater than that of a recreational performer, and thus the two types of patients should be treated differently.

The participants' perceptions that their bodies are objects to be manipulated are, while not explicit, a product of post-industrial society (Turner 1996) and allow them to be influenced by medical professionals. Elite sporting participants begin working towards a fitness regime that disciplines the body in a manner that will allow it to perform at ever-increasing levels. This drive makes inevitable the increased potential for injury. The need for medical attention thus increases with elite sporting participants' desire to achieve *optimum* fitness. In this context, after long discussions with performers, it is felt that optimum fitness is that level which would guarantee a starting position on the national squad in their chosen sport. Because of the subjective nature of selection and limits to individual skill, this level may never be reached. This is not to suggest that increased training always brings an increase in the rates of injury, but my observations suggest that there is indeed a strong correlation.[1] It is therefore the change in attitude towards fitness that has led to a need for better preventive and curative injury treatment. This is for two reasons. First, the elite sporting performer may need more curative treatment as a result of an injury sustained in attempting to enhance performance. Second, the availability of a clinic may encourage the participant to adopt a preventive medical approach, an approach that may have become incorporated into their training regime. Adopting a preventive approach to injury means that risk, though ever-present in elite sport, is minimised.

Physical pain is the indicator of a sporting injury and also a clear sign that a decision about the risks involved with elite sporting participation needs to be addressed. Once pain surfaces in the body, the body itself becomes the focus of attention. By contrast, when the body is in an injury-free state, it is normally absent from the sportsperson's view during training or in a match. It has been shown that pain, injury and risk are very closely related. In the process of dealing with this triad, the shift in attitudes towards participants' bodies has been emphasised throughout this volume. This shift has made an impact on how the sports highlighted in the case studies will be transformed over the long term. Every time an elite sporting performer is confronted with pain, the social environment surrounding the sport or the local risk culture surrounding the individual gives them a number of avenues in which to deal with it. They can play through it, reduce their level of activity, and/or consult a medical practitioner. The manner in which a participant deals with this triad can be affected as much by life experience as by the sporting habitus of which they are a part.

Advances in the treatment of injury by sports medicine practitioners have been the catalyst for the shift from amateur to professional sport as a result of the link between the commercial desires of sporting authorities and the fragility of the human body. If sporting participants wish to be involved in a professional sport environment, with all the benefits and costs that this entails, they must take greater control over their bodies.

The treatment of sports injuries is a practical process that is informed by the theoretical investigation of sports medicine derived from controlled environments such as laboratories. For the most part, the medical treatment administered to sports participants is curative in nature. Preventive medical treatment has increasingly become important, as has the use of massage therapy to improve suppleness, which builds on simple training regimes that all elite sporting performers are encouraged to engage in. The participants initiate these preventive techniques in order that their performance will be enhanced so that they can increase their fitness level in a marketplace that is becoming increasingly competitive. Competition for place in elite squads has therefore initiated the desire of the elite sporting performer to prevent injury and increase their level of performance. The desire for success is mirrored by the management's commitment to getting the medical staff who can provide the services the participants need. This has been clearly illustrated in my fieldwork, by the shift away from volunteers who were minimally trained as treatment staff, towards the enlisting of the services of a sports medicine clinic staffed by qualified practitioners. For example, Valley RFC secured the services of the commercial medical insurance company's manager of physiotherapy in South Wales and made him a key member of their treatment team. Such an association was established initially by the club signing up each player to be covered by their insurance scheme. As the structure of the game of rugby union (and for that matter both athletics and Paralympic sport) continues to evolve, the methods of insuring athletes will become more comprehensive and more complex. In fact, in both athletic and Paralympic sport the participant is likely to receive comprehensive medical support only if they are good enough to be one of those being helped by their government's funding for national teams.

Clubs, sponsors and agencies are now paying performers for their services, and this may result in trouble for the performers in the future, since the more responsibility you give a participant, the less responsibility associated organisations have to take upon themselves. My observations suggest that because of the nature of the habitus of both the runners and the rugby players highlighted in this book, the self-management given to participants may pose problems for insurance companies in the future as they struggle to assess risk in sporting performances or cultures. Such risk is dependent not only on the nature of the activity but also on how talented and susceptible to injury the sports performer is, as well as how the habitus of the club is structured. It is important to realise that medicine is not an exact science and that sports medicine is in its infancy. There are a number of reasons for this. The patient–practitioner relationship is different in sports medicine as compared with in other forms of medicine. While modern society has adopted a more understanding approach to the body, especially in the light of the fitness boom of the past thirty years, elite sporting performers have always had a far greater understanding of their embodied self, as the construction of lay knowledge of injury treatment attests. Throughout the case studies the elite performers were in a constant struggle with themselves with regard to their identity as physical objects that can be manipulated by a structured training regime designed to make their bodies ever more competitive. Because elite sporting performers are more aware of their body than are the general population (Leder 1990), this gives the relationship with medical staff a unique twist. It appears that the treatment of injuries is a process of elimination, especially if the injury is new and is due to the overuse of a particular part of the body. When the injury has been treated on an earlier occasion, the rate of success in treating it again (and, importantly, getting the performer ready for action) has, in my observation, been greatly improved. Whether a result of too much running on uneven surfaces or the fact that the Paralympian (in the case of those with cerebral palsy) lacks balance in basic running movements, the nature of overuse injury is difficult to pinpoint even for experienced medically trained individuals.

The pressures on elite sporting performers that may come from the social environment surrounding the transition from amateur pastime to professional occupation will increase, as the money now openly available in the sports of rugby union, athletics and the Paralympics may be seen as a neutraliser of risk. This is evident in the development of cost culture, where decision making about risk becomes individualised. Before money was openly available, the objective of elite participants may have been to look after themselves physically, yet now these individuals, especially towards the end of their career, may be tempted to risk serious disablement in order to put money in the bank. Ultimately, though, it is the performer who has the final say in the game of risk. In spite of its solid social foundations, the habitus of Valley RFC and the distance runners' training group are not completely immune to risk culture and other social constructs that may alter their diachronic development. It is hoped that having developed a better understanding of their bodies, the players in these clubs will become less the victims of risk culture and more able to use it to benefit their performances in competition and in their post-athletic lives and careers.

Changes in the laws of rugby union

Amendments to the laws of the game to be implemented in the Northern Hemisphere from 1 September 1996

Law 4: Players' dress

The whole of this law has been rewritten. The important points are that:

Players' dress consists of the following items: Jerseys, shorts and undergarments, socks and boots.

(1) **A player may wear**
- a mouth guard
- shin guards provided that they have no sharp edges
- soft thin pads of cotton wool, sponge rubber or similar soft material, provided that they are attached **to the body** by adhesive tape **and are not sewn into the jersey, shorts or undergarments**
- a scrum cap or strips of adhesive tape as a protection for the ears or against abrasions from hard ground provided that the scrum cap is made of soft lightweight unreinforced fabric or leather without additional padding and has no projections
- mitts
- bandages or a dressing to cover an open or bleeding wound sustained during the match.

(2) **A player may not wear**
- shoulder pads of the harness type
- braces or supports which include any rigid or reinforced material
- protective garments on any part of the body except as in Section (1)
- helmets or head guards except as in Section (1)
- undergarments which include padding
- clothing which has become bloodstained during the match
- gloves
- dangerous projections such as buckles or rings.

I thank the Welsh Rugby Union for providing this information.

Changes in the laws of rugby union

Amendments to the laws of the game effective as of 4 November 1996

Law 1: Ground

Delete Note (i) which states – Advertising painted on the surface of the playing area is not permitted.

Law 3: The number of players and the replacement and substitution of players

Number of players in a team

(1) A team shall comprise:
   (a) no more than fifteen players on the playing area
   (b) a number of players for replacement/substitution as authorised by the Laws of the Game.

(2) When a Union authorises matches to be played with fewer than fifteen players per team, the Laws of the Game shall apply except that there will be no fewer than three players per team in the scrummage at all times.

   Note: Seven-a-Side games are covered by the standard set of variations adopted for this type of game.

(3) Any objection by either team as regards the number of players in a team may be made to the referee at any time but objections shall not affect any score previously obtained.

Nomination of players for replacement/substitution

(4) For international matches a Union cannot nominate more than six replacements/substitutes except for Under 21 teams where the maximum is seven.

For other matches the number of replacements/substitutes is the responsibility of the Union having jurisdiction over the match provided they otherwise comply with the Laws of the Game.

Nominated players and replacements/substitutes of a team

(5) Any team must include suitable trained/experienced players as follows:

(a) If a team nominates 21 players, it should have five players who can play in front row positions.

(b) If a team nominates 22 players, it should have five players who can play in front row positions and three in lock positions.

(c) If a team nominates more than 22 players it should have six players minimum who can play in front row positions so that each position i.e. loose head prop, hooker, tight head prop is covered by two players, and three players minimum who can play in lock positions.

(d) If a team nominate 19 or 20 players it should have five players who can play in front row positions.

(e) If a team nominates 16, 17 or 18 players it should have four players who can play in front row positions.

Injured player and his replacement

(6) An injured player should stop playing and be replaced as follows:

(a) On the account of a bleeding or open wound the player must leave the playing area until such time as the bleeding is controlled and the wound is covered or dressed; the replacement of the player is temporary but, if he is unable to resume playing, the replacement becomes permanent.

(b) On the account of any other type of injury: If the referee is advised by a doctor or other medically trained person or for any other reason considers that a player is so injured that it would be harmful for him to continue playing, the referee shall require the player to leave the playing area. For this purpose the referee may also require a player to leave the field to be examined medically.

(7) An injured player who has been permanently replaced must NOT resume playing.

(8) The replacement of an injured player may be made on the following advice:

(a) in matches in which a national representative team is playing, by a medical practitioner only.

(b) in other matches, by a medically trained person, or if a medically trained person is not present, by a request from the team's captain to the referee.

Substituted players

(9) The replacement of an injured player shall be made only when the ball is dead and with the permission of the referee. The referee should not permit a player to resume until the ball is dead.

(10) Up to two substitutes of front row players and up to three substitutes of the other players may be made for any reason only when the ball is dead and with the permission of the referee.

(11) Players who have been substituted may not re-enter the match even to replace an injured player except in the case of a player having a bleeding or open wound.

Special circumstances

(12) In the event of a front row forward being ordered off, the referee, in the interests of safety, will confer with the captain of his team to determine whether another player is suitably trained/experienced to take his position; if not the captain shall nominate one other forward to leave the playing area and the referee will permit a substitute front row forward to replace him. This may take place immediately or after another player has been tried in the position.

When there is no other front row forward available due to a sequence of players ordered off or injured or both, then the game will continue with non-contestable scrummages which are the same as normal scrummages except that:

- there is no contest for the ball
- the team putting in the ball must win it
- neither team is permitted to push
- the formation of both teams must be 3-4-1
- if one team is one player short, then its scrummage must be in a 3-4 formation
- if one team is two players short, then its scrummage must be in a 3-2-1 formation
- if one team is three players short, then its scrummage must be in a 3-2 formation.

From a facsimile from IRFB Services LTD dated 25 October 1996.

High-risk situations in rugby union

When an analysis is made of the mechanism of rugby injuries, certain factors stand out.

General

1   *Mismatch.* When opponents are roughly the same size and strength for their position, they are usually able to cope with the stresses of the game. When this is not the case, such as in schoolboys versus adults rugby matches, then the risks increase. This is especially pertinent to school rugby, where children should be matched by size and not age.
2   *Incorrect equipment.* No player should be allowed to take the field or to participate in opposed training in incorrect or inadequate kit; for example, a forward using track shoes in a scrum instead of boots is 50 per cent more at risk.
3   *Unfit or inexperienced player.* Not infrequently, a veteran, who may be unfit, is asked at the last minute to play or practise against strong opposition. Once, on an Irish tour in Australia, an assistant manager, who was a past international forward, packed down in the front row without boots against the test side to illustrate a point. He emerged from the top of the scrum with two broken ribs – a sorry sight and a very chastened man.
4   *Horseplay or foul tactics.* There are still, unfortunately, individuals playing rugby who appear to derive pleasure from injuring their opponents. It is the duty of club members and selection committees to weed these people out, as they have no place in the game.

Specific

The set scrum. Serious neck injuries can occur in association with the set scrummage. The front-row players are primarily at risk. In the set scrum the danger times are:

1   When the scrums pack down and the front rows collide, shoulder to shoulder. Faulty timing of one player may cause his head to collide against his opponent's head or shoulder with obvious risk of injury.

2   *Collapsing scrum.* When the scrum has settled after the impact of the two sets of forwards, it may collapse unintentionally or be collapsed deliberately. There are many ways in which a scrum can be made to collapse which are not in this brief. The most obvious is the prop forward pulling down his opponent. With experienced players this is not usually dangerous, as most competent front-row players have practised how to fall. It is usually when there is a mismatch in physique or experience between opposing front rows that injuries occur. The most dangerous part of a collapse situation occurs when the second and back rows continue to push while the heads and necks of the front-row players are trapped against the ground. This can be prevented by the education of players and the prompt whistle of the referee.

3   *Aerial scrum.* This is one of the most frightening and dangerous experiences for front-row players. It may happen when an entire front row is lifted off the ground by the superior technique of their opposition, while their own second row continue to push. The trapped players risk severe damage to their cervicothoracic spine, and any forward who has been in this situation speaks of his helplessness and fear. It is also the situation where 'sprung ribs', or fractures at the costochondral junction, may occur.

Methods of reducing risks of injury

1   Players:
    (a) must be fit;
    (b) always wear correct equipment;
    (c) do not play out of position;
    (d) do not indulge in horseplay or foul play.

2   The coach:
    (a) does not select unfit players;
    (b) ensures that the skills of the game are learned and practised; this includes tackling, falling and scrummaging.

3   The referee:
    (a) must stop the play at once when a set scrum collapses;
    (b) must stop the play at once if a loose scrum becomes a fight or collapses;
    (c) should punish severely (sending off, followed by club disciplinary action) repeated use of illegal techniques such as the short-arm tackle.

4   Administrators have a duty to keep the laws of the game under constant review with a view to improving safely for players and taking into account the evidence available from relevant research.

Source: Kennedy, K.W. (1992) 'The Team Doctor in Rugby Union Football', in S.D.W. Payne (ed.) *Medico-legal Hazards of Rugby Union*. Oxford: Blackwell Special Projects, pp. 9–17.

Pain relief

What should the doctor do when asked to provide pain relief to enable an athlete to continue competition? There can be no hard and fast rules here, each situation requiring individual appraisal. Factors to be considered include:

1　Is the injury likely to get worse if the pain is masked? (Broken nose or severe ankle sprain.)
2　Does the athlete really want to continue, or is he or she being psychologically pressured by family, team mates or coach?
3　How important is the competition to the individual – is it his/her last chance for a British title, or just the street championships?
4　What other measures can be taken, e.g. equipment modification, changes in technique, protective taping?
5　Is the athlete intelligent enough to understand the risks and give informed consent?
6　Does the sport forbid or place restrictions on the contemplated practice?

Source: Anstiss, T.J. (1992) 'Uses and Abuses of Drugs in Sport: The Athlete's View', in S.D.W. Payne (ed.) *Medico-legal Hazards of Rugby Union*. Oxford: Blackwell Special Projects, pp. 89–125.

Contents of the medical kitbag as used at Valley RFC

1 Airway
Elastoplast   5 cm (× 3), 2.5 cm (× 3)
Rigid tape rolls   2 inches (× 1), 1.5 inches (× 1), 0.5 inch (× 1)
1 tin PR spray
1 small Vaseline
1 tube embrocation
1 small hand mirror
1 solid rubber gag
2 dozen gauze swabs
4 packets of Kaltostat
1 smelling salts
2 pairs of scissors
1 cervical collar
1 water bottle
1 waterproof container for sponge in ice water
1 hand towel
spare contact lens sets
pair of laces
spare club shorts and shirt

Notes

Introduction

1   In an elite sporting environment that is becoming increasingly commercialised (see Polley 1998; Smith and Porter 2000), tension may not be reduced by the act of playing a sport if one's livelihood depends upon it.
2   For further details, see Chapter 3 in this volume and Jarvie and Maguire (1994).
3   Ingham and Donnelly (1997) have outlined the development of sport sociology in the North American context.
4   By this I mean there are certain things in every culture that members of the cultural groups concerned know explicitly but if interviewed or questioned would more often than not fail to articulate accurately because within their cultural environment everyone knows these 'facts'.
5   The value of this type of data should not be underestimated, and, contrary to suggestions by anthropologists such as Sands (1999c), these data have just as much of a role to play in constructing 'social reality' as do the data collected by the use of the ethnographic method.

1   Investigating sports medicine: medical anthropology in context

1   The 'magic sponge' was a traditional treatment for ailments that were considered non-serious. Basically it was a bucket full of icy water that was applied to the injured party using a sponge. If a participant got a knock or cut, the sponge was used to deaden the pain. Obviously the level of hygiene was not particularly good, as all players were treated with the same sponge using the same water, and therefore such treatment measures are frowned upon today.
2   See Chapter 6 on risk culture in this book.
3   Creatine is a naturally occurring substance that can be found in red meat. A diet loaded with creatine therefore can be seen as not dissimilar to the diets of sportsmen over a hundred years ago, which largely comprised raw meat.

2   Amateur pastime to professional spectacle

1   With the exception of Chapter 9, which is a case study of pain and injury in Paralympic sport and therefore has an international focus.
2   The rugby league code is played with thirteen players instead of the fifteen used in rugby union. Emphasis is not on scrums and line-outs, but on recycling the ball for the next play as safely and as quickly as possible after the tackle. This provides a game that is explosive and very spectator-friendly.

3 In North America the league structure is different, with no demotion or promotion in elite professional team sports. What happens as a result is often to the detriment of community ties. If the sporting franchise is not making money, it will move to a city where it feels it can, with no regard for its supporters.

4 This development can have as many negative as positive connotations, but ultimately the codifying of the game set limits on what was considered acceptable in the game. The rules have been altered greatly over the past century. For current rules of the game, see *Laws of the Game of Rugby Football*. Rule changes appear to have been more frequent since the advent of professionalism in the sport.

5 Participation in the national squad has for a long time taken this philosophy for granted. It is the depth of commitment even in lower divisions that is unique to the present era.

6 The Union, since it was established, in 1880, has been charged with upholding the amateur values on which the game was founded. Therefore, its control of finances did originally have a value, but today, in the open era, this role is in question.

7 For more on the risk involved in sport, see Chapter 6.

3 Sporting bodies: mortal engines

1 Some sports are more dependent than others on improvisation. In rugby, improvisation can be beneficial, whereas in figure skating it is not.

2 A panopticon is an architectural structure that involves maximum supervision with minimum effort. Such structures were incorporated into the design of Victorian hospitals and prisons. The importance of the panopticon was first articulated by Jeremy Bentham, but more recently the idea has been used effectively in the work of Erving Goffman (1961) on asylums, in which he explores the concept of total institutions.

3 The body politic, according to Scheper-Hughes and Lock (1987) is the body that the state controls, in order to maintain social stability. Therefore, if this body is ill or in pain, it follows that the society exhibits the same condition.

4 Pain and injury: signal and response

1 Sporting equipment, for an elite sporting performer, becomes part of the body. Because very few participants are actually involved in the manufacture of sporting equipment (though they may advise), they have only their bodies to enhance through training.

2 Pathology is the science of bodily disease that explores the symptoms of the disease. In the sporting context, pain and injury manifest themselves in much the same way as a disease.

3 To the individual without a medical background this might be expressed as an active imagination leading to some form of mental disorder.

4 Schedules for the healing of injuries vary considerably and are heavily dependent on lifestyle.

5 It is possible to objectify pain using laboratory conditions and equipment to measure the physiological response of the nerves to hurt (Good *et al.* 1992: 9). However, these conditions do not exist during competition or training and therefore the measurement of pain I am discussing is the subjective response of the sportsperson.

6 When I give coaching clinics I refer to this as 'Zatopekian' pain – after the gold medallist in the 5,000 metres, 10,000 metres and marathon at the 1952 Olympic

games, Emil Zatopek, who legend states had the most punishing of training regimes.

7   This means a decrease in mileage from 100/week to 70/week with an increased focus placed on intense track sessions accompanied by less volume on the hard days.

5   The importance of injury in the commercialised world of sport

1   The sin bin is where a player in rugby is sent if he has committed an infraction of the laws of the game that is serious enough for him to be sent off the field of play. In this respect, the sin bin is similar to the penalty box in hockey, though a player usually has to sit out for ten minutes of the match.

2   It is rather unfortunate for Hitler that a man named Jesse Owens did not perform according to this racist, nationalist agenda.

3   The use of illicit drugs has been one of the tools that nations are willing to resort to in order to maintain their superiority (Waddington 1996, 2000). More broadly, it is the issue of a risk that exists in elite sporting environments, to which the focus of the book will turn in Chapter 6.

6   Risk culture as a 'product'

1   For example, the good capitalist and the bad communist, as Olympic competition was often portrayed by Western media.

2   A participant is often known as 'slippery fingers' if he or she has the ability to work hard for the team but lacks the physical gifts to contribute effectively to the team's good performance very often. Lacking good skills but having a big heart is the hallmark of such individuals.

3   It has been argued that the fitness boom is really a push for consumers to sell more 'fashion' products (Cole 1998).

7   Distinctive community: the Welsh rugby club

1   The expression 'kicking to touch' literally means to kick the ball out of play. In essence, if a player does this outside his 22-metre line without allowing the ball to bounce before it leaves the field, the other team takes possession of the ball from where it was kicked.

2   It is evident from the nature of the game that the more the ball is in play, the more likely it is that an injury is going to occur.

3   Canadian football is similar to the American game and until recently was the most popular field sport in high schools across Canada. As equipment has become too expensive, many schools have switched to rugby. In this manner the game of rugby has been able to develop a unique Canadian style, with uncharacteristically hard-hitting large forwards.

4   Touch rugby is a form of rugby in which tackling is illegal. The game is like rugby sevens in that there are seven players a side on the pitch at any one time.

5   Lifting has been allowed in the game since the 1995 World Cup, in part to make the decisions of referees less problematic, and to heighten the spectacle of the line-out.

6   A failing of many players is the lack of care taken in the warm-up/warm-down segment of any training session.

7   Of course, because I was not feeling the pains myself it is difficult to determine their severity.

8   For more detail of the injury, see the full case in Chapter 5 (p. 92).
9   Although my comments about pain are based on observation, they cannot be proved, as it was not possible to collect accurate quantitative data on overuse injuries.

8   Elite distance runners

1   Few elite distance runners can make a living out of the sport, so the notion of retirement is unofficial in the sense that it simply means that an athlete stops training and racing with the same intensity. Even in retirement, few runners give up the physical benefits associated with running.
2   In the case of this training group, banter, a form of social discourse, was felt to be full of irony, sarcasm and four-letter words.
3   A 'niggle' is a sore, stiff feeling in part of the body. It does not limit training but may be an indication that more severe pain and injury are just around the corner. In the case of distance runners, niggles usually show up in the lower extremities.
4   These are devices that are inserted into shoes to control the movement of the legs when a foot strikes the ground.

9   Bodily dysfunction: the Paralympics as an arena for risk

1   For a detailed look at the number of different classes, see DePauw and Gavron (1995).
2   Boccia is a game of skill similar to lawn bowls, played by athletes with severe cerebral palsy. In the context of the Paralympic Games it is confined to an indoor gymnasium. This shift away from the main stadium where either swimming or athletics takes place could imply that the competition in boccia is liminal to the larger spectacle of the Paralympic Games.
3   In some federations the classification team is different. The International Blind Sports Federation (IBSA) only requires the knowledge of an ophthalmologist. The Cerebral Palsy International Sport Recreation Association (CP-ISRA) requires a medical doctor, a sports technical official and a physiotherapist.
4   In the current climate, formal classification protests are becoming less frequent. Classification teams are now given the opportunity to watch athletes in competition several times before they receive permanent status – the idea being that an athlete is less likely to hide his or her functional ability on the field of play.
5   As impaired sporting culture develops, new image ideals are beginning to become apparent. On the one hand this is a positive step: it shows acceptance of the impaired form. On the other, more severely impaired individuals might continue to be marginalised because they cannot meet this ideal either.
6   'Pushing' a wheelchair means that the user is propelling it with his or her own arms.

Conclusion

1   My observations indicate that players at Valley RFC who were not dedicated to fitness when I arrived at the club but began to increase their training, perhaps as a result of the pressure from other players on their squad position, became more frequent visitors to the physiotherapist's treatment room.

Bibliography

Aaron, J., Rees, T., Betts, S. and Vincentelli, M. (eds) (1994) *Our Sisters' Land: The Changing Identities of Women in Wales*. Cardiff: University of Wales Press.

Adams, J. (1995) *Risk*. London: UCL Press.

Allison, L. (2001) *Amateurism in Sport*. London: Cass.

Andrews, D.L. (1991) 'Welsh Indigenous! and British Imperial? Welsh Rugby, Culture and Society, 1890–1914', *Journal of Sport History*, 18: 335–349.

—— (1993) 'Desperately Seeking Michel: Foucault's Genealogy, the Body, and Critical Sport Sociology', *Sociology of Sport Journal*, 10: 148–167.

—— (1996) 'Sport and the Masculine Hegemony of the Modern Nation: Welsh Rugby, Culture and Society, 1890–1914', in J. Nauright and T.L.J. Chandler (eds) *Making Men: Rugby Masculine Identity*. London: Frank Cass.

Andrews, D.L. and Howell, J.W. (1993) 'Transforming into a Tradition: Rugby and the Making of Imperial Wales, 1890–1914', in A.G. Ingham and J.W. Loy (eds) *Sport in Social Development: Traditions, Transitions and Transformations*. Leeds: Human Kinetics.

Anstiss, T.J. (1992) 'Uses and Abuses of Drugs in Sport: The Athlete's View', in S.D.W. Payne (ed.) *Medico-legal Hazards of Rugby Union*. Oxford: Blackwell Special Projects.

Armstrong, G. (1998) *Football Hooligans: Knowing the Score*. Oxford: Berg.

Armstrong, G. and Giulianotti, R. (eds) (1997) *Entering the Field: New Perspectives on World Football*. Oxford: Berg.

Babić, Z., Mišigoj-Duraković, M., Matasić, H. and Jančić, J. (2001a) 'Croatian Rugby Project Part I: Anthropometric Characteristics, Body Composition and Constitution', *Journal of Sports Medicine and Physical Fitness*, 41: 250–255.

Babić, Z., Mišigoj-Duraković, M., Matasić H. and Jančić, J. (2001b) 'Croatian Rugby Project Part II: Injuries', *Journal of Sports Medicine and Physical Fitness*, 41: 392–398.

Bale, J. (1986) 'Sport and National Identity: A Geographical View', *British Journal of Sports History*, 3: 18–41.

—— (1994) *Landscapes of Modern Sport*. London: Leicester University Press.

Bale, J. and Sang, J. (1996) *Kenyan Running: Movement Culture, Geography and Global Change*. London: Cass.

Bates, M. (1987) 'Ethnicity and Pain: A Bio-cultural Model', *Social Science and Medicine*, 24: 47–50.

Bateson, G. (1972) 'A Theory of Play and Fantasy', in G. Bateson (ed.) *Steps to an Ecology of Mind*. New York: Random House.

BBC (1994) *On the Line: Disability for Dollars*. Video shown 11 July.

Beck, U. (1992) *Risk Society*. London: Sage.

Bendelow, G. (1993) 'Pain Perceptions, Emotions and Gender', *Sociology of Health and Illness*, 15(3): 273–294.

Bendelow, G. and Williams, S.J. (1995) 'Transcending the Dualism: Towards a Sociology of Pain', *Sociology of Health and Illness*, 17: 139–165.

Benjamin, I.S. (1992) 'The Case against Anabolic Steroids', in S.D.W. Payne (ed.) *Medico-legal Hazards of Rugby Union*. Oxford: Blackwell Special Projects.

Benson, H. and Friedman, R. (1996) 'Harnessing the Power of the Placebo Effect and Renaming It "Remembered Wellness" ', *Annual Review of Medicine*, 47: 193–199.

Berryman, J. (1992) 'Exercise and the Medical Tradition from Hippocrates through Antebellum America: A Review Essay', in J. Berryman and R. Park (eds) *Sport and Exercise Science: Essays in the History of Sports Medicine*, Chicago: University of Illinois Press.

Berryman, J.W and Park, R.J. (eds) (1992) *Sport and Exercise Science: Essays in the History of Sports Medicine*, Chicago: University of Illinois Press.

Bickford, R.G. (1939) 'The Fibre Dissociation Produced by Cooling Human Nerves', *Clinical Science*, 4: 159–165.

Binder, A., Hodge, G., Greenwood, A.M. and Hazleman, B.L. (1985) 'Is Therapeutic Ultrasound Effective in Treating Soft Tissue Lesions?', *British Medical Journal*, 290: 512.

Blake, A. (1996) *The Body Language: The Meaning of Modern Sport*. London: Lawrence and Wishart.

Blanchard, K. (1995) *The Anthropology of Sport: An Introduction*. London: Bergin and Garvey.

Bordo, S. (1990) 'Reading the Slender Body', in M. Jacobs (ed.) *Body/Politic: Women and the Discourses of Science*. London: Routledge.

Bourdieu, P. (1977) *Outline of a Theory of Practice*, Cambridge: Cambridge University Press.

—— (1984) *Distinction: A Social Critique of the Judgement of Taste*. London: Routledge.

—— (1988) 'Program for the Sociology of Sport', in S. Kang, J. MaAloon and R. DaMatta (eds) *The Olympics and Cultural Exchange*. Hanyang Ethnology Monograph No. 1: Hanyang University Press.

—— (1990) *In Other Words: Essays towards a Reflective Sociology*. London: Polity Press.

—— (1992) *The Logic of Practice*. Cambridge: Polity.

—— (1993) *Sociology in Question*. London: Sage.

Bowie, F. (1993) 'Wales from Within: Conflicting Interpretations of Welsh Identity', in S. MacDonald (ed.) *Inside European Identities*. Oxford: Berg.

Boyce, S.H. and Quigley, M.A. (2001) 'Sports Medicine Clinics on the NHS: A Patient Survey', *British Journal of Sports Medicine*, 35: 281.

Brook, N. (1986) *Mobility Training*. Birmingham, UK: British Athletics Federation.

Brown, W.M. (2001) 'As American as Gatorade and Apple Pie: Performance Drugs and Sports', in W.J. Morgan, K.V. Meier and A.J. Schneider (eds) *Ethics in Sports*. Leeds: Human Kinetics.

Burry, H.C. and Calcinai, C.J. (1988) 'The Need to Make Rugby Safer', *British Medical Journal*, 296: 149–150.

Camilleri, J.M. (1999) 'Disability: A Personal Odyssey', *Disability and Society*, 14(6): 845–853.

Caplan, R.L. (1984) 'Chiropractic', in J.S. Salmon (ed.) *Alternative Medicines: Popular and Policy Perspectives*. London: Tavistock.

Carmichael, K. (1988) 'The Creative Use of Pain in Society', in R. Terrington (ed.) *Towards a Whole Society*. London; Fellowship Press.

Chalmers, D.J. (1994) 'New Zealand's Injury Prevention Research Unit: Reducing Sport and Recreational Injury', *British Journal of Sports Medicine*, 28: 221–222.

Chick, G. (1998) 'Leisure and Culture: Issues for an Anthropology of Leisure', *Leisure Sciences*, 20: 111–133.

Clément, J.-P. (1995) 'Contributions of the Sociology of Pierre Bourdieu to the Sociology of Sport', *Sociology of Sport Journal*, 12: 147–157.

Clifford, J. (1988) *The Predicament of Culture: Twentieth-Century Ethnology, Literature and Art*. London: Harvard University Press.

Clifford, J. and Marcus, G. (1986) *Writing Culture: The Poetics and Politics of Ethnography*. London: University of California Press.

Clutton, G. (1996a) 'Welsh Clubs May Sue for Euro Cash', *Western Mail*, 28 March.

—— (1996b) 'Welsh Player Tests Positive for Steroids', *Western Mail*, 28 September.

Coe, P. (1996) *Winning Running: Successful 800m and 1500m Racing and Training*. Marlborough, UK: Crowood Press.

Cole, C. (1999) 'Faster, Higher, Poorer', *National Post*, 28 August.

Cole, C.J. (1998) 'Addiction, Exercise, and Cyborgs: Technologies of Deviant Bodies', in G. Rail (ed.) *Sport and Postmodern Times*. New York: SUNY Press.

Collings, A.F. (1988) 'Blood Doping: How, Why and Why Not', *Excel*, 4(3): 12–16.

Collins, T. (1996) 'Rugby's Road to 1895', *Sporting Heritage*, 1: 36–51.

—— (1998) *Rugby's Great Split: Class, Culture and the Origins of Rugby League Football*. London: Cass.

Cooper, P. (1998) *The American Marathon*. Syracuse, NY: Syracuse University Press.

Corrigan, A.B. (1968) 'Sports Injuries', *Hospital Medicine*, 2: 1328–1334.

Crossley, N. (2001) *The Social Body: Habit, Identity and Desire*. London: Sage.

Curry, T.J. (1991) 'Fraternal Bonding in the Locker Room: A Profeminist Analysis of Talk about Competition and Women', *Sociology of Sport Journal*, 8: 119–135.

Curry, T.J. and Strauss, R.H. (1994) 'A Little Pain Never Hurt Anybody: A Photo-Essay on the Normalization of Sport Injuries', *Sociology of Sports Journal*, 11: 195–208.

Curtis, J. and McTeer, W. (1981) 'Towards a Sociology of Marathoning', *Journal of Sports Behaviour*, 4(2): 67–81.

Curtis, T. (ed.) (1986) *Wales the Imagined Nation: Essays in Cultural and National Identity*. Bridgend, UK: Poetry Wales Press.

DaMatta, R. (1988) 'Hierarchy and Equality in Anthropology and World Sport: A Perspective from Brazil', in S. Kang, J. MaAloon and R. DaMatta (eds) *The Olympics and Cultural Exchange*. Hanyang Ethnology Monograph No. 1: Hanyang University Press.

Davies, C.A. (1989) *Welsh Nationalism in the Twentieth Century: Ethnic Option and the Modern State*. New York: Praeger.

Davies, J.E. (1990) 'The Team Doctor in International Rugby', in E. Simon and S.D.W. Payne (eds) *Medicine, Sport and the Law*. Oxford: Blackwell Scientific.

—— (1992) 'The Team Doctor in International Rugby Football', in S.D.W. Payne (ed.) *Medico-legal Hazards of Rugby Union*. Oxford: Blackwell Special Projects.

Davies, J.E. and Gibson, T. (1978) 'Injuries in Rugby Union Football', *British Medical Journal*, 2(6154): 1759–1761.

Davis, C. (1992) 'Body Image, Dieting Behaviours, and Personality Factors: A Study of High-Performance Female Athletes', *International Journal of Sport Psychology*, 23: 179–192.

Davis, R.W. and Ferrara, M.S. (1995) 'Sports Medicine and Athletes with Disabilities', in K. DePauw and S. Gavron (eds) *Disability and Sport*. Leeds: Human Kinetics.

De Garis, L. (1998) 'Experiments in Pro Wrestling: Toward a Performative and Sensuous Sport Ethnography', *Sociology of Sport Journal*, 16: 65–74.

DePauw, K. (1997) 'The (In)Visibility of DisAbility: Cultural Contexts and "sporting bodies" ', *Quest*, 49: 416–430.

—— (2000) 'Social–Cultural Context of Disability: Implications for Scientific Inquiry and Professional Preparation', *Quest*, 52: 358–368.

DePauw, K. and Gavron, S. (1995) *Disability and Sport*. Leeds: Human Kinetics.

Descartes, R. (1978) *A Discourse on Method, Meditation and Principles*. London: J.M. Dent.

Digel, H. (1992) 'Sport in Risk Society', *International Review for Sociology of Sport*, 27: 3.

Dirix, A. (1988) 'Classes and Methods', in A. Dirix, H.G. Knuttgen and K. Tittel (eds) *The Olympic Book of Sports Medicine*. Oxford: Blackwell.

Douglas, M. (1966) *Purity and Danger: An Analysis of Concepts of Pollution and Taboo*. London: Routledge & Kegan Paul.

—— (1985) *Risk Acceptability According to the Social Sciences*. New York: Russell Sage Foundation.

—— (1992) *Risk and Blame: Essays in Cultural Theory*. London: Routledge.

Douglas, M. and Wildavsky, A. (1982) *Risk and Culture*. London: University of California Press.

Donahoe, T. and Johnson, N. (1988) *Foul Play: Drug Abuse in Sports*. Oxford: Blackwell.

Donnelly, P. (1993) Subcultures in Sport: Resilience and Transformation', in A.G. Ingham and J.W. Loy (eds) *Sport in Social Development: Traditions, Transitions and Transformations*. Leeds: Human Kinetics.

Dougherty, N., Auxter, D., Goldberger, A.S. and Heinzmann, G.S. (1994) *Sport, Physical Activity, and the Law*. Leeds: Human Kinetics.

Druckman, D. and Bjork, R.A. (eds) (1991) *In the Mind's Eye: Enhancing Human Performance*. Washington, DC: National Academic Press.

Dubin, C. (1990) *Commission of Inquiry into the Use of Drugs and Banned Practices Intended to Increase Athletic Performance*. Canadian Government Publishing Centre.

Dunning, E. and Sheard, K. (1979) *Barbarians, Gentlemen and Players: A Sociological Study of the Development of Rugby Football*. Oxford: Martin Robinson.

Dunning, E., Maguire, J.A. and Pearton, R. (eds) (1993) *The Sport Process: A Comparative and Developmental Approach*. Leeds: Human Kinetics.

Dyck, N. (2000) 'Parents, Kids and Coaches: Constructing Sport and Childhood in Canada' in N. Dyck (ed.) *Games, Sport and Cultures*. Oxford: Berg.

Dyson, M. (1985) 'Therapeutic Applications of Ultrasound', in W.L. Nyborg and M.C. Ziskin (eds) *Biological Effects of Ultrasound*. New York: Churchill Livingstone.

Evans, J. (1994) *How Real Is My Valley? Post-modernism and the South Wales Valleys*. Pontypridd, UK: Underground Press.

Ewald, K. and Jiobu, R.M. (1985) 'Explaining Positive Deviance: Becker's Model and the Case of Runners and Bodybuilders'. *Sociology of Sport Journal*, 2: 144–156.

Falk, P. (1994) *The Consuming Body*. London: Sage.

Featherstone, M. (1991) 'The Body and Consumer Culture', in M. Featherstone, M. Hepworth and B. Turner (eds) *The Body: Social Process and Cultural Theory*. London: Sage.

Featherstone, M., Hepworth, M. and Turner, B. (1991) *The Body: Social Process and Cultural Theory*. London: Sage.

Ferrara, M.S. and Peterson, C. (2000) 'Injuries to Athletes with Disabilities: Identifying Injury Patterns', *Sports Medicine*, 30(2): 137–143.

Ferstle, J. (1999) 'Nandrolone', *Athletics Weekly*, 15 September.

Firth, R. (1931) 'A Dart Match in Tikopia', *Oceania*, 1: 64–97.

Fitzsimons, P. (1996) *The Rugby War*. London: HarperCollins.

Foley, D. (1990) *Learning Capitalist Culture*. Philadelphia: University of Pennsylvania Press.

Foucault, M. (1975) *The Birth of the Clinic: An Archeology of Medical Perception*. London: Vintage Books.

—— (1979) *Discipline and Punish: The Birth of the Prison*. Harmondsworth, UK: Penguin.

Frankenberg, R. (1957) *Village on the Border: A Social Study of Religion, Politics and Football in a North Wales Community*. London: Cohen & West.

—— (1993) 'Risk: Anthropological and Epidemiological Narrative of Prevention', in S. Lindenbaum and M. Lock (eds) *Knowledge, Power and Practice: The Anthropology of Medicine and Everyday Life*. London: University of California Press.

Frecknell, T. (1993) 'The Chinese Puzzle Solved', *Athletics Weekly*, 46(36): 48–49.

Frey, J.H. (1991) 'Social Risk and the Meaning of Sport', *Sociology of Sport Journal*, 8: 136–145.

Fung, L. (1992) 'Commitment to Training among Wheelchair Marathon Athletes', *Intenational Journal of Sport Psychology*, 21: 138–146.

Gains, P. (2002) 'Is Blood Doping Back?', *Athletics Weekly*, 5 June: 30.

Gallup, E.M. (1995) *Law and the Team Physician*. Leeds: Human Kinetics.

Gardner, R. (1989) 'On Performance-Enhancing Substances and the Unfair Advantage Argument', *Journal of the Philosophy of Sport*, 16: 59–73.

Garraway, W.M., Macleod, D.A.D. and Sharp, J.C.M. (1991) 'Rugby Injuries: The Need for a Case Register', *British Medical Journal*, 303: 1082–1083.

Geertz, C. (1973) *The Interpretation of Cultures*. New York: Basic Books.

Gerrard, D.F., Waller, A.E. and Bird, Y.N. (1994) 'The New Zealand Rugby Injury and Performance Project: 2', *British Journal of Sports Medicine*, 28: 229–233.

Gerschick, T.J. and Miller, A.S. (1995) 'Coming to Terms: Masculinity and Physical Disability', in D. Sabo and F. Gordon (eds) *Men's Health and Illness: Gender, Power, and the Body*. London: Sage.

Glassner, B. (1992) *Bodies: The Tyranny of Perfection*. Los Angeles: Lowell House.

Gledhill, N. (1981) 'Blood Doping and Related Issues: A Brief Review', *Medicine and Science in Sport and Exercise*, 14(3): 183–189.

Gledhill, N. and Froese, A.B. (1979) 'Should Research on Blood Doping Be Continued?', *Modern Athlete and Coach*, 17(1): 23–25.

Goffman, E. (1961) *Asylums: Essays on the Social Situation of Mental Patients and Other Inmates*. London: Anchor Books.

Good, B.J. (1994) *Medicine, Rationality, and Experience: An Anthropological Experience*. Cambridge: Cambridge University Press.

Good, M.J.D., Brodwin, P.E., Good, B.J. and Kleinman, A. (eds) (1992) *Pain as Human Experience: An Anthropological Perspective*. Los Angeles: University of California Press.

Gorn, E.J. (1986) *The Manly Art: The Lives and Times of the Great Bare-Knuckle Champions*. London: Cornell University Press.

Gramsci, A. (1971) *Selections from the Prison Notebooks*. New York: International.

Grayson, E. (1992) 'Sports Medicine and the Law', in S.D.W. Payne (ed.) *Medicolegal Hazards of Rugby Union*. Oxford: Blackwell Special Projects.

—— (1999) *Ethics, Injuries and the Law in Sports Medicine*. Oxford: Butterworth-Heinemann.

Green, R.M. (1951) *A Translation of Galen's 'Hygiene'*. Springfield, IL: Charles C. Thomas.

Gruneau, R. (1983) *Class, Sports and Social Development*. London: University of Massachusetts Press.

—— (1993) 'The Critique of Sport in Modernity: Theorising Power, Culture, and the Politics of the Body', in E. Dunning, J.A. Maguire and R. Pearton (eds) *The Sport Process: A Comparative and Developmental Approach*. Leeds: Human Kinetics.

Guttmann, A. (1986) *Sports Spectators*. New York: Columbia University Press.

—— (1988) *A Whole New Ball Game: An Interpretation of American Sports*. Chapel Hill, NC: University of North Carolina Press.

—— (1993) 'The Diffusion of Sports and the Problem of Cultural Imperialism', in E. Dunning, J.A. Maguire and R. Pearton (eds) *The Sport Process: A Comparative and Developmental Approach*. Leeds: Human Kinetics.

Gwyer, D. (1990) *Sport in Pontypridd*. Pontypridd, UK: Historical and Cultural Centre.

Gwyther, M. (1995) 'Tackling Injury', *The Sunday Times: Style*, 28 May.

Hahn, H. (1984) 'Sports and the Political Movement of Disabled Persons: Examining Nondisabled Social Values', *Arena Review*, 8(1): 1–15.

Haley, B. (1978) *The Healthy Body and Victorian Culture*. Cambridge, MA: Harvard University Press.

Hall, G.S. (1904) *Adolescence, Its Psychology and its Relations to Physiology, Anthropology, Sociology, Sex, Crime, Religion and Education*. New York: Appleton.

Hall, M.A. (1996) *Feminism and Sporting Bodies*. Leeds: Human Kinetics.

Hammersley, M. (1992) *What Is Wrong with Ethnography?* London: Routledge.

Haraway, D. (1991) *Simians, Cyborgs and Women: The Reinvention of Nature*. London: Routledge.

Hargreaves, Jennifer (1994) *Sporting Females: Critical Issues in the History and Sociology of Women's Sport*. London: Routledge.

—— (2000) *Heroines of Sport: The Politics of Difference and Identity*. London: Routledge.

Hargreaves, John (1986) *Sport, Power and Culture: A Social and Historical Analysis of Popular Sports in Britain.* Oxford: Polity Press.

—— (1987) 'The Body, Sport and Power Relation', in J. Horne, D. Jary and A. Tomlinson (eds) *Sports, Leisure and Social Relations.* London: Routledge & Kegan Paul.

—— (1992) 'Sport and Socialism in Britain', *Sociology of Sport Journal*, 9: 131–153.

Hargreaves, John and Tomlinson, A. (1992) 'Getting There: Cultural Theory and the Sociological Analysis of Sport in Britain', *Sociology of Sport Journal*, 9: 207–219.

Hawkins, R.D., Hulse, M.A., Wilkinson, C., Hodson, A. and Gibson, M. (2001) 'The Association Football Medical Research Programme: An Audit of Injuries in Professional Football', *British Journal of Sports Medicine*, 35: 43–47.

Hechter, M. (1975) *Internal Colonialism: The Celtic Fringe in British National Development, 1536–1966*, Berkeley, CA: University of California Press.

—— (1985) 'Internal Colonialism Revisited', in R. Rogowski and E.A. Tirakian (eds) *New Nationalisms of the Developed West*, Boston: Allen & Unwin.

Heil, J. (ed.) (1993) *Psychology of Sport Injury.* Leeds: Human Kinetics.

Helal, B., King, J.B. and Grange, W.J. (1986) *Sports Injuries and Their Treatment.* London: Chapman & Hall.

Helman, C. (1990) *Culture, Health and Illness*, 2nd edn. London: Butterworth-Heinemann.

Henschen, K.P., Hovat, M. and Roswal, G. (1992) 'Psychological Profiles of the United States Wheelchair Basketball Team', *International Journal of Sport Psychology*, 23: 128–137.

Hey, V. (1986) *Patriarchy and Pub Culture.* London: Tavistock.

Hilbert, R.A. (1984) 'The Acultural Dimensions of Chronic Pain: Flawed Reality Construction and the Problem of Meaning', *Social Problems*, 31: 365–378.

Hoberman, J. (1992) *Mortal Engines.* New York: Free Press.

—— (2001) 'Listening to Steroids', in W.J. Morgan, K.V. Meier and A.J. Schneider (eds) *Ethics in Sports.* Leeds: Human Kinetics.

Hobsbawm, E. (1983) 'Introduction: Inventing Traditions', in E. Hobsbawm and T. Ranger (eds) *The Invention of Tradition.* Cambridge: Cambridge University Press.

Holowchak, M.A. (2002) 'Ergogenic Aids and the Limits of Human Performance in Sport: Ethical Issues, Aesthetic Consideration', *Journal of the Philosophy of Sport*, 29: 75–86.

Holt, R. (1989) *Sport and the British: A Modern History.* Oxford: Clarendon Press.

Horwill, F. (1982) 'When Things Go Wrong', in D. Watts, H. Wilson and F. Horwill (eds) *The Complete Middle Distance Runner.* London: Stanley Paul.

Howe, P.D. (1997) 'Commercialising the Body, Professionalising the Game: The Development of Sports Medicine at Pontypridd Rugby Football Club', unpublished PhD thesis, University College London.

—— (1999) 'Professionalism, Commercialism and the Rugby Club: From Embryo to Infant at Pontypridd RFC', in T.L.C. Chandler and J. Nauright (eds) *The Rugby World: Race, Gender, Commerce and Rugby Union.* London: Cass.

—— (2001) 'An Ethnography of Pain and Injury in Professional Rugby Union: The Case of Pontypridd RFC', *International Review of Sport Sociology*, 35(3): 289–303.

Howe, P.D. and Reeves, M. (1999) 'Read All About It! Representation of a Distinctive Community: The Printed Media, Sport and Disability', paper given at Leisure Studies Association Annual Conference, Cheltenham.

Hróbjartsson, A. (1996) 'The Uncontrollable Placebo Effect', *European Journal of Clinical Pharmacology*, 50: 345–8.

Hughes, B. (2000) 'Medicine and the Aesthetic Invalidation of Disabled People', *Disability and Society*, 15(4): 555–568.

Hughson, R. (1980) 'Sports Injuries and the Marathon Runner', *Canadian Runner*, November: 23.

Huizenga, R. (1994) *You're Okay, It's Just a Bruise: A Doctor's Sideline Secrets about Pro Football's Most Outrageous Team*. New York: St Martin's Griffin.

Huizinga, J. (1950) *Homo Ludens: A Study of the Play Element in Culture*. Boston: Beacon Press.

Illich, I. (1975) *Medical Nemesis*. London: Calder & Boyars.

Ingham, J. and Loy, J.W. (eds) (1993) *Sport in Social Development: Traditions, Transitions, and Transformations*, Leeds: Human Kinetics.

Ingham, A. and Donnelly, P. (1997) 'A Sociology of North American Sociology of Sport: Disunity in Unit, 1995–1996', *Sociology of Sport Journal*, 14(4): 362–418.

International Paralympic Committee (IPC) (2000) *The Paralympian: Newsletter of the International Paralympic Committee*. Special Edition, October.

—— (2001a) *The Paralympian: Newsletter of the International Paralympic Committee*, no. 1.

—— (2001b) *The Paralympian: Newsletter of the International Paralympic Committee*, no. 3.

James, A., Hockey, J. and Dawson, A. (1997) 'Introduction: The Road from Santa Fe', in A. James, J. Hockey and A. Dawson (eds) *After Writing Culture: Epistemology and Praxis in Contemporary Anthropology*. London: Routledge.

Jarvie, G. (1993) 'Sport, Nationalism and Cultural Identity', in L. Allison (ed.) *The Changing Politics of Sport*. Manchester: Manchester University Press.

Jarvie, G. and Maguire, J. (1994) *Sport and Leisure in Social Thought*. London: Routledge.

Jenkins, R. (1992) *Pierre Bourdieu*. London: Routledge.

Jennings, A. and Simson, V. (1992) *The Lords of the Rings: Power, Money and Drugs in the Modern Olympics*. London: Simon & Schuster.

Jokl, E. (1964) *Medical Sociology and Cultural Anthropology of Sport and Physical Education*. Springfield IL: C.C. Thomas.

Jones, S. (1993) 'End of an Era', *Rugby News*, October: 22–23.

Jorgenson, D.E. and Jorgenson, C.B. (1981) 'Perceived Effects of Running/Jogging: A Social Survey of Three Clubs', *International Review of Sport Sociology*, 16(3): 75–83.

Joyce, P. (2001) 'Governmentality and Risk: Setting Priorities in the New NHS', *Sociology of Health and Illness*, 23(5): 594–614.

Kennedy, K.W. (1992) 'The Team Doctor in Rugby Union Football', in S.D.W. Payne (ed.) *Medico-legal Hazards of Rugby Union*. Oxford: Blackwell Special Projects.

Kew, F. (1997) *Sport, Social Problems and Issues*. Oxford: Butterworth-Heinemann.

King, J.B. (1983) 'Second Injury Syndrome', *British Journal of Sports Medicine*, 17: 59–60.

Klatell, D. and Marcus, N. (1988) *Sports for Sale: Television, Money and the Fans*. Oxford: Oxford University Press.

Kleiber, D.A. and Brock, S.C. (1992) 'The Effect of Career-Ending Injuries on the Subsequent Well-Being of Elite College Athletes', *Sociology of Sport Journal*, 9: 70–75.

Klein, A. (1991) *Sugarball: The American Game, the Dominican Dream*. London: Yale University Press.

—— (1993) *Little Big Men: Bodybuilding Subculture and Gender Construction*. Albany: State University of New York.

—— (1995) 'Life's Too Short to Die Small: Steroid Use among Male Bodybuilders', in D. Sabo and F. Gordon (eds) *Men's Health and Illness: Gender, Power, and the Body*. London: Sage.

Kleinman, A. (1986) 'Concepts and a Model for the Comparison of Medical Systems as Cultural Systems', in C. Currer and M. Stacey (eds) *Concepts of Health, Illness and Disease: A Comparative Perspective*. Oxford: Berg.

—— (1988) *The Illness Narratives: Suffering, Healing and the Human Condition*, New York: Basic Books.

—— (1991) 'Pain and Resistance: The Delegitimation and Relegitimation of Local Worlds', in M.J. Good, P. Brodwin, B. Good and A. Kleinman (eds) *Pain and Human Experience: An Anthropological Perspective*. Oxford: University of California Press.

Kotarba, J.A. (1983) *Chronic Pain: Its Social Dimensions*. London: Sage.

Labanowich, S. (1988) 'A Case for the Integration of the Disabled into the Olympic Games', *Adapted Physical Activity Quarterly*, 5: 264–272.

Laberge, S. and Sankoff, D. (1988) 'Physical Activities, Body Habitus, and Lifestyles', in J. Harvey and H. Cantelon (eds) *Not Just a Game: Essays in Canadian Sport Sociology*. Ottawa: University of Ottawa Press.

Lance, L.M. and Antshel, D. (1981) 'Social Factors Associated with Adoption of Running as a Sport Innovation', *International Review of Sport Sociology*, 16(1): 79–85.

Last, M. (1981) 'The Importance of Knowing about Not Knowing', *Social Science and Medicine*, 158: 387–392.

Laura, R.S. and White, S.W. (eds) (1991) *Drug Controversy in Sport: The Socio-ethical and Medical Issues*. Sydney: Allen and Unwin.

Leder, D. (1984/5) 'Towards a Phenomenology of Pain', *Review of Existential Psychology and Psychiatry*, 19: 255–266.

—— (1998) 'A Tale of Two Bodies', in D. Welton (ed.) *Body and Flesh*. Oxford: Blackwell.

—— (1990) *The Absent Body*. London: University of Chicago Press.

Lee, A.J., Myers, J.L. and Garraway, W.M. (1997) 'Influence of Players' Physique on Rugby Football Injuries', *British Journal of Sports Medicine*, 31: 135–138.

Lesser, A. (1933) *The Pawnee Ghost Dance Hand Game: A Study of Cultural Change*, Columbia University Contributions to Anthropology 16. New York: Columbia University Press.

Lock, M. (1993) 'Cultivating the Body: Anthropology and Epistemologies of Bodily Practice and Knowledge', *Annual Review of Anthropology*, 22: 133–155.

Loland, S. (1992) 'The Mechanics and Meaning of Alpine Skiing: Methodological and Epistemological Notes on the Study of Sport Technique', *Journal of the Philosophy of Sport*, 19: 55–77.

Loveday, C. (1992) 'HIV Disease and Sport', in S.D.W. Payne (ed.) *Medico-legal Hazards of Rugby Union*. Oxford: Blackwell Special Projects.

Lupton, D. (1999) *Risk*. London: Routledge.

Lüschen, G., Cockerham, W. and Kunz, G. (1996) 'The Sociocultural Context of Sport and Health: Problems of Causal Relations and Structural Interdependence', *Sociology of Sport Journal*, 13: 197–213.

Lyng, S. (1990) 'Edgework: A Social Psychological Analysis of Voluntary Risk Taking', *American Journal of Sociology*, 95(4): 851–886.

MacAloon, J. (1992) 'The Ethnographic Imperative in Comparative Olympic Research', *Sociology of Sport Journal*, 9: 104–130.

Macauley, D. (1991) *Sports Medicine*. Sports Council of Northern Ireland.

—— (1997a) 'Will Money Corrupt Sports Medicine?', *British Journal of Sports Medicine*, 31: 1.

—— (1997b) 'Family Doctors: Players or Spectators in the Future?', *British Journal of Sports Medicine*, 31: 91.

—— (1998) 'Lawyers on the Touchline', *British Journal of Sports Medicine*, 32: 191–192.

MacClancy, J. (ed.) (1996) *Sport, Identity and Ethnicity*. Oxford: Berg.

McIntosh, M.J. and Morford, W.R. (1993) 'Sport and the Victorian Gentlemen', in A.G. Ingham and J. Loy (eds) *Sport in Social Development: Traditions, Transitions and Transformations*. Leeds: Human Kinetics.

Mackinnon, L.T. (1994) 'Current Challenges and Future Expectations in Exercise Immunology: Back to the Future', *Medicine and Science in Sports and Exercise*, 26: 191–194.

McLatchie, G.R. (1993) *Essentials of Sports Medicine*. London: Churchill Livingstone.

Macleod, D.A.D. (1992) 'The Doctor's Contribution towards Safety in Sport: An Exercise in Preventative Medicine', in S.D.W. Payne (ed.) *Medico-legal Hazards of Rugby Union*. Oxford: Blackwell Special Projects.

Maguire, J. (1993) 'Bodies, Sportscultures and Societies: A Critical Review of Some Theories in the Sociology of the Body', *International Review for Sociology of Sport*, 28(1): 33–50.

—— (1999) *Global Sport: Identities, Societies, Civilisation*. Oxford: Polity Press.

Mansfield, A. and McGinn, B. (1993) 'Pumping Irony: The Muscular and the Feminine', in D. Morgan and S. Scott (eds) *Body Matters*. London: Falmer Press.

Maran, A.G.D. (1998) 'Performing Arts Medicine', *British Journal of Sports Medicine*, 32: 5.

Marcus, G. and Fischer, M. (1996) *Anthropology as Cultural Critique: An Experimental Moment in Human Sciences*. Chicago: University of Chicago Press.

Martin, D.E. and Coe, P.N. (1991) *Training Distance Runners*. Leeds: Human Kinetics.

Mead, G. (1967) *Mind, Self and Society*. Chicago: University of Chicago Press.

Meir, R.A., McDonald, K.N. and Russell, R. (1997) 'Injury Consequences from Participation in Professional Rugby League: A Preliminary Investigation', *British Journal of Sports Medicine*, 31: 132–134.

Melzack, R. and Wall, P. (1982) *The Challenge of Pain*. New York: Penguin.

Mennesson, C. (2000) ' "Hard" Women and "Soft" Women: The Social Construction of Identity among Female Boxers', *International Review for the Sociology of Sport*, 35(1): 21–33.

Merleau-Ponty, M. (1962) *Phenomenology of Perception*, London: Routledge and Kegan Paul.

—— (1964) *Sense and Non-Sense*. Evanston, IL: Northwestern University Press.

—— (1965) *The Structure of Behaviour*. London: Methuen.

Messner, M.A. (1990) 'When Bodies Are Weapons: Masculinity and Violence in Sport', *International Review for the Sociology of Sport*, 25: 203–220.

—— (1992) *Power at Play: Sports and the Problem of Masculinity*. Boston: Beacon Press.

Milburn, P.D. (1993) 'Biomechanics of Rugby Union Scummaging: Technical and Safety Issues', *Sports Medicine*, 16: 168–179.

Miller, T., Lawrence, G., McKay, J. and Rowe, D. (2001) *Sport and Globalization: Playing the World*. London: Sage.

Monaghan, L. (2001) *Bodybuilding, Drugs and Risk*. London: Routledge.

Morris, D.B. (1991) *The Culture of Pain*. Berkeley: University of California Press.

Morse, R. (1972) *Exercise and the Heart*. Springfield, IL: Charter C. Thomas.

Mottram, D.R. (1988) 'Introduction: Drugs and Their Use in Sport', in D.R. Mottram (ed.) *Drugs and Their Use in Sport*. London: E. & F.N. Spon.

Mrozek, D.J. (1992) 'The Scientific Quest for Physical Culture and the Persistent Appeal of Quackery', in J.W. Berryman and R.J. Park (eds) *Sport and Exercise Science: Essays in the History of Sports Medicine*. Chicago: University of Illinois Press.

Muir, R., McDonald, K. and Russell, R. (1997) 'Injury consequences from participation in professional rugby league: a preliminary investigation', *British Journal of Sports Medicine*, 31: 132–134.

Munnings, F. (1987) 'What Is Sportsmedicine?', *The Physician and Sportsmedicine*. 15(1): 41.

Murdoch, B. (1997) 'Ready to Pick Welsh Bones', *Sport on Sunday, Wales on Sunday*, 12 January: 20.

Murphy, K. (1992) 'The Role of the Physiotherapist in Club and International Rugby Football', in S.D.W. Payne (ed.) *Medico-legal Hazards of Rugby Union*. Oxford: Blackwell Special Projects.

Murphy, R.F. (1987) *The Silent Body*. London: Norton.

Nauright, J. (1991) 'Sport, Manhood and Empire: British Responses to the New Zealand Rugby Tour of 1905', *International Journal of the History of Sport*, 8: 239–255.

Nauright, J. and Chandler, T.J.L. (1996) *Making Men: Rugby and Masculine Identity*. London: Cass.

Nettleton, S. (1992) *Power, Pain and Dentistry*. Milton Keynes: Open University Press.

—— (1995) *The Sociology of Health and Illness*. Oxford: Polity Press.

Nixon, H.L. (1989) 'Reconsidering Obligatory Running and Anorexia Nervosa as Gender Related Problems of Identity and Role Adjustment', *Journal of Sport and Social Issues*, 13: 14–24.

—— (1992) 'A Social Network Analysis of Influences on Athletes to Play with Pain and Injuries', *Journal of Sport and Social Issues*, 16: 127–135.

—— (1993a) 'Accepting the Risks of Pain and Injury in Sport: Mediated Cultural Influences on Playing Hurt', *Sociology of Sport Journal*, 10: 183–196.

—— (1993b) 'Social Network Analysis of Sport: Emphasizing Social Structure in Sport Sociology', *Sociology of Sport Journal*, 10: 315–321.

—— (1996) 'The Relationship of Friendship Networks, Sports Experiences, and Gender to Express Pain Thresholds', *Sociology of Sport Journal*, 13: 78–86.

Noakes, T.D. (1991) *Lore of Running: Discover the Science and Spirit of Running*, 3rd edn. Leeds: Human Kinetics.

—— (2000) 'Medical Considerations for Runners', in J.A. Hawley (ed.) *Handbook of Sports Medicine and Science: Running*. Oxford: Blackwell Science.

Noakes, T.D. and Granger, S. (1990) *Running Injuries*. Oxford: Oxford University Press.

Nuzzo, N.A. and Waller, D.P. (1988) 'Drug Abuse in Athletes', in J. Thomas (ed.) *Drugs, Athletes and Physical Performance*. London: Plenum.

O'Brien, C.P. (1992) 'Retrospective Survey of Rugby Injuries in the Leinster Province of Ireland, 1987–1989', *British Journal of Sports Medicine*, 26: 243–244.

—— (1993) 'Alcohol and Sport: Impact of Social Drinking on Recreational and Competitive Sports Performance', *Sports Medicine*, 15: 71–77.

O'Donoghue, D.H. (1984) *Treatment of Injuries to Athletes*, 4th edn. Philadelphia: W.B. Saunders.

Oliver, M. (1996) *Understanding Disability*. London: Macmillan.

O'Toole, M.L. (1998) 'Overreaching and Overtraining in Endurance Athletes', in R.B. Kreider, A.C. Fry and M.L. O'Toole (eds) *Overtraining in Sport*. Leeds: Human Kinetics.

Pargman, D. (ed.) (1999) *Psychological Basis of Sports Injuries*, 2nd edn. Morgantown, WV: Fitness Information Technology.

Park, R.J. (1992a) 'Athletes and Their Training in Britain and America, 1800–1914', in J.W. Berryman and R.J. Park (eds) *Sport and Exercise Science: Essays in the History of Sports Medicine*. Chicago: University of Illinois Press.

—— (1992b) 'Physiologists, Physicians, and Physical Educators: Nineteenth-Century Biology and Exercise, Hygienic and Educative', in J.W. Berryman and R.J. Park (eds) *Sport and Exercise Science: Essays in the History of Sports Medicine*. Chicago: University of Illinois Press.

Pavelka, E. (1985) 'Olympic Blood Boosting: How American Cyclists Sweated Blood, Literally, to Win', *Bicycling*, April: 32–39.

Payne, S.D.W. (ed.) (1992) *Medico-legal Hazards of Rugby Union*. Oxford: Blackwell Special Projects.

Pearce, J.M.S. (1995) 'The Placebo Enigma', *Quarterly Journal of Medicine*, 88: 215–220.

Perkin, H. (1989) 'Teaching the Nations How to Play: Sport and Society in the British Empire and Commonwealth', *International Journal of the History of Sport*, 6: 145–155.

Polley, M. (1998) *Moving the Goalposts: A History of Sport and Society since 1945*. London: Routledge.

—— (2000) ' "The Amateur Rules": Amateurism and Professionalism in Post-war British Athletics', in A. Smith and D. Porter (eds) *Amateurs and Professionals in Post-war British Sport*. London: Cass.

Pomerleau, O.F. (1982) 'A Discourse on Behavioral Medicine: Current Status and Future Trends', *Journal of Consulting and Clinical Psychology*, 50(6): 1030–1039.

Ponomaryov, N.I. (1981) *Sport and Society*. Moscow: Progress Publishers [original 1974; translation by J. Riordan].

Porter, D. and Smith, A. (2000) 'Introduction', in A. Smith and D. Porter (eds) *Amateurs and Professionals in Post-war British Sport*. London: Cass.

Powell, D. (1996) *Victorian Pontypridd*. Frome, UK: Merton Priory Press.

Quarrie, K.L., Handcock, P., Toomey, M.J. and Waller A.E. (1996) 'The New Zealand Rugby Injury and Performance Project. IV. Anthropometric and Physical Performance Comparisons between Positional Categories of Senior A Rugby Players', *British Journal of Sports Medicine*, 30: 53–56.

Quarrie, K.L., Alsop, J.C., Waller, A.E., Bird, Y.N., Marshall, S.W. and Chambers, D.J. (2001) 'The New Zealand Rugby Injury and Performance Project. VI. A Prospective Cohort Study of Risk Factors for Injury in Rugby Union Football', *British Journal of Sports Medicine*, 35: 157–166.

Rail, G. and Harvey, J. (1995) 'Body at Work: Michel Foucault and the Sociology of Sport', *Sociology of Sport Journal*, 12: 164–179.

Rees, P. (1995) 'The Great Strip Teaser', *Wales on Sunday*, 22 January.

—— (1996) 'It's Cardiff PLC', *Wales on Sunday*, 31 March.

—— (1997) 'Clubs Demand Peace in TV Cash Row', *Wales on Sunday*, 20 April.

Richter, K.J. (1993) 'Integrated Classification: An Analysis', in R.D. Steadward, E.R. Nelson and G.D. Wheeler (eds) *Vista '93: The Outlook. Proceedings of the International Conference on High Performance Sport for Athletes with Disabilities*, Jasper, Alberta: Rick Hansen Centre.

—— (1999) 'The Wheelchair Classification Debate', paper given at CP-ISRA STC, Ottawa, September.

Richter, K.J., Adams-Mushett, C., Ferrara, M.S. and McCann, B.C. (1992) 'Integrated Swimming Classification: A Faulted System', *Adapted Physical Activity Quarterly*, 9: 5–13.

Riordan, J.W. (1991) *Sport, Politics and Communism*. Manchester: Manchester University Press.

Roberts, G. (1997) 'Europe, Here We Come!', *Western Mail*, 5 May.

Roderick, M. (1998) 'The Sociology of Risk, Pain and Injury: A Comment on the Work of Howard L. Nixon II', *Sociology of Sports Journal*, 15(1): 64–79.

Roderick, M., Waddington, I. and Parker, G. (2000) 'Playing Hurt: Managing Injuries in English Professional Football', *International Review for the Sociology of Sport*, 35(2): 165–180.

Rowe, D. (1999) *Sport, Culture and the Media*. Buckingham, UK: Open University Press.

Ryan, A.J. (1989) 'Sports Medicine in the World Today', in A.J. Ryan and F.L. Allman (eds) *Sports Medicine*. San Diego, CA: Academic Press.

Ryle, G. (1949) *The Concept of Mind*. Harmondsworth, UK: Penguin.

Sands, R. (1999a) 'Anthropology and Sport', in R. Sands (ed.) *Anthropology, Sport and Culture*. London: Bergin and Garvey.

Sands, R. (ed.) (1999b) *Anthropology, Sport and Culture*. London: Bergin and Garvey.

Sands, R. (1999c) *Sport and Culture: At Play in the Fields of Anthropology*. Needham Heights, MA: Simon & Schuster.

Satterthwaite, P., Norton, R., Larmer, P. and Robinson, E. (1999) 'Risk Factors for Injuries and Other Health Problems Sustained in a Marathon', *British Journal of Sports Medicine*, 33: 22–26.

Scarry, E. (1985) *The Body in Pain: The Making and Unmaking of the World*. Oxford: Oxford University Press.

Schantz, O.J. and Gilbert, K. (2001) 'An Ideal Misconstrued: Newspaper Coverage of the Atlanta Paralympic Games in France and Germany', *Sociology of Sport*, 18(1): 69–94.

Schell, L.A. and Rodriguez, S. (2001) 'Subverting Bodies/Ambivalent Representations: Media Analysis of Paralympian, Hope Lewellen', *Sociology of Sport*, 18(1): 127–135.

Scheper-Hughes, N. and Lock, M. (1987) 'The Mindful Body: A Prolegomenon to Future Work in Medical Anthropology', *Medical Anthropology Quarterly*, 1(1): 6–41.

Scher, A.T. (1991) 'Catastrophic Rugby Injuries of the Spinal Cord: Changing Patterns of Injury', *British Journal of Sports Medicine*, 25: 57–60.

Seidler, V.J. (1997) *Man Enough: Embodied Masculinities*. London: Sage.

Sharp, J.C.M., Murray, G.D. and Macleod, D.A.D. (2001) 'A Unique Insight into the Incidence of Rugby Injuries Using Referee Replacement Reports', *British Journal of Sports Medicine*, 35: 34–37.

Shephard, R.J. and Shek, P.N. (1994) 'Potential Impact of Physical Activity and Sport on the Immune System: A Brief Review', *British Journal of Sports Medicine*, 28: 247–255.

Sherrill, C. and Williams, T. (1996) 'Disability and Sport: Psychosocial Perspectives on Inclusion, Integration, and Participation', *Sport Science Review*, 5(1): 43–64.

Shilling, C. (1993) *The Body and Social Theory*. London: Sage.

Shogan, D. (1998) 'The Social Construction of Disability: The Impact of Statistics and Technology', *Adapted Physical Activity Quarterly*, 15: 269–277.

—— (1999) *High-Performance Athletes: Discipline, Diversity, and Ethics*. Toronto: University of Toronto Press.

Sigerist, H.E. (1956) *Landmarks in the History of Hygiene*. London: Oxford University Press.

Simon, R.L. (2001) 'Good Competition and Drug-Enhanced Performance', in W.J. Morgan, K.V. Meier and A.J. Schneider (eds) *Ethics in Sports*. Leeds: Human Kinetics.

Sinclair, S. (1997) *Making Doctor: An Institutional Apprenticeship*. Oxford: Berg.

Skey, F.C. (1867) 'Athletics', *The Times*, 10 October: 9.

Smith, A. (2000) 'Civil War in England: The Clubs, the RFU, and the impact of Professionalism on Rugby Union', in A. Smith and D. Porter (eds) *Amateurs and Professionals in Post-war British Sport*. London: Cass.

Smith, A. and Porter, D. (eds) (2000) *Amateurs and Professionals in Post-war British Sport*. London: Cass.

Smith, D. (1981) 'People's Theatre: A Century of Welsh Rugby', *History Today*, 31(3): 31–36.

Smith, D. and Williams, G. (1980) *Fields of Praise: Official History of the Welsh Rugby Union, 1881–1981*. Cardiff: University of Wales Press.

Smith, S.L. (1998) 'Athletes, Runners, and Joggers: Participant-Group Dynamics in a Sport of "Individuals" ', *Sociology of Sport Journal*, 15: 174–192.

Sparks, J.P. (1985) 'Rugby Football Injuries, 1980–1983', *British Journal of Sports Medicine*, 19: 71–75.

Sperryn, P.N. (1983) *Sports Medicine*. London: Butterworth.

Sperryn, P.N. and Williams, J.G.P. (1975) 'Why Sports Injuries Clinics?', *British Medical Journal*, 3: 364–365.

Steadward, R. (1996) 'Integration and Sport in the Paralympic Movement', *Sport Science Review*, 5(1): 26–41.

Stebbins, R.A. (1992) *Amateurs, Professionals and Serious Leisure*. London: McGill-Queen's University Press.

Stone, S.D. (1995) 'The Myth of Bodily Perfection', *Disability and Society*, 10(4): 413–424.

Sugden, J. (1996) *Boxing and Society: An International Analysis*. Manchester: University of Manchester Press.

Szerszinski, B., Lash, S. and Wynne B. (1996) 'Introduction: Ecology, Realism and Social Sciences', in S. Lash, B. Szerszinski and B. Wynne (eds) *Risk, Environment and Modernity: Towards a New Ecology*. London: Sage.

Tawd Vale (1969) 'The Malaise of Rugby League', *The Rugby Leaguer*, 31 January: 3.

Thomas, C. (1999) *Female Forms: Experiencing and Understanding Disability*. Buckingham, UK: Open University Press.

Tittel, K. and Knuttgen, H.G. (1988) 'The Development, Objectives and Activities of the International Federation of Sports Medicine', in A. Dirix, H.G. Knuttgen and K. Tittel (eds) *The Olympic Book of Sports Medicine*. Oxford: Blackwell.

Todd, T. (1987) 'Anabolic Steroids: The Gremlin of Sport', *Journal of Sport History*, 14: 87–107.

—— (1992) 'Anabolic Steroids and Sport', in J. Berryman, and R. Park (eds) *Sport and Exercise Science: Essays in the History of Sports Medicine*. Chicago: University of Illinois Press.

Tuck, J. (1996) 'Patriots, Barbarians, Gentlemen and Players: Rugby Union and National Identity in Britain since 1945', in *One Day in Leicester* (2nd Journal of the Association of Sports Historians: Sporting Heritage Series).

Turner, B.S. (1991) 'Recent Developments in the Theory of the Body', in M. Featherstone, M. Hepworth and B. Turner (eds) *The Body: Social Process and Cultural Theory*. London: Sage.

—— (1992) *Regulated Bodies: Essays in Medical Sociology*. London: Routledge.

—— (1995) *Medical Power and Social Knowledge*, 2nd edn. London: Sage.

—— (1996) *The Body and Society*, 2nd edn. London: Sage.

—— (1997) 'Foreword: From Governmentality to Risk: Some Reflections on Foucault's Contribution to Medical Sociology', in A. Petersen and R. Bunton (eds) *Foucault: Health and Medicine*. London: Routledge.

Turner, J.A., Deyo, R.A., Loeser, J.D., Von Korff, M. and Fordyce, W.E. (1994) 'The Importance of Placebo Effects in Pain Treatment and Research', *Journal of the American Medical Association*, 271(20): 1609–1614.

Turner, V. (1967) *The Forest of Symbols: Aspects of Ndembu Ritual*. Ithaca, NY: Cornell University Press.

Tylor, E.B. (1896) 'On American Lot Games as Evidence of Asiatic Intercourse before the Time of Columbus', *International Archives for Ethnographia*. Supplement to vol. 9: 55–67.

Vanlandewijck, Y.C. and Chappel, R.J. (1996) 'Integration and Classification Issues in Competitive Sports for Athletes with Disabilities', *Sport Science Review*, 5(1): 65–88.

Videman, T. and Rytömaa, T. (1977) 'Effects of Blood Removal and Autotransfusion on Heart Rate Response to a Submaximal Workload', *Journal of Sports Medicine*, 17: 387–390.

Vrancken, M. (1989) 'Schools of Thought on Pain', *Social Science and Medicine*, 29(3): 435–444.

Wacquant, L. (1995) 'Pugs at Work: Bodily Capital and Bodily Labour among Professional Boxers', *Body and Society*, 1: 65–93.

Waddington, I. (1996) 'The Development of Sports Medicine', *Sociology of Sport Journal*, 13: 176–196.

—— (2000) *Sport, Health and Drugs: A Critical Sociological Perspective*. London: E. and F.N. Spon.

Waddington, I. and Murphy, P. (1992) 'Drugs, Sport and Ideologies', in E. Dunning, and C. Rojek (eds) *Sport and Leisure in the Civilising Process*. London: Macmillan.

Waddington, I., Roderick, M. and Naik, R. (2001) 'Methods of Appointment and Qualifications of Club Doctors and Physiotherapists in English Professional Football: Some Problems and Issues', *British Journal of Sports Medicine*, 35: 48–53.

Waddle, G.I. and Hainline, B. (1989) *Drugs and the Athlete*. Philadelphia: F.A. Davis.

Walk, S. (1997) 'Peers in Pain: The Experience of Student Athletic Trainers', *Sociology of Sport Journal*, 14(1): 22–56.

Waller, A.E., Feehan, M., Marshall, S.W. and Chalmers, D. (1994) 'The New Zealand Rugby Injury and Performance Project: 1', *British Journal of Sports Medicine*, 28: 223–228.

Ward, T. (1999) 'Pee Now, Pay Later', *Athletics Weekly*, 11 August.

Watts, D., Wilson, H. and Horwill, F. (eds) (1982) *The Complete Middle Distance Runner*. London: Stanley Paul.

Weightman, D. and Browne, R.C. (1974) 'Injuries in Association and Rugby Football', *British Journal of Sports Medicine*, 8: 183–187.

Wekesa, M., Asembo, J.M. and Njororai, W.W.S. (1996) 'Injury Surveillance in a Rugby Tournament', *British Journal of Sports Medicine*, 30: 61–63.

Welchew, E. (1995) *Patient Controlled Analgesia*. London: BMJ Publishing Group.

Welsby, B. (1995) *Creatine: Food for Prolonged Energy*. Peterborough, UK: Be-Well Nutritional Products.

Welsh Rugby Union (1996) *Laws of the Game of Rugby Football with Instructions and Notes on the Laws*. Cardiff: WRU.

Whannel, G. (1992) *Fields in Vision: Television Sport and Cultural Transformation*. London: Routledge.

Wheaton, B. (1997) 'Covert Ethnography and the Ethics of Research: Studying Sport Subcultures', in A. Tomlinson and S. Fleming (eds) *Ethics, Sport and Leisure: Crises and Critiques*. Aachen, Germany: Meyer and Meyer.

—— (2000) 'Just Do It: Consumption, Commitment, and Identity in Windsurfing Subculture', *Sociology of Sport Journal*, 17(3): 254–274.

Wheaton, B. and Tomlinson, A. (1998) 'The Changing Gender Order in Sport? The Case of Windsurfing Subcultures', *Journal of Sport and Social Issues*, 22(3): 252–274.

White, P.G., Young, K. and McTeer, W.G. (1995) 'Sport, Masculinity and the Injured Body', in D. Sabo, and F. Gordon (eds) *Men's Health and Illness: Gender, Power, and the Body*. London: Sage.

Whorton, J.C. (1992a) ' "Athlete's Heart": The Medical Debate over Athleticism, 1870–1920', in J.W. Berryman and R.J. Park (eds) *Sport and Exercise Science: Essays in the History of Sports Medicine*. Chicago: University of Illinois Press.

—— (1992b) 'Muscular Vegetarianism: The Debate over Diet and Athletic Performance in the Progressive Era', in J.W. Berryman and R.J. Park (eds) *Sport and Exercise Science: Essays in the History of Sports Medicine*. Chicago: University of Illinois Press.

Wigglesworth, N. (1996) *The Evolution of English Sport*. London: Cass.

Willan, F. (1867) 'The University Boat Race', *The Times*, 14 October: 10.

Williams, Gareth (1983) 'From Grand Slam to Great Slump: Economy Society and Rugby Football in Wales during the Depression', *Welsh History Review*, 13: 338–357.

—— (1985) 'How Amateur Was My Valley: Professional Sport and National Identity in Wales, 1890–1914', *British Journal of Sports History*, 2: 248–269.

—— (1988) 'From Popular Culture to Public Cliche: Images and Identity in Wales, 1890–1914', J.A. Magan (ed.) *Pleasure, Profit and Proselytism: British Culture and Sport at Home and Abroad, 1700–1914*. London: Cass.

—— (1991) *1905 and All That: Essays on Rugby Football and Welsh Society*. Llandysul, UK: Gomer Press.

—— (1994) 'The Road to Wigan Pier Revisited: The Migration of Welsh Rugby Talent since 1918', in J. Bale and J. Maguire (eds) *The Global Sports Arena*. London: Cass.

Williams, Gwyn A. (1985) *When Was Wales?* London: Penguin.

Williams, H. (1981) *Pontypridd: Essays on the History of an Industrial Community*. Cardiff: University of Wales Press.

Williams, J.G.P. (1962) *Sports Medicine*. London: Arnold.

—— (1990) 'The Nature and Incidence of Injury in Sport', E. Simon and S.D.W. Payne (eds) *Medicine, Sport and the Law*. Oxford: Blackwell Scientific.

—— (1992) 'The Nature and Incidence of Injury in Sport', in S.D.W. Payne (ed.) *Medico-legal Hazards of Rugby Union*. Oxford: Blackwell Special Projects.

Williams, J.G.P. and Sperryn, P.N. (1976) *Sports Medicine*, 2nd edn. London: Arnold.

Williams, S.J. and Bendelow, G. (1998) *The Lived Body: Sociological Themes, Embodied Issues*. London: Routledge.

Williams, S.J. and Calnan, M. (eds) (1996) *Modern Medicine: Lay Perspectives and Experiences*, London: UCL Press.

Wyatt, D. (1995) *Rugby Disunion: The Making of Three World Cups*. London: Vista.

Young, K. (1993) 'Violence, Risk, and Liability in Male Sports Culture', *Sociology of Sport Journal*, 10: 373–396.

Young, K., White, P. and McTeer, W. (1994) 'Body Talk: Male Athletes Reflect on Sport, Injury and Pain', *Sociology of Sport Journal*, 11: 175–194.

Zola, I.K. (1972) 'Medicine as an Institution of Social Control', *Sociological Review*, 20(4): 487–504.

Index